HERE IS WHAT ROSALIE AND HOWARD MINKOW
HAVE TO SAY ABOUT PAYING TAXES:
**You are the only one who can get your
money back from the IRS. It is up to you to
file your return in the way that allows you the
largest number of deductions. Our assertion
is that you can get three years' worth of refunds back from the IRS. How to do this is
what this book is all about.**

THE FOUR BASIC RULES ARE:
- If it isn't a deduction, don't spend it.
- Take advantage of all deferrals of income.
- Keep impeccable tax records
  with documentation.
- Do tax planning every day.

THE COMPLETE
LIST OF IRS TAX
DEDUCTIONS

explains exactly how to make the most of your
money—by giving the least amount of it away
to the government. You can no longer afford to
be ignorant of your tax rights. An absolutely
indispensable guide!

By Rosalie and Howard Minkow
The Complete List of IRS Tax Deductions
(1981 Edition)

By Rosalie Minkow
Money Management for Women

THE COMPLETE LIST OF IRS TAX DEDUCTIONS

ROSALIE AND HOWARD MINKOW

PLAYBOY
PAPERBACKS

This book is dedicated to our children:
Ellen, Lynn, and David

CONTENTS

9

FOREWORD

"'It was as true,' said Mr. Barkis, '. . . as taxes is. And nothing's truer than them.'"

—Charles Dickens, *David Copperfield*

We would have to concur with Mr. Barkis. However, many people, although they too know that taxes are indisputably a fact of life, do not know how to save money on them. As a matter of fact, many accountants do not know either.

Today's inflation has made taxes an even more onerous burden. With that thought in mind we decided that it was time we shared our knowledge with the general public, with a book that is both complete and easy to understand. Our goal is to illustrate how you can maintain your life-style as well as save on taxes by remembering the four rules outlined in Chapter 2 and explained in Chapter 3. The result of our efforts was the 1981 edition of *The Complete List of IRS Tax Deductions*.

The feedback from readers of our 1981 edition was indeed gratifying.

The division manager of a Southern department store chain who travels a great deal on business discovered so many on-the-job travel expenses previously unknown to him that he received a refund of several hundred dollars on his return.

13

A bachelor lawyer realized a saving when he filed the cheaper head-of-household rate. He had not known that although his mother was in a nursing home he could claim her as a dependent.

A young psychiatric social worker who was filing for divorce discovered that she could deduct tax-related fees incurred during the process.

A young mother found that she could go back to work with an easy mind because she could leave her infant with her mother. Her mother was delighted to realize the income from baby-sitting her grandchild, especially when she found that Social Security did not have to be taken out.

A teacher who has to wear special elastic hose for her phlebitis was gratified to learn that she could deduct the cost of the hose from her medical.

When a sudden storm blew down several trees on their property, the homeowners whose house was now devalued learned they could file for a casualty loss.

A daughter who received a considerable inheritance and wanted to conserve the principal while receiving income from it saw the wisdom of tax-free municipal bonds.

A businessman learned how to take his wife to conventions tax free.

A former Ivy Leaguer determined that he was able to make a handsome contribution to his alma mater by selling some stocks on which he had been losing money.

Our book even helped the sex life of one young couple! They were able to afford sex therapy after reading that it would be tax deductible.

Our up-to-date 1982 edition contains a table of medical deductions as well as nondeductibles. We have also introduced a section on tax-free property swaps and explained exactly what it means for you. There are many more replications of schedules and forms with which you should be familiar. Included also in this 1982 edition is formerly top secret information recently released under the Freedom of Information Act which tells in detail how your return is processed and screened for possible audit. It will intrigue you and also help you to avoid tax trouble.

You will see that our book not only deals with deductions but also with exemptions and credits. To clarify what each is in the tax structure: a deduction is an amount that may be subtracted from your adjusted gross income; an exemption is the amount you are allowed to deduct from gross income for each dependent; a credit is a dollar-for-dollar amount you can deduct from the final tax bill.

As you read this book you may possibly come across tax-saving strategies which you may not be able to implement for your 1981 taxes because it is too late. Don't be disheartened. Better late than never. Tuck this book into a handy space and use it as your tax reference "bible" through '82!

As we went to press, the Economic Recovery Act of 1981 was signed by President Reagan. How will this affect you and your 1981 taxes? It means a cumulative tax rate reduction of 1¼% for 1981. It means that if you sold your house after January 30, 1980, you can defer the gain if you purchase or construct a new home within *two years* (extended from 18 months). Also, for those fifty-five and older selling a home after July 20, 1981, the one-time exclusion of gain has been upped to $125,000. (It was formerly $100,000.)

The top tax rate on long-term capital gains has been changed to 20%, effective retroactively for sales occurring after June 9, 1981.

If you purchased an "all-savers" certificate after October 1, 1981, you can look forward to a $1,000 total exclusion of interest if you are single; $2,000 if you file jointly.

Greater tax benefits will be yours for 1982 and future years. To make the most of the new tax law, pack as many deductions as you can into 1981 (when tax brackets are higher than they are going to be) and try to defer income to next year (when your tax bracket will be lowered) by delaying a year-end bonus or postponing interest income.

What do you have to look forward to for 1982 taxes? Income will be taxed 10% less for those in income brackets under 50%; up to 29% less in brackets above 50%. The top tax bracket will be 50% (rather than 70% as formerly).

Individual Retirement Accounts (IRAs) will be permitted for all employees next year even if your company already has a pension for you. You will be able to contribute up to $2,000 per year to an IRA. Keogh retirement plans for self-employed will allow up to $15,000 or 15% of net self-employment income—whichever is less. This is double that of the previous allowance.

Starting with 1982, the new tax law phases in a special deduction for two-income married couples. By 1983, the deduction will be 10% of the first $30,000 earned by the lower-income spouse, for a maximum of $3,000. For 1982, the limits are 5% and $1,500.

Also beginning in 1982, the foreign earned-income exclusion will be increased, dependent care credit will be liberalized, and depreciation on real estate and business assets will be more generous.

Beginning in 1985, the individual income tax brackets, the personal exemption, and the zero bracket amount (standard deduction) will be adjusted for inflation according to the Consumer Price Index. This should avoid "bracket creep" after 1984.

Bleak note: Starting in February 1982, interest will conform to within 100% of the prime interest rate.

Note: 1981 forms are not made available until late December or early January; too late to reach us as we go to press. Therefore, we have used 1980 forms, which differ only slightly from the 1981 forms.

CHAPTER 1

Don't Give It Away
to the IRS

"Every Friday," confided Jim M. to us, "I take it easy. I figure the IRS takes one-fifth withholding from my salary. So I figure that one day out of five I am working for the IRS. Why should I knock myself out if none of that money goes to me? I make Friday my IRS day."

It doesn't matter which day you consider your IRS day if you follow Jim's way of thinking. It could be Monday, Tuesday, Wednesday, Thursday, or Friday. It is true that if you have withholding taken from your paycheck, you are working one day a week for the IRS. AND, if you are in the highest earnings bracket, it could be two and a half days a week.

On top of that, some of that money is not entirely due the IRS. Some of that money is yours due you on a refund if you know how to get it back.

AND what couldn't you do with a refund!

A recent divorcée used her $800 refund check toward plastic surgery to enhance her new image as a "single."

A Long Island member of a ham radio club spent his check on a new radio setup so that he could keep up with the other ham radio aficionados. "It's twice the fun having your own rather than having to share with some other member," he told us.

A cosmetologist in Chicago planned to use her $600 tax refund for a cruise on a Maine schooner. "I've always wanted to see Cape Cod," she glowed.

A Midwest retail shop owner and his wife were going to buy a used car for their son with their $1,200 check. "It will mean a great relief to my wife. No more juggling her car time with our son. He will have his own car now."

Some people used all of their check for pleasure buying, some used their check to pay for their past pleasures—wiping their debts slate clean. Some refundees used part of their check to pay old debts and put part into savings.

What couldn't you do with a refund check—a really fat one? Put it toward a new gas-efficient auto? Treat yourself to a ski vacation in the Rockies? Help it finance your child's college education?

You can get yourself a fat refund check from the IRS, too. After all, aren't you just applying for money that is rightfully yours? That money was withheld from your paycheck.

The problem for most people is how to get that money back. Millions of refunds go by the boards for millions of taxpayers simply because they don't know how to get a refund—LEGALLY!

The purpose of this book is to show you how to get it back through taking the biggest and the most deductions on your 1040. Even that august and revered judge, Learned Hand, said:

> There is nothing sinister in so arranging one's affairs to keep taxes as low as possible. Nobody owes any public duty to pay more than the law demands; taxes are enforced exactions, not voluntary contributions. To demand more in the name of morals is mere cant.

However, you must remember that the IRS is not obligated in any way to tell you how to get your own money back from them or show you how to apply for a refund, nor does it do it for you. YOU MUST DO IT FOR YOURSELF!

As a matter of fact, you cannot even rely on the IRS's free tax-preparation services to do your tax return properly. For the past five years a major New York newspaper has done a survey before April 15. It sends a reporter out with the same set of circumstances and income figures and a fictitious W-2 to accountants, private tax services, and the IRS tax service. Each year all the IRS tax-assistance agents miss the boat with several hundred dollars in overpayments!

You are the only one who can get your money back from the IRS. It is up to you to file your return in such a way as to take the largest number of deductions. However, you can't, as some people do, deduct everything but the kitchen sink. That is inviting an audit. Your deductions must be *legal* deductions. You cannot take a deduction simply because it seems unfair to you that your son's college tuition is so high that it's breaking the family bank, and how the heck does the government expect you to educate your kid on the $1,000 exemption they give for him?

Congress has allowed for legal deductions. Again, the emphasis is on *legal*. You must remember that the deductions must face the scrutiny of a possible audit. False claims will result in IRS computers spitting out your return for audit, which might mean you will be paying that tax with interest and penalties, and if you have hidden income, the horrendous claim of fraud, resulting in a heavy fine or jail term or both. Moreover, when the agent is examining your return on one deduction claim and finds it false, he is liable to be very curious about what other deductions on your return he can nail down as being too presumptuous on your part.

Read, and maybe you can actually get money back from the government in the form of a refund, legally. Think aggressively, and you may be able to file amended returns for past years and get refunds for them. The IRS code allows three years from the time you filed your return to amend it and claim deductions you might have overlooked.

Our assertion is that you *can* get three years' worth of refunds back from the IRS. How to do this is what this book is all about.

CHAPTER 2

Four Basic Rules
You Should Always
Keep in Mind

Your rich cousin Willie never bothers about what goes on his tax return. He boasts: "I have the biggest tax-accounting firm in the United States doing my return. I don't have to know a thing about tax laws. My accountant does everything for me."

What rich cousin Willie is not telling you is that only he can supply the accountant with the information to make up his return. True, rich cousin Willie does not have to know about tax law, but he does follow his CPA's directions on some basic rules that must be adhered to if his accountant is going to do the best for him on his return.

Even rich cousin Willie's accountant, if he is going to do the best for Willie on his return by reducing his taxes to the bare minimum, cannot do it all by himself. Rich cousin Willie, just as you and I, must arrange his investments and sources of income and keep records of expenditures so that his CPA can compute the least tax for him. If Willie did not do this he would not have given his accountant, even though he is a member of the most top-notch firm in the United States, enough to work with, and his accountant could do nothing but follow the strict outlines of Willie's 1040. Rich cousin Willie would not be getting his money's worth from his accountant. You can be sure that Willie's accountant has instructed him on some basic rules to follow.

As a result of many tax seasons, we have come up with four basic rules that we request all our clients to follow. Our clients have learned, because of many a refund, that doing things our way brings results.

What are the four basic rules we ask our clients to follow?

The four basic rules are:

1. IF IT ISN'T A DEDUCTION, DON'T SPEND IT.
2. TAKE ADVANTAGE OF ALL DEFERRALS OF INCOME.
3. KEEP IMPECCABLE TAX RECORDS WITH DOCUMENTATION.
4. DO TAX PLANNING EVERY DAY.

In the following chapter we explain what each basic rule means.

CHAPTER 3

More About
the Basic Rules

Remember our No. 1 rule: If it isn't a deduction, don't spend it? It may seem an impractical rule, and it may be in many cases. After all, you say your weekly food bill is not deductible. But wait, it may be! Tax law allows the cost of food and beverages prescribed by your doctor for medicinal purposes in addition to normal diet.

One senior citizen was allowed to write off his evening brandy because he was instructed by his physician that it was required to pep up a slow heartbeat.

An allergist and his wife were severely allergic to chemicals in most ordinary supermarket foods. They were required, because of their conditions, to purchase much of their food at a health-food store, where they could get natural, organic foods to alleviate their severely allergic reactions. The couple attested that comparable food prices at their local supermarket were much lower. They proved that it cost them twice as much to eat than it would had they not had their allergic conditions. The IRS allowed them the difference between the cost of the foods at the supermarket and the cost of the foods at the health-food store.

A patient who was in a mentally depressed state was found to suffer from hypoglycemia (abnormally low blood sugar). Her doctor advised eating protein six to eight times per day and to abstain from eating carbohydrates and processed foods. The high-quality protein was necessary to treat her disease. It was also very expensive. She deducted the additional expense incurred for this particular diet over the amount spent on a normal diet as a medical expense, and the IRS allowed the deduction.

Clothing, another basic necessity of life, may be deductible for you. If it is required for your job and is not suitable for wearing off duty or away from work, your clothing is deductible, and so are dry cleaning costs or any other costs of maintenance. For instance: Nurses and airline pilots wear uniforms to work that they cannot or would not wear in civilian life; commercial fishermen may deduct the cost of protective clothing—oil slickers, rubber boots, and work gloves. But the law does not simply apply to uniforms and protective clothing. Take the case of a fashion coordinator. She purchased clothing to wear at fashion shows and meetings of fashion experts. She argued that her high-style outfits were necessary for her work and were not the type of clothing she would don for ordinary street wear, and she won a deduction.

The third basic necessity of life, shelter, may be partially deductible for you. If you are self-employed and have an office at home—we will go into this situation in a later chapter—there are big deductions for you. However, even if you are an employee or self-employed and have your main office away from home, mortgage interest and the Energy Tax Act of 1978 (which we will also go into later) give you some leeway in paying the costs of home ownership. In certain states you can take off for property taxes included in your rent as a deduction.

Our rule No. 2: Take advantage of all deferrals of income. Postpone them into lower earnings years, or even better, postpone them into your retirement years, when you probably will have little or no active income to pay tax on.

You can have your employer defer a bonus from a

fat salary year to a leaner salary year, when you will be in a lower tax bracket.

If self-employed, you might defer billing at the end of a higher-earnings year, postponing it into the new year.

By all means, take advantage of IRA (Individual Retirement Account) if you are an employee or a Keogh plan if self-employed to defer income into the lower tax brackets of retirement years.

Recall our No. 3 rule: Keep impeccable tax records with documentation? You might have the very best and valid right to a deduction, but if you face a tax audit without proper and thorough records, you will not pass the rigors of the audit. After all, would you argue a case in a court of law without documentation and expect to win?

Documenting all your financial transactions makes sense for another reason. You never know when there may be a change in the tax laws that will be favorable to you in a certain transaction. You will need those financial records to substantiate your claim for a tax write-off.

How to keep proper tax records? Get yourself a business diary. In this, write in detail what each deduction was, what it was for, whom it involved, and how much it was for.

Hold on to monthly statements and canceled checks for other than business purposes. Supposing you have decided to take advantage of the Energy Tax Act and are reinsulating your house. Hold on to those papers related to that work. What specific papers? Keep the estimate, receipted bill, and your canceled check. They are your proofs to the IRS that work was actually done and that you are owed a tax deduction.

Many people ask, "How long should I keep tax records?" The law says that for ordinary tax audits you need *detailed* records for three years. That means both bills and canceled checks. But for liability purposes, the statute of limitations is six years to prove that you paid the bill.

We say this: Keep financial records that have to do with anything that is a permanent investment that you still own, such as a house, stocks and bonds, jewelry, or autos. You should keep papers related to those as long as you own them, because you may need the records in case of a sale or loss to prove their worth for a deduction.

Rule No. 4: Do tax planning every day. Read your daily newspaper. Keep abreast of what is happening in the economy and with tax rulings so that you may base daily decisions on current events and get the best deductions. When you are spending money you should be conscious of what is happening today as it relates to you and the economy and revenue rulings. The tax laws are always changing. What was not a deduction yesterday may be one today.

Now we shall go on to show you how different facets of your life may include a tax deduction and a fat refund check for you!

CHAPTER 4

On-the-Job Deductions
That May Be Yours

You say that your work life does not give you many deductions because you are not in business for yourself?

Look at this IRS rule: The performance of services as an employee constitutes the carrying on of a trade or business. Therefore, the rule that allows deductions that are ordinary and necessary for a business also allows deductions of expenses that are ordinary and necessary for doing your job.

Let's explore several cases in which expenses you might have thought came out of pocket and were strictly not deductible yielded high deductions and refunds for other taxpayers.

Take a look at the case of Jeff R. Jeff was an advertising space salesman for a national magazine. He disagreed with their management policies and decided to look for a similar position at a magazine whose policies were more to his liking. He knew that the IRS allows a deduction for job-hunting expenses whether or not you get a particular job, so long as you are looking for work in the same field and it is not your first job. Furthermore, in order to deduct job-hunting expenses, you need not quit your present job while looking for another one.

Jeff wrote up a résumé and had it professionally typed. The typing cost was deductible. He kept a record (remember the business diary we mentioned in Chapter 3?) of all interview travel expenses, including buses, subways, taxis, gas, tolls, and parking, as well as a plane trip from his home in Massachusetts to Los Angeles for an interview. He even deducted the cost of a few lunch tabs he picked up for personnel people.

After a number of months, Jeff landed a job in Minneapolis. His plane transportation and moving expenses were not reimbursed by his new employer. Jeff took them as deductions.

Jeff settled into a home and his job in Minneapolis. He subscribed to magazines related to advertising (deductible), and to a daily newspaper that carried advertising news (deductible). He joined an ad salesman's organization and deducted his dues. He also thought that it might be beneficial for business goodwill to join the local Rotary (dues deductible).

Traveling between customers, he had to use his auto. That meant that his gas, repairs, tolls, and parking were deductible for his trips between customers. He was also allowed a percentage depreciation on his car because it was necessary for him to do business. Public transportation between customers was sparse and inefficient.

To keep the goodwill of his customers, he often picked up lunch tabs. If it was toward the end of the day, he would treat the client to cocktails (deductible). He also sent gifts (not exceeding the IRS legal limit of $25 to each person) to good customers. Often he would present a secretary, who could smooth the way for him with a customer, a bottle of her favorite perfume (deductible).

At the end of the year, Jeff had hefty deductions and applied for and got a refund.

Annette T. was a high school English teacher. She was required to pay dues to the state teachers' union. She also belonged to an English teachers' organization. Dues on both were deductible because they were necessary and ordinary for her profession. She went back to school one summer to study Chaucerian English. The cost of her books, tuition, room, and board at the college were deductible. The IRS calls it enhancement of job skills. Another summer, for enhancement of job skills, she took a trip to Britain's Stratford country, where Shakespeare wrote his plays. Her travel expenses, meals, and lodging were allowed.

During the school year, Annette—who also teaches drama at her high school—goes to the theater quite often. She holds on to the ticket stubs and notes and theater programs, and documents her business diary for a whopping deduction.

A chemistry professor friend, Grant H., does much research on his own in his field of expertise. Expenses include the use of a lab and lab materials. He hopes to gain recognition on his discoveries related to drugs and foods that affect the human fetus. He is permitted to deduct these research expenses and depreciation on his equipment because they are in his field of expertise. Grant also lectures on the effect of drugs and foods on embryonic life. Expenses related to his traveling on his lecture tours are written off on his 1040.

Robbie L. commutes to work every day to his job as a television marketing expert. His office is located in a very prestigious glass-and-steel building in New York City. His corporation provides the minimum in office decor. Robbie has many important people come to see him. At his own expense, he bought a floor lamp and comfortable chair for his visitors, plus some colorful throw rugs and a few important prints. He was allowed a deduction on those expenses.

Carol C. was a pension planning expert. She decided that a law school degree study program taken at night would enhance her knowledge of pensions and trusts, though she had no intention of practicing law. Because she was using her law school studies as enhancing a skill she already had, and she was not preparing herself for new employment, she got a deduction on tuition and books. (Had she studied law for the purposes of *new* employment—say, as a legal expert—the school expenses would have been disallowed.

Steven L. worked for a boatyard as an all-around yardhand. Usually he wore blue jeans and a work shirt for painting boat bottoms and for other chores. However, when the boats were in the water, he was also required to clean barnacles and other marine life from boat bottoms. This necessitated his wearing a wet suit. Because this apparel came under the "ordinary and necessary" rule for his job, Steve was able to deduct the cost of this expensive outfit. Steve also had to haul heavy tools from the garage of his home, where he stored them for the boatyard twenty-five miles away, every day to work. He applied for and got a deduction on his auto commuting that included gas, repairs, and a percentage of depreciation, because it was imperative for him to haul the equipment, and using public transportation for hauling the equipment was impractical.

Lisa G. was a psychiatric social worker. She had herself psychoanalyzed. Ordinarily, the IRS would not have allowed her a deduction for her psychoanalyst's bills as a business deduction. They would have argued that she was undergoing psychoanalysis to prepare herself for her profession. Lisa's analyst wrote a statement that Lisa did indeed have some mild form of paranoia which did not interfere with her functioning as a normal, happy human being. However, because of her condition, analysis was an ordinary and necessary expense so that she could function professionally without neurosis. Lisa was therefore able to take off her analyst's bill as a business deduction. She won her case with the IRS.

Lisa had a job during the week working for a family-service agency. She also had a private practice all day Wednesdays and Saturday mornings at an office in her home. She was able to deduct a percentage of her home mortgage interest and depreciation relating to the use of her home office, the cost of light and heat in the office, and the cost of a cleaning service and supplies for the office lavatory. Even though all home interest is deductible in any event, it was a tax saving in Lisa's case to allocate the interest expense against her income earned in her private practice.

The popular magazines Lisa subscribed to for her waiting room, as well as technical magazine subscriptions relating to her field, were also deductible.

At least once a year, Lisa went to conventions in Chicago and San Francisco that related to psychiatric social work. She fully deducted the cost of plane transportation from her Maryland home, meals, and lodging.

Did you recognize some job situations similar to yours in the foregoing cases? Think about the deductions those job holders took on their taxes. You might relate those same deductions to your job and your tax return and get a fat refund from on-the-job deductions.

The rest of our book will go into various aspects of your life and tell you in explicit detail how you will be able to whittle down your taxable income. The first step for you is to examine your filing status. This is discussed in the next chapter.

CHAPTER 5

Filing and
Marital Status

The way in which you fill out the very first box of your 1040 return may determine whether you will receive a refund or not, and how big a refund. It is the box labeled Filing Status. There are five choices. You check one: Single, Married Filing Joint Return, Married Filing Separate Return, Head of Household, Qualifying Widow(er) with Dependent Child.

Okay, you say, I'll check the cheapest, and we don't blame you. However, the government has regulations on qualifications for each of those categories.

How will the way you file affect the outcome of your return? For each of those filing-status categories there is a different tax rate in the government's tax-rate schedule. Let us illustrate.

John Langston is a computer programmer. He is single. According to IRS definition he was not married at the end of the tax year, nor was he engaged in a common-law marriage recognized by his state. His taxable income is $20,000. John would pay $3,565 on $18,200 in taxes plus 34% of the amount of his income over $18,200. John's tax bill is $4,177.

Tom Rowton owns an auto supply store. His taxable income is also $20,000. Tom checks Married Filing Joint Return. According to tax law that means that on the last day of the tax year one of the following applies: He is married and living as husband with a wife, or he is living in a common-law marriage recognized by the state in which the common-law marriage was entered, or he is married and living apart from his wife but he is not legally separated under a decree of divorce or separate maintenance, or he and his wife are separated under an interlocutory decree of divorce.

The advantage for Tom of being a married person filing a joint return is that he gets the "split-income benefit" reflected in the tax rates. The tax table and tax-rate schedules for married couples filing jointly split the income and reflect the tax at a lower rate.

Tom's wife stays home to take care of the house. She is not employed outside the home. She has no other income except what Tom brings home. Tom will owe $2,565 on his taxable income of $16,000 plus 24% of the amount over $16,000. Tom's tax bill is $3,225.

Richard Clark, an assistant editor, also has a taxable income of $20,000. Richard is also married, but Richard's wife, Julie, is employed as an interior designer. Her taxable income is equal to Richard's. That makes a combined taxable income of $40,000. Filing a joint return, according to the tax-rate tables, the Clarks must pay $8,162 plus 43% of the amount over $35,200. The Clarks have a combined tax bill of $10,226.

Remember John Langston, our single? His tax bill was $4,177. Richard Clark is actually paying $936 more on his taxable income for the privilege of being married to Julie ($10,226 divided in half is $5,113, or $936 more than John Langston's tax bill of $4,177 on his taxable income of $20,000!).

It hardly seems fair, does it? A few years ago, CBS-TV's *60 Minutes* showed its viewers how couples with relatively equal incomes, who felt they were being taxed unfairly for being married, combined vacations and tax avoidance by securing quickie Caribbean divorces before the end of the tax year and marrying again at the beginning of the next tax year, thus saving themselves a whopping tax bill. However, the IRS caught up with this practice before there threatened to become a national epidemic of divorce and remarriage by passing Revenue Ruling 76-255: "Couple that gets foreign divorce only for tax avoidance with intent to remarry early in next year will still be considered married for tax purposes."

There is an alternative to Married Filing Joint Return, and that is Married Filing Separate Return. Will this reduce your taxes? In some cases it will. If both you and your wife have income, you should figure your tax both jointly and separately to make sure you are using the method that will result in the lesser tax.

Here is an example for husband and wife using equal incomes of $20,000 each, wherein using the Married Filing Separate Return category actually did save money. Bob Barker made his $20,000 taxable income as an assistant art director. His wife, Alicia, made her $20,000 taxable income as a bookkeeper. One day while crossing the street, Bob was hit by a car. Non-reimbursable medical expenses amounted to $5,000. The IRS allows the excess of 3% of adjusted gross income as a medical deduction. If the Barkers file jointly on their next tax return, they will be allowed $3,800 as a medical deduction. The calculation goes: Three percent of $40,000 (their combined incomes) is $1,200; subtract the $1,200 from that $5,000 medical bill, and the Barkers have a medical deduction of $3,800.

Now look at this. The Barkers decide to try filing separately. They find that 3% of Bob's $20,000 income is $600. That $600 subtracted from the $5,000 medical bill gives Bob a medical deduction of $4,400. That's $600 more on his medical deduction than if he had filed using the category Married Filing Joint Return.

However, if the Barkers had had unequal incomes—say, Bob made $30,000 and Alicia $10,000—they might have lost the "split-income benefit" that filing jointly gives to couples with unequal incomes. When Bob went to the Married Filing Separate Return tax table he would find that he was being taxed at a much greater rate than if he had stuck to the Married Filing Joint Return category. The higher tax rate might cancel out gains made on his medical deduction by filing a separate return.

There is another instance wherein married filing separately might be more advantageous than married filing jointly. Suppose, as in the following example, both husband and wife earn comparable incomes. One of them has a long-term gain on sale of property, and the other has a short-term loss on sale of property.

Ricardo and Carmela Juarez each earned $30,000. Ricardo had a long-term gain of $10,000. His wife Carmela had a short-term loss of $7,000. If they were to file jointly, the short-term loss would offset the gain and therefore there would be a gain of $3,000 ($10,000 − $7,000 = $3,000). This would be taxed at 40%, and the result would be taxable income of $1,200 ($3,000 × 40% = $1,200). Now, if Ricardo and Carmela filed separately, Ricardo's gain would be taxed at $4,000 ($10,000 × 40% = $4,000), and Carmela could take a loss of $3,000. The result would be taxable income of $1,000 instead of $1,200, or a savings of tax on $200.

As we said before, work out your tax return both ways—Married Filing Joint Return and Married Filing Separate Return—before making a decision as to which will give you the greatest tax saving.

If you are not married but maintain a household, you may qualify for (unmarried) Head of Household filing. Though this category is not as favorable with its tax rate as that for marrieds, it is a lesser rate than filing as a single. How does one qualify for this filing status?

1. You must be unmarried at the end of the tax year.
2. You file a separate return.
3. You must have paid more than half the costs to keep up your home in the tax year. By costs, the IRS means such expenses as property taxes, mortgage interest, rent, utility charges, upkeep and repair of property, property insurance, and food. The IRS ex-

cludes the cost of clothing, education, medical expenses, vacations, life insurance, transportation, rental value of home, and the value of services rendered by you or a member of the household in its counting of household costs.

4. Your spouse did not live with you at any time during the tax year.

5. For more than six months of the tax year your home was the main home of your child or stepchild whom you can claim as a dependent. This category can be used by married people who are *not* legally separated.

Legally separated or never married or divorced or widowed taxpayers may *also* qualify as unmarried heads of household if they meet certain qualifications. The taxpayer's child, grandchild, stepchild, or adopted child who is not married at the end of the tax year must live in the taxpayer's home.

Marie Lawrence was a widow. Her son and his wife and their child, Marie's grandchild, lived with her. Though her son and his wife rightfully claimed the child as a dependent, Marie was still able to file under the Head of Household category because she paid more than half the costs of maintaining the household according to the IRS's definition and therefore was maintaining a home for her unmarried grandchild.

You may be considered a head of household if your child, grandchild, stepchild, or adopted child who is married at the end of the taxable year and is also a dependent (you provide more than half toward their support) lives in your household *and* does not file a joint return with his or her spouse.

A taxpayer may also be considered head of household if certain relatives live with him whom the taxpayer is entitled to call dependents (again, he provides more than half of their support). Those certain relatives, according to the IRS's dictum, would be:

brother or sister (whole or half-blood), stepbrother, stepsister, parent, grandparent or any other ancestors of parents, stepparent (but not foster parent), nephew, niece, uncle, aunt, son-in-law, or brother-in-law. Note that even if you are providing more than half of their support and they live with you, your Cousin Louie is not included, nor that deprived teen-age youngster you have taken under your wing.

Not more than one person can claim one of those relatives as a dependent to qualify as head of household. Also, a person who claims status as head of household must also maintain as principal place of living that home for the person who qualifies him as head of household and must live in the same household with that person.

There is one exception wherein you may claim status as head of household and still not live in the same household with the person who qualifies you as head of household. That is in the case of parents. You may maintain a separate household for your parent or parents and still qualify. That separate residence could be a nursing home or a rest home. If you paid more than half the costs for your parent or parents in the nursing home or rest home, you would qualify for status as head of household.

Though you and your dependent must live together for you to qualify as head of household (with the exception of parents), the household does not have to be in the same place all during the tax year.

Roger Carter was a bachelor who kept a home for himself and his maiden aunt. During the course of the tax year, Roger moved from Concord, New Hampshire, to Miami and then to Tucson. He took his aunt with him to each of his homes. Because his aunt, who qualified him as head of household, went with Roger to each of his homes and lived in them with him during the tax year, he was still able to qualify as head of household because the IRS says that you need not live in the same domicile during the tax year to qualify as head of household as long as the relative who qualifies you as head of household stays with you.

If your husband or wife died last year or the year before that, you may be able to figure your current tax using joint-return rates as a qualifying widow or widower. You must meet four tests:

1. You maintain your home for your child, adopted child, or stepchild for the entire year and pay more than half the costs of maintaining the household.
2. You are entitled to claim the child as a dependent.
3. In the year your spouse died, you could have filed a joint return.
4. You did not marry before the end of the current tax year.

You must be prepared to prove your claim to status as head of household or to status as qualifying widow or widower. You must be prepared to prove that you furnished more than half the support for a dependent and that you were the one who maintained the household. (Remember what we said earlier in the chapter about what constitutes household maintenance?) That means you must remember one of our basic rules: KEEP IMPECCABLE TAX RECORDS WITH DOCUMENTATION. We don't care if you keep your canceled checks and receipts in a cardboard shoebox or an ostrich leather file from Mark Cross; just remember to keep them!

In this chapter we have talked about marital status and how you should file to best advantage. Some of you may be divorced and now in the single state; some of you may be divorced and remarried. In either case, you will want to read the next chapter to learn about how you can manage divorce and alimony (if you are paying or receiving it) to the best of your tax-knowledge ability.

CHAPTER 6

Divorce, Alimony, and Child Support

Divorce ranks near the top of stress scales by psychiatrists. Moreover, the strain on finances exacerbates the stress of separating from a spouse. However, by astute arrangement of your divorce settlement and by keeping records (there we go again with the importance of keeping tabs on things by good record keeping), you may be able to garner a few tax deductions for yourself.

Legal fees and court costs for obtaining a divorce are nondeductible personal expenses. But legal fees paid for tax advice in connection with divorce are deductible. Legal fees to obtain alimony are also deductible for the spouse receiving it. How can you separate deductible charges from your lawyer on your divorce from nondeductible charges?

1. You may have a second law firm handle tax aspects of your divorce. This firm's fee would be separately stated to you.
2. The law firm handling your divorce might refer tax matters of the divorce to a separate department within the firm that specializes in taxation. The firm's bill would allocate the amount of fee that was attributable to the tax department.
3. If you use the same lawyer for both nontax and tax matters relating to your divorce,

have him allocate his fee between the tax advice and the nontax matters based on time he has spent on each, fees customarily charged for such services, and the results obtained in the divorce negotiations.

Legal fees for a spouse who is seeking to obtain or collect alimony are deductible. The rationale by the IRS: Alimony is declared as income by the recipient, and those legal fees to obtain or collect it are considered ordinary and necessary expenses for the production or collection of income. By the way, the tax code is not sexist. It recognizes that husbands as well as wives may receive alimony.

Alimony is deductible to the spouse giving it and taxable as income for the spouse receiving it. Though it may be difficult to discern at times, there is a basic logic to the tax laws referring to alimony. That basic logic goes something like this: Alimony payments are not a deduction in the usual sense, in that alimony is not an *itemized* deduction. It is a deduction taken off gross income. It is an adjustment to income that is subtracted from gross income on page 1 of your 1040. Previous to January 1, 1978, alimony payments were stated as itemized deductions. The result was that many who did not have enough other deductions to itemize lost out on tax relief for alimony payments by having to take the standard deduction. Now, because alimony is deducted from gross income, whether you have enough deductions to itemize or not, you will get to write off those alimony payments. The deductibility of alimony payments is a recognition of a reassignment of gross income. It is really an exclusion of income for the spouse paying it, and income to the spouse receiving it.

Alimony is paid periodically. If instead of alimony a spouse decides to give a single sum all at once—a lump-sum settlement—or even monies in a few installments, the income amount the wife receives is *not* considered as income to her. The money making up a lump sum will probably come from the spouse (let's for simplicity's sake call that spouse the husband and the other the wife)—the husband's savings or other assets—and will already have been included in his income and will already have been taxed by the federal government. If it were declared income to the wife, it would be subject to tax again. Because the federal government sees a lump sum as a division of accumulated assets, the lump-sum settlement is not regarded as income to her. Then, too, if the lump-sum settlement were viewed as income to the wife, she would have to pay a large tax because she is receiving a large amount of money in one year or in just a few years. However, if she received alimony payments—payments over a period of ten years or more—she is more likely to be getting income coming from her husband's yearly income. He will be able to deduct that income from his income, thereby reducing his income and tax liability. She will be paying a tax upon receiving it. Because payments are spread over a number of years, payments will be smaller, and therefore the tax burden will be easier for her to bear.

The alimony-paying spouse must be sure that he meets IRS requirements in order to take his deduction. There are four requirements:

1. Payments must be required under the decree of divorce or separation, or a written instrument incident to that decree.
2. Payments must be based on the marital or family relationship.
3. Payments must be paid after the decree.
4. Payments must be periodic.

If payments are made when there is no divorce (there is a legal separation, or the final decree of divorce is pending), alimony payments are deductible providing you do not file a joint return with your spouse for the year you are claiming the deduction.

Now that all sounds clear, except that rule No. 4—payments must be periodic—is misleading. The usual meaning of "periodic" is that something occurs at regular intervals, as do phases of the moon. The IRS has its own definition of the word "periodic" when it comes to tax laws concerning alimony.

According to IRS dictum, periodic payments are payments of a fixed amount (for example, $100 a month) for an indefinite period, or payments of an indefinite amount (for example, 10% of a fluctuating income) for either a fixed or an indefinite period. They need not be made at regular intervals.

The definition of "periodic" becomes easier if we break it up into examples.

Gordon Kyle obtains a divorce decree from his wife, Lorna. The divorce decree stipulates that he must pay her $400 a month for life. The payments are considered periodic. Gordon is paying a fixed amount, the $400 a month, for an indefinite period, Lorna's lifetime.

Donald Lynch obtains a divorce decree from his wife, Madeline. The divorce decree stipulates that he must pay her one third of his fluctuating yearly income for a period of six years. The payments are considered periodic. Donald is paying an indefinite amount, one third of his fluctuating yearly income, for a fixed period, six years.

Philip Manley obtains a divorce decree from his wife, Alice. The divorce decree stipulates that he must pay her one fourth of his fluctuating yearly income until Alice remarries. The payments are considered periodic. Philip is paying an indefinite amount, one fourth of his fluctuating yearly income, for an indefinite period, until Alice remarries. Note: In all the cases of periodic payments, payments need not be made at regular intervals, such as on the first of every month, to be considered periodic.

We said previously that lump-sum payments are not deductible to the spouse paying or taxable as income to the spouse receiving. The lump-sum rule is different, however, if that single amount is to be paid over a period of more than ten years in approximately equal amounts. How come? The rationale is that if the wife is paid over a period of more than ten years, the money is more likely to be coming from the husband's yearly income, and so tax liability is shared. Then, too, the tax on the smaller annual amount won't be so difficult for the wife to bear. The spouse making payments may deduct them, and the spouse receiving payments must include them in taxable income, as she would periodic payments. In any one year, the wife may never include in her income, nor the husband deduct from his, more than 10% of the principal sum.

Sam Matthews's divorce decree specified that he must pay his wife, Sara, $150,000 in installments of $20,000 a year for five years, and $5,000 a year for the following ten years. Sam may deduct only 10% of the $150,000, or $15,000, during each of the first five years. During the last ten years Sam may deduct the entire $5,000 paid each year because it is less than 10% of the $150,000 settlement.

The 10% of total settlement being deductible in one-year limitation applies to installment payments made in advance, but not to delinquent installment payments received during your spouse's tax year.

Kenneth Duane's divorce decree specifies that he must pay his wife, Gale, $200,000 in installments of $10,000 for twenty years. The third year after the decree, business was bad, and he made no payments. He could take no deduction for that year and, of course, Gale had no tax to pay on alimony payments. The next year business picked up and he paid Gale the back alimony plus what he owed for that year—total, $20,000. Kenneth deducted the $20,000 on that year's return, and Gale paid tax on the $20,000 received.

Paul Simon's divorce decree specified that he must pay his wife, Emily, $300,000 in installments of $20,000 for fifteen years. The second year after the divorce decree, Emily complained that she was deeply in debt because of expenses in furnishing her new "singles" apartment. Paul agreed to help her out by giving her $25,000 ($20,000 was for her second-year alimony, and the extra $5,000 was toward the third-year alimony). Paul later regretted what he had done when he found that he could deduct only $20,000 of the $25,000 in that tax year. The $5,000 he advanced Emily was not deductible at all. It was more than 10% of the total.

Your divorce decree or agreement might specify that you pay your spouse's medical and dental expenses. If so, you may deduct those expenses as alimony. Your spouse must include those medical and dental payments in declaring her gross income. However, if she itemizes deductions on her return, she may deduct those payments as medical expenses.

Your divorce decree may demand that you carry a life-insurance policy that is absolutely assigned to your former spouse and on which she is the irrevocable beneficiary. The premiums paid on that policy would be taxable income to your former spouse but deductible to you. On the other hand, if the policy is not assigned and you own the policy, it is not taxable income to your wife and not a deduction for you.

Suppose you have children for whom you give your wife child support. Is that deductible? The answer is "No." Neither are child-support payments considered taxable income for your wife. However, you might very well be concerned about which of you may claim the $1,000 exemption for your child. And if you have a number of children, you may be even more concerned about who gets the exemptions for the children, because that will amount to several thousand more in exemptions.

The basic rule on child support is that the parent who has custody of the child for more than half the year gets the exemption. However, if there is an agreement or decree that the other spouse will get the exemption, and that spouse pays more than $600 for each child's support, that spouse gets the exemption.

If the spouse not having custody and no exemption privilege in an agreement or decree provides at least

$1,200 support for each child, and the spouse having custody cannot prove that her expenses exceed that, the noncustodial spouse can claim the exemption. If you decided to take that route, be prepared to prove it. There very well may be a dispute between mother and father over who provided the greater amount of support. Mother and father will have to exchange itemized statements of support. This again is where you will have to be careful to save canceled checks and receipts to back up your claim. Attach your statement and your spouse's to your tax return in case the IRS decides to dispute your claim. In the case where a wife (or if it is a husband having custody) does not cooperate in sending you this statement, attach your statement anyway to your return. In that way, if the IRS disputes your claim, you will have a defense against negligence penalties that could be levied by the IRS.

The following is what your itemized statement should include:

1. The name of the child being claimed as dependent; the names of both parents, their addresses and Social Security numbers.
2. The number of months the child lived in each parent's home or the home of person other than parent during the year.
3. If the child owned taxable income, state how much.
4. The total amount of support furnished the child, including amounts furnished by persons other than the parents.
5. Specified amounts spent during the year by you. They should be for items that constitute support, which are: food, shelter, clothing, medical and dental care, education, recreation, and transportation.

What if you are a grandparent who has custody of your grandchild? Would you get the exemption for your grandchild? The IRS rule is that when someone other than either parent has custody of the child, the $600 or $1,200 tests do not apply. Rather, the person who provides more than 50% of the child's support gets the exemption. So if you are providing more than 50% as well as having custody, you get the exemption. If you have custody, but the father provides more than 50% of the child's support, he gets the exemption; and if it is the mother providing more than 50% of the child's support, she gets the exemption.

If a third party contributing to the support of the child is the new spouse of the mother or father (the child's stepparent), that stepparent's contribution is treated as a contribution by the parent he is married to.

Charles and Rita are divorced. Their child Maria lives with Rita. Rita remarries to Sam. Maria's support totaled $3,000 per year. Her father, Charles, contributed $1,350; Rita contributed $1,000; and Sam, the new stepfather, $650. Charles does not get the exemption for his child. It goes to Rita, because her contribution is combined with her new husband's, which together total more than Charles's.

You see, the IRS does allow tax savings on your children. For information on how the IRS will allow further savings, read the next chapter.

CHAPTER 7

Your Children and Your Exemptions and Deductions

You may have convinced yourself that it is as cheap for two to live as one, but when baby makes three, the costs of your living take a steep climb—up. You may find some relief from the government not in the form of family bonuses, as in some European countries, but with some concessions on your tax return.

First off, the federal government gives a $1,000 exemption for each child. Even if your child is born on December 31, you are entitled to a tax exemption for the entire year. Your child may be an adopted child, a stepchild, a child placed in your household by an authorized adoption agency pending final adoption, or a foster child, providing he lived with you for the entire year. You must contribute more than one half of the support for the child. To enable you to take the exemption, your child's gross income must be less than $1,000, except if he is nineteen years or younger or is a full-time student.

What does the IRS mean by "full-time student"? The rules say that the child must attend school for five months during the tax year. Night school does not qualify. However, if the child is taking some courses at night in conjunction with other full-time courses, he qualifies as a dependent. Correspondence schools do not qualify as educational institutions so far as the IRS is concerned. If your child is learning to be an electrician via a mail-order course, unless he is under nineteen, there is no exemption.

If your child is married and files a joint return with his spouse, you will get no exemption even if you contributed to his support. One exception: If the married children file a joint return for the sole purpose of receiving a refund, you may still take your child as an exemption.

Julius Hagen contributed over half to the support of his daughter Eileen. Eileen was married and a student at college. She and her husband, Eric, had summer jobs. They earned less than $2,500 each. They filed separate returns. Because they filed separately, Julius was still able to take Eileen as a dependent on his return and claim an exemption of $1,000 on her.

Suppose your child is given a scholarship. Are you still entitled to an exemption? If it is for study in an educational institution and if the scholarship is not contingent on the child's working for the institution and if you are still providing more than one half of his support, the IRS says you can still take him as a dependent.

Howard Irving had a son and daughter. His son was an intern at a general hospital. His daughter was in nurses' training at the same hospital and received room and board. Howard took both children as his dependents. The IRS said he could not take his intern son. Interns are considered employees of a hospital, not students—even though they are getting training. The IRS did allow a deduction for Howard's daughter. She was considered to be a student at the hospital's nurses' training school.

In the previous chapter, we discussed what constituted support of a child, according to IRS regulations. Usually, support items are: food, clothing, shelter, medical and dental care, education, recreation, and transportation. However, sometimes the IRS can dispute your claim on some of those items even if you did pay for them. Take transportation, for instance.

Automobile expenses for transporting your child to dancing lessons might be considered support. Transporting the child to and from your home while exercising visitation rights might not be. On the other hand, the IRS was very munificent with the transportation item in calculating support for one taxpayer. He had paid $4,000 for a car for his son, who was in the custody of his former wife. His wife claimed support and the exemption for the boy. The father countered with the $4,000 car item, which he said was ordinary for a boy in his son's milieu. With the car included, the father's total support was greater than that claimed by the mother. The IRS allowed the car purchase as a support item, and the father got the exemption.

On the other hand, one taxpayer who bought a boat for his teen-ager was not permitted to use it as a support item. The IRS did not consider a boat necessary for a child's support. Expenditures made on behalf of the child and considered support items by the IRS have included: baby-sitters, TV sets, music and drama lessons, school supplies, school lunches and extra milk, parochial school tuition, toys, bicycle repairs, summer camp, swimming pool fees, haircuts, vitamins, and the child's wedding apparel and accessories, wedding reception, and flowers for the wedding party, church, and reception.

Spurred on by the women's liberation movement, child-care credit is another concession the government has given to families. Child-care credit enables parents to take as a tax credit 20% of the expenses paid for a dependent under fifteen years of age if the payments were necessary to enable the taxpayer to work. One parent may be working full time and the other may be working part time or be a full-time student, or both parents may be working part time or one spouse may be incapacitated. The 20% credit is based on a maximum of $2,000 of care expenses for one child or $4,000 for two or more children. Married couples must file jointly, and the children must be dependents. (The one case where a parent may take the child-care credit even if the child cannot be counted for exemption as a dependent is when the parent has custody of the child for more than half the year.) The 20% credit for one child, therefore, could amount to $400 (20% of $2,000), or $800 for two or more children (20% of $4,000).

Of course, the IRS is not going to let you make a profit on this child-care credit by your holding down a part-time job for three hours a week at three dollars an hour and having a housekeeper take care of your child while you indulge yourself shopping the department stores the rest of the time while your housekeeper is taking care of the child. The IRS says you cannot deduct more in expenses than what you are making or, if you are filing a joint return, you cannot deduct more than what the spouse who is making the lesser amount of money is making. So it would work this way: Even if the husband is making $30,000 a year and the wife is making $600 a year on her little part-time job, they cannot deduct the $400 for that full-time maid who is getting $5,200 a year. That couple would have to figure 20% of the wage of the spouse making the lesser amount—in this case, $600. The result is a $120 child-care credit (20% of $600 equals $120).

If the situation is reversed and the wife is making the $30,000 and the husband is working part time, the tax credit would be figured in the same way. The IRS does not discriminate when it comes to gender.

In the case of a spouse who is a student, to be able to take the child-care credit, the spouse must be a full-time student. Simply taking a pottery course in someone's basement four hours a week will not qualify. By "full-time student" the IRS means that the spouse must be attending a qualified educational institution full time for five months of the year (though they need not be five consecutive months). Some of the courses may be taken in the evening as part of a full-time program, but attendance at night school will not make it. It might pay for a spouse to switch from a night course to a full-time day course to get the child-care credit, especially if it qualifies the spouse for her degree earlier and gets her in the work force and earning income in shorter time.

The IRS puts a figure of $166 a month equivalent earnings for the spouse who is a full-time student if there is one child, and $333 a month if there are two or more children. The same figure of $166 a month equivalent earnings for an incapacitated spouse for one child and $333 a month for two or more children is allocated by the IRS.

Your wife breaks both legs in a skiing accident and is confined to bed and then a wheelchair for nine months. You have two preschoolers. Obviously, your wife is in no condition to cook and clean for them, to say nothing of running after them to see what they are up to. You must hire a housekeeper for the nine months your wife is incapacitated. The IRS considers your incapacitated wife to be earning $333 per month (the earnings figure put on the spouse who is incapable of child care in determining child-care credit for two or more children). Your wife is given a figure earning of $2,997 by the IRS for the nine months (9 times $333).

Supposing you are in this situation. You are a woman with custody of your two children. You share a home with another divorced mother, who has custody of her three children. You are both employed full time. You have hired a housekeeper to take care of cleaning and to look after the five children. The housekeeper gets $6,000 per year. You pay one third and the other mother pays two thirds. One third of $6,000 is $2,000— your share. You are permitted to deduct 20% for child-care credit. That gives you a deduction of $400. She deducts 20% of her share for child-care credit, too, or $800.

Even if you employ a relative to take care of your child, you may claim the child-care credit providing the relative is not a dependent, such as in the case of an older child taking care of a younger child. Previous to 1978, that relative's payments had to be subject to Social Security contributions. However, now you may employ your parents, sister, aunt, niece, or nephew without making Social Security contributions for them.

Baby-sitting expenses may count for child-care credit even if they are performed outside the home. If you are sending your child to boarding school so that you may work, that part of the payment to the school that may be considered child care would count in determining your child-care credit. You would first make an allocation between tuition costs and child-care costs.

Sally Reynolds is a widow with a fourteen-year-old son, Marc. She was working as an assistant buyer for a Houston department store when she was told that she was being promoted to buyer. As a buyer, she would be required to jet to Europe on buying trips several times a year. Marc, too old for a baby-sitter, was also too young to leave at home alone. Sally decided to send Marc away to boarding school. The cost for the year was $6,000. Because Marc was still under fifteen and still could qualify Sally for child-care credit, she had the school in a letter break down its costs into an allotment for tuition and an allotment for Marc's care. The school estimated tuition as being $2,500, $2,000 for room and board, and the rest of the school's fee, $500, as child care. Sally kept the school's letter in her tax files, and although she could only deduct the maximum of $400 for child-care credit for one child on her tax return, she figured that was $400 in her pocket!

Though meals provided are not part of child-care costs for older children, on the other hand, if you have a child attending nursery school so that you as a parent are able to work, there is no need to make allocations even though meals may be included in the costs. Meals in nursery school may be considered in with child care. You can take 20% of that nursery school tuition up to $2,000 for one child ($400); 20% of up to $4,000 ($800) for two or more children.

Did you know that there are tax benefits in hiring your own child? We don't mean for doing household chores, but if you perform a service or are in business, hiring your child can give you tax benefits. If he is old enough, he may work for you during school vacations and after school. You pay him what you would reasonably pay anyone else in the same job. You deduct the cost of his employment on your Schedule C return (self-employment return). Even if your child makes more than the $3,300 amount, which means he will have to file a tax return, he will be taxed in a lower bracket than yours. If he is under nineteen or a full-time student, he can use what he is making to help support himself without your losing him as a dependent!

If your child works for you or for someone else, he will have to file a return if his gross income is $3,300 or more. He may be a minor, but his income is not included on your tax return. He must file his own return, and you as his parent or guardian are responsible for the filing and for any tax that may be due on his return. You should inform your child that even if he does not have to pay taxes, if he is due a refund he must file a return to receive it.

One of the biggest expenses you will have in your lifetime is your children's college education. It's roughly $6,000 a year now for an out-of-town college. That's $24,000 for a total of four years before your child gets his degree! How are you ever going to afford it? Here's a way that can make it possible while you save on taxes.

Set up a trust fund for your child. If you can set it up by the time he is seven years old, so much the better. Each year you put part of your savings into the trust; as long as the trust money is not used for support of the child, it is taxed at a lower rate. If it is a ten-year trust, the money will be there when he is ready for college. It is important not to state on the trust that the trust is aimed at paying for your child's college education. Why not? Because in some states, if you are in an income bracket that supposedly can afford it, you are obligated to provide your child with a college education as part of his support. As we said before, the trust money is taxable at a lower rate only if it is not used for the support of your child. Just to be safe, the trust should end before the child starts college, and then he can withdraw the money from the bank or cash in the bonds you have bought in trust for him and pay the college expenses himself. If in your state children are no longer considered minors at eighteen and are considered emancipated and responsible for their own support, you do not have to worry about the breakup of the trust then.

The Uniform Gift to Minors Act also enables you to siphon off income to your children tax free. This is how it works. You are permitted, if filing a single return, to gift each child with $3,000 per year. If you file a joint return with your spouse and have her consent, you can make that double—$6,000. Your gift does not even go onto your tax return. If you are a grandparent, you may also take advantage of the Uniform Gift to Minors Act. If you have several grandchildren, you will have the satisfaction of passing on money to them without its being subjected to estate taxes after you die. There is no limit as to how many children you may give the $3,000 per year to, so that if you have eleven grandchildren and $33,000 a year ($3,000 times 11) to spare, you do not have to worry about slighting any of them. You can take care of all of them. If you file a joint return with your wife, you can give each grandchild $6,000!

Suppose you say, "Yes, I will avoid paying tax on that income of gift money, but suppose my child 'blows' that money on foolish expenditures instead of a college education, or for starting up a business, or for whatever purpose I have in mind for him?" All we can say is that you have to chance that. If you have faith that you brought up that child to have some sense, keep the faith!

Did you know that your child may be able to set up a mini-Keogh with perhaps a little help from you?

A mini-Keogh is for the self-employed person whose earnings are low. He may put into the mini-Keogh

100% of his yearly earnings or $750, whichever is less. Not only can the amount be deducted from gross income on his tax return, but the mini-Keogh also allows one to accumulate tax-free dividends, interest, and capital gains.

Many youngsters are earning substantial amounts of money today with newspaper routes, cutting grass, working as lifeguards, removing snow, baby-sitting, etc. At college they often find even better-paying freelance jobs. Now, Keogh monies cannot be withdrawn until age 59½ without substantial penalties, and many young people may not have the patience to wait until then. However, here is a gimmick to solve that problem: You, the parent(s) or grandparent(s), can reimburse the child for the money he deposits in his Keogh account. There is nothing in the law that prevents you from doing that. (Of course, if your child is earning a great deal of money, he might want to go to a regular Keogh, which allows 15% of yearly income up to $7,500, whichever is less, to be deposited in the account. The amount would be deducted on your child's 1040.)

If you can afford to give the child the monies for his Keogh, you will be providing for his retirement, thereby reducing the amount of money he will have to set aside as an adult. In addition, the Keogh plan is a partial substitute for life insurance; if the Keogh holder dies, the money goes to the spouse and children at advantageous rates.

Here's an example of how a Keogh tax-free accumulation of dividends, interest, and capital gains would grow over many years.

Your child, a real hustler, earns $2,000 a year during high school. At college he earns more—$4,000 a year for four years. You decide you can afford to give him the equivalent of 15% for a Keogh. That is a total of $1,200 in high school years and $2,400 in college years, or $3,600 in all. His Keogh plan might conceivably grow to $5,000 at age twenty-two when he graduates from college. His Keogh money is invested at, say,

9%. Compounded at 9%, money doubles in eight years. If he had $5,000 in the plan at age twenty-two, the sum would grow to $10,000 at age thirty; $20,000 at age thirty-eight; $40,000 at age forty-six; $80,000 at age fifty-four. If he wanted to retire at age sixty-two, he would have $160,000 from that original $5,000.

You may also be helping a parent keep his head above water. The next chapter tells how you can reduce your taxes if you are contributing to your mother or father's support.

CHAPTER 8

Your Parents
and Exemptions
and Deductions

What with advances in medical science and nutrition, people are living longer these days. Whereas in our day it was highly unusual to have known all four grandparents, it is not unusual today, and many children even have great-grandparents whose laps they crawl into.

Longer life-spans would be cause for rejoicing if along with that went assurances of income that would keep up with living costs. Unfortunately, that is not the case. Social Security, which was conceived as a partial means of support for the elderly, has not been able to keep pace with inflation. Inflation has even diminished hard-earned pension dollars and savings of the elderly.

More and more, younger people will have to help out in the supporting of their parents to assure them a decent standard of living. They have been good to us in the past, and now we want to be good to them. However with our own children to take care of, it can be rough on the pocketbook. If there is any way we can contribute to the support of parents and get tax deductions, we certainly want to know about it. We cannot afford to overlook those deductions.

Not only your mother and father, but also your mother-in-law or father-in-law, may qualify as your dependent. You may claim your mother-in-law and father-in-law as dependents if you are still supporting them, even after death of or divorce from your spouse. After death of or divorce from your spouse, because you are now single, you may file under the Head of Household category, which we have discussed in a previous chapter. It gives you an advantage on the tax-computation table. Of course, if you never married and you are supporting one parent or two parents, you are also entitled to status as head of household.

Your dependent parent qualifies you for a $1,000 exemption on your tax return. Even if a parent dies during the year, if you had provided more than half support for him during the part of the year he was alive, you are entitled to the whole $1,000 exemption.

Randy Halpern's mother died on February 5. Randy had paid her rent and given her an allowance for food and clothing and paid her medical bills. What he gave to her was substantially more than what she contributed to her own support from her meager savings and what she received from Social Security. Though his mother did not live out the whole year, Randy may claim a $1,000 exemption for the whole year on his return.

For you to take the $1,000 exemption for a parent or parents, they must meet the following four tests:

1. Support test.
2. Gross-income test.
3. Relationship test.
4. Citizenship or residency test.

Let's take those four tests one by one. First, the support test. If your parent has no income from any sources outside of minimum Social Security payments, which almost everyone is entitled to, and you were the sole provider of support, you clearly have contributed more than half to your parent's support and don't have to concern yourself further about meeting the support test.

To determine whether you meet the support test—by providing more than 50% to your parent's total support—calculate first how much money was spent during the year for your parent's total support from all sources, including from your parent's own funds. Then calculate how much you spent for your parent's support. If that amount is more than 50%, you get the exemption.

The total cost, not the period of time you contributed payments, is crucial as to whether you provided more than 50% of support.

Clara Winslow sent her widowed mother, who had no means of support, $200 a month starting in January. Clara had sent her $2,000 by October, when her mother incurred some medical bills that Clara could not afford to cover. She asked her brother Jerry to take over contributing to Mother. Jerry sent Mother $3,000 during November and December. Who got to take Mother as a dependent? Jerry. Though Clara sent her mother support money over a period of ten months and Jerry provided support only the last two months of the year, the amount he contributed—$3,000—was more than half of the total support of $5,000 that both he and Clara sent.

What if several children are supporting your parent? You have sisters and brothers who help. Who then gets to take the $1,000 exemption when none of you individually meets the more-than-50% support test? Not one of you, unless you file a Multiple Support Declaration (Form 2120).

Multiple Support Declarations are just for such cases, wherein two or more children are supporting a parent. Together they must be providing more than 50% support, though each one may or may not be contributing equal amounts. The children agree that one of them will get the exemption. The child who is designated to get the exemption for a particular tax year files the Multiple Support Declaration with his tax return. The other children must sign the part of the declaration that states they are not claiming an exemption for the parent they are helping to support. One stipulation for the child who files the Multiple Support Declaration: That child must have contributed more than 10% to the support of the parent for the tax year.

Alan Maxwell gives 45% to the support of his mother in one tax year. His brother Gordon contributes 35%. Their sister Kay gives 10%, and their sister Kim gives another 10%. They all agree that Alan will file the Multiple Support Declaration for that year. Gordon will file a written statement that he will not claim the exemption for their mother. Neither of the sisters can claim the exemption because they do not contribute *more than* 10%. Because they do not contribute more than 10%, they do not have to file a disclaimer of support either.

Children can take turns claiming the exemption. The only stipulation is that the child filing the Multiple Support Declaration and claiming the exemption must have contributed more than 10% of the more than 50% support given by the children to the parent's support.

We have used the term "support" a great deal. You might have your idea of what it means, but what is the IRS's definition of support? Before determining whether you provided more than half the support for a parent, you must know what constitutes *total* support.

Total support is the sum of:

1. The fair rental value of housing for the dependent. Housing could be the room, apartment, or house in which the dependent lives. It includes a reasonable estimate for furnishings, heat, and other utilities. An easy way to estimate fair rental value is to figure the amount you could reasonably expect to receive from a stranger for the same type of housing.

2. All items of expenses paid or incurred directly by or for the dependent. This includes clothing, recreation, transportation (this might include your buying a car for your dependent or paying maintenance costs of a car

he or she owns), appliances, and TV sets. It also includes medical costs. However, basic Medicare benefits are considered to be support that your parent provides himself or herself; you must attribute basic Medicare benefits to your parent's contribution when you calculate total support. On the other hand, if you contribute *supplementary* Medicare benefits, you may total those amounts as your share of total support.

3. Total support includes a proportionate share of expenses that cannot be attributed directly to a particular individual, such as cost of food for the entire household. To determine cost of food you furnish a dependent parent, first calculate cost of food for the entire household, then divide by the number of members of the household. Example: You spend $5,000 per year for food for you, your spouse, two children, and your mother. Dividing $5,000 by 5, the number in your household, you get $1,000—the amount you may attribute to the cost of feeding your mother.

Do you recall several pages back our mentioning the gross-income test you must meet in order to take the $1,000 exemption for a parent? That means that no matter how much you contribute to the support of your parent, if she or he has more than $1,000 in income in the form of money, property, and services that is not exempt from tax, you cannot take your parent as a dependent.

You spent $5,000 to support your mother this year. She received $3,000 in Social Security payments. She had no other income at all. Does that mean you don't get an exemption for her? No. Because Social Security payments are exempt from tax, you pass the gross-income test. Other income your parent might have coming that is exempt from tax might be:

Accident and health insurance proceeds

"Black lung" benefits

Disability payments

Federal Employees' Compensation Act payments

Gifts, bequests, or inheritances

Life insurance proceeds

Payments to beneficiary of deceased employee

Railroad Retirement Act pensions

Railroad Retirement Act lump-sum payments

Tax-exempt interest

Veteran's benefits

Workmen's compensation

Welfare benefits

Important: Though the foregoing constitute tax-exempt income, it is still counted as support that your parent provides for himself or herself out of his or her total support. Take this case, for instance.

Kitty Reilly's widowed mother receives $2,500 in Social Security benefits. Kitty gives her mother $2,000 in additional monies. Total support of Mother is $4,500. The Social Security income is counted as support Kitty's mother provides for herself. Kitty's $2,000 does not come to more than 50% of her mother's total support. Kitty does not get to take her as a dependent.

Suppose Kitty contributed $3,000 to her mother's support to supplement the Social Security benefits. Would Kitty be able to take her mother as a dependent? Yes. Though her mother is collecting Social Security of more than $1,000, Kitty passes the gross-income test because Social Security is not taxable income. Kitty's contribution is more than half of Mother's total support of $5,500.

There are cases we have come across wherein a parent collecting Social Security payments is totally supported by a child. The parent banks the Social Security payments, building up an estate. The child is able to take the parent as a dependent; the child has provided total support. The parent is not obligated by law to use the Social Security payments for his own support.

The support test can get complicated because there are variations. To help make it clearer, we will illustrate with a number of cases.

Case of Parent Living with Children. Sophie Slater, mother of Connie Stearns, lives with Connie and her husband, Elliot, and their two children. Sophie receives a survivor's annuity of $1,500, which she spends for clothing and recreation. Only $500 of this annuity represents gross income to Sophie; the rest is excluded from her income as a recovery of cost. Elliot paid total food expenses for the entire household for the year—$3,000. He paid Sophie's medical and drug expenses of $275. The fair rental value of the room furnished Sophie is, the Stearnses figure, $960 per year (the amount they estimate they could get if they were to rent the room to a stranger). Sophie's total support is computed as follows:

Fair rental value of room		$ 960
Direct expenses paid by Sophie	$1,500	
Direct expenses paid by Elliot (medical)	275	1,775
Pro rata share of food (⅕ of $3,000)		600
Total support		$3,335

Since the support Elliot furnishes ($960 for room plus $275 for medical expenses plus $600 for food equals $1,835) is more than half of the $3,335 total support and Sophie has less than $1,000 gross income, Elliot may claim Sophie as a dependent.

Case of Two Parents Living with Children. Barney and Stella Evans lived with Andrew Evans, his wife, Audrey, and their two children in a house that Andrew and Audrey rented. Andrew figured that his parents' room was worth $2,000 per year in support. His father received a nontaxable pension of $3,200, which he spent equally for himself and Andrew's mother on clothing and recreation. Andrew's total food expense for the household is $3,000; Andrew's heat and utility bills amount to $1,200. His mother had hospital and medical expenses of $600, which Andrew paid during the year. Andrew computed his parents' total support this way:

	Support Furnished	
	FATHER	MOTHER
Fair rental value of room	$1,000	$1,000
Pension spent for their support	1,600	1,600
Pro rata share of food (⅙ of $3,000)	500	500
Medical expenses for mother		600
Parents' total support	$3,100	$3,700

Andrew furnished $1,500 ($1,000 room, $500 food) of his father's total support of $3,100—less than half. Andrew furnished his mother $2,100 ($1,000 room, $500 food, $600 medical)—more than half of her total support of $3,700. Andrew may claim his mother as a dependent, but not his father. Heat and utilities costs were included in determining the fair rental value of their quarters and are not considered separately.

Case of Parents Not Living with You, but You Pay Part of Housing Costs. Eric VanDusen's parents live rent free in a house Eric owns. It has a fair rental value of $2,400 a year unfurnished and $3,600 furnished, not including heat and utilities. The house is completely furnished with furniture and appliances belonging to Eric's parents. Eric's father receives nontaxable pension payments of $1,000, which he spends equally for himself and Eric's mother. Eric pays $900 for their groceries and $600 for their utilities. Utilities are not customarily furnished in rented houses in the area where Eric's parents live. Therefore, Eric considers the total fair rental value of the house as $4,200 ($2,400 for rental value of unfurnished house; $600 cost of utilities; $1,200 allowance for furniture provided by parents). Total support of Eric's parents is computed as follows:

Fair rental value of house	$4,200
Expenses paid by father	1,000
Food furnished by Eric	900
Parents' total support	$6,100

The $3,900 support Eric gives ($2,400 for the fair rental value of the house plus $600 for the cost of utilities equal $3,000 housing plus $900 food) is more than half the $6,100 total support, so Eric may claim both parents as dependents to the tune of $2,000.

Another Case of Parent Not Living with Child, but Child Providing Housing Costs. Betsy Billings helps support both her parents. Her case is similar to Eric's except that she spends $550 for her father's clothing and does not give them food money. Her mother buys $900 worth of food with savings. The total support of Betsy's parents is:

	Support Furnished		
	FATHER	MOTHER	TOTAL
Fair rental value of housing	$2,100	$2,100	$4,200
Expenses paid by father	500	500	1,000
Father's clothing	550		550
Food bought by mother	450	450	900
Total	$3,600	$3,050	$6,650

The $3,550 support Betsy gives ($3,000 for housing plus $550 for clothing) is more than half the $6,650 total support of her parents. However, the IRS says the dependency status of each dependent must be determined separately. In figuring the amount of support Betsy gives each, she must divide the contribution for their mutual benefit between them. Therefore, the amount she gives her mother, $1,500 (one half of the $3,000 housing), is less than half of her mother's total support of $3,050. Betsy may not claim her mother as her dependent. However, she does furnish more than one half the support for her father ($1,500 for housing plus $550 for clothing) and therefore gets a $1,000 exemption for Dad.

Case of Dependent Living in Own Home. Keith Parkerson contributes $2,000 to the support of his father. His father lives alone in a house he himself owns. It has a fair rental value of $4,500 a year, including an allowance for furniture and appliances and utilities. Keith's father spends $1,500 of his savings for taxes, utilities, and upkeep of his home. His total support is $6,500 ($2,000 plus $4,500). Keith's contribution of $2,000 is less than half his father's total support, so Keith cannot claim his father as a dependent. The $1,500 that his father spends for taxes, utilities, and upkeep on his home is not considered separately, since it is spent on items included in determining fair rental value. The total fair rental value of Keith's father's home is considered as support he himself contributes for himself.

Case of Parent Living in Own Home That Child Helps to Maintain. Fred Cooper contributes $2,000 cash to his father's support during the year, when he lives in his own home, which has a fair rental value of $2,400 a year. He uses $500 of the money Fred gives him to help pay his real estate taxes. His total support is computed as follows:

Cash contributed by Fred	$2,000
Fair rental value of house contributed by father to his own support, $2,400 reduced by $500 for taxes	1,900
Father's total support	**$3,900**

Since Fred contributed more than half to his father's support, Fred may claim him as a dependent. If Fred lived with his dependent father rent free in his father's home, the amount of Fred's contribution to his father's support would be offset by the fair rental value of lodging furnished him.

We have covered three of the four tests for you to meet to take a parent or parents as dependent: support test, gross-income test, and relationship test. The last test is the citizenship test, which requires that your parent or parents must be a citizen or resident of the United States, including Puerto Rico, or of Canada or Mexico, in order for you to take an exemption for them. Even if you send your mother an allowance that covers all her needs, if she is not a U.S. citizen and lives, say, in Italy, you cannot claim that $1,000 exemption. However, if you bring your mother to the United States and she has lived here for at least one year, she would be considered a resident.

Often a child misses getting the exemption for a parent because the child is just a few dollars shy of that more than one-half total support. Figure your parent's support well ahead of the end of the year. If you are short of the more than one-half support, it may very well pay for you to increase your parent's allowance, or to gift your parent with a television set if that brings you up to more than one half of the parent's support. One hundred or two hundred dollars more, say, toward your parent's support will produce a $1,000 exemption for you.

It may be necessary to put your parent in a nursing home. If you are contributing more than one half the cost of what it costs the nursing home to keep your parent (and possibly you are also picking up extras such as special nursing and special drugs), you are entitled to the $1,000 exemption.

Furthermore, the courts have recently ruled that if you are single and contributing more than one half to the support of a parent in a nursing home, you may file as head of household just as if you were supporting your parent in your home or in his or her own home. As we have said before, filing as head of household rather than as a single person will give you a substantial reduction in the tax-table rates.

The next chapter will discuss the possibility of taking a medical deduction for your parents as well as for yourself and the rest of your family.

Form **2120** (Rev. Oct. 1980)	Department of the Treasury—Internal Revenue Service **Multiple Support Declaration**	For instructions see other side.

During the calendar year 19 ..... , I paid more than 10% of the support of

.. ..
(Name of person)

I could have claimed this person as a dependent except that I did not pay more than 50% of his or her support.

I understand that this person is being claimed as a dependent on the income tax return of

(Name)

(Address)
, and

I agree not to claim an exemption for this person on my Federal income tax return for any tax year beginning in this calendar year.

(Signature)   (Social security number)

(Date)   (Address)

CHAPTER 9

Deductions and Your Health and Physical Maintenance

There's no enjoying the world without good health. Who can put a price on it? You can—on your tax return. The government realizes that everyone gets sick once in a while, and everyone—well, almost everyone— buys Band-Aids and toothpaste. Those are everyday expenditures and not deductible, but when it comes to the point where health and physical-maintenance costs are so expensive as to become a hardship, the government feels the taxpayer needs relief. That is why it has allowed the medical deduction.

Medical expenses are usually deductible in the year in which they are paid. The government has a complicated calculation for helping you arrive at your deduction. Basically, it is this: Medical expenses are deductible only to the extent that they exceed 3% of your adjusted gross income. However, even if you have no medical bills or don't have bills that exceed 3% of your adjusted gross income, you can still deduct one half of your medical insurance up to $150.

You say that your employer takes care of all your medical insurance premiums? You may be overlooking "hidden" medical insurance premiums that you pay. If you have homeowner's insurance or auto insurance, is medical insurance included in those policies? If there is no allocation of costs in your premium for the medical insurance parts of those policies, ask your insurance agent to make an allocation for you so that you may include it in your possible deduction of one half of your medical insurance up to $150. Also, if you have a child going to a school or camp and the health insurance fee is stated separately from other costs, add that fee to the rest of the family's health insurance.

If you are collecting Social Security payments, don't forget to include Medicare insurance, which is part of your Social Security payments.

. If there is a balance left on your medical insurance, it can be added in with your medical, subject to the 3% qualification. Medical expenses also include drugs and medicines that exceed 1% of adjusted gross income. If the total cost of drugs and medicines is 1% or less of adjusted gross income, it does not count as part of your medical deduction.

Joan and Arthur Harper paid the following medical expenses during the year:

$195.60 for hospitalization insurance

$80.40 for medical and surgical insurance

$125.00 for medicines and drugs

$240.35 for hospital bills

$39.00 for doctor bills for themselves.

In addition, they paid $200 for doctors and $75 for medicines and drugs for Sylvia Kramer, Joan's mother, who is their dependent. Arthur's young sister, Eileen Harper, is also a dependent. She had doctor bills of $350, and $100 in bills for medicines. The hospital and doctor bills paid are after reimbursements from the Harpers' insurance. Their adjusted gross income is $21,030.30.

This is how Joan and Arthur computed their medical-expense deduction:

Insurance

Hospitalization	$ 195.60	
Medical and surgical	80.40	
Total insurance	$ 276.00	

Insurance deductible

Outright (½ of $276)	$138.00

Medicine and drugs

Joan and Arthur Harper	$ 125.00
Sylvia Kramer (mother)	75.00
Eileen Harper (sister)	100.00
	$ 300.00
Less 1% exclusion	210.30
	$ 89.70

Balance of insurance | $ 138.00 |

Other medical and dental

Joan and Arthur Harper (doctors)	$ 39.00	
Sylvia Kramer (mother—doctors)	200.00	
Eileen Harper (sister—doctors)	350.00	
Joan and Arthur Harper (hospitals)	240.35	
	$1,057.05	
Less 3% exclusion	630.91	426.14
Total amount deductible		$564.14

This is how the Harpers filled out their medical and dental expenses:

Schedules A&B
(Form 1040)

Itemized Deductions AND Interest and Dividend Income

Department of the Treasury
Internal Revenue Service

▶ Attach to Form 1040.   ▶ See Instructions for Schedules A and B (Form 1040).

1980
08

Name(s) as shown on Form 1040   Arthur and Joan Harper

Your social security number   516 | 04 | 1492

Schedule A—Itemized Deductions (Schedule B is on back)

Medical and Dental Expenses (not paid or reimbursed by insurance or otherwise) (See page 16 of Instructions.)

1 One-half (but not more than $150) of insurance premiums you paid for medical care. (Be sure to include in line 10 below.) ▶	138	00
2 Medicine and drugs	300	00
3 Enter 1% of Form 1040, line 31	210	30
4 Subtract line 3 from line 2. If line 3 is more than line 2, enter zero	89	70
5 Balance of insurance premiums for medical care not entered on line 1	138	00
6 Other medical and dental expenses:		
a Doctors, dentists, nurses, etc.	589	00
b Hospitals	240	35
c Other (itemize—include hearing aids, dentures, eyeglasses, transportation, etc.) ▶		
7 Total (add lines 4 through 6c)	1057	05
8 Enter 3% of Form 1040, line 31	630	91
9 Subtract line 8 from line 7. If line 8 is more than line 7, enter zero	426	14
10 Total medical and dental expenses (add lines 1 and 9). Enter here and on line 23 ▶	564	14

Taxes (See page 17 of Instructions.)
Note: Gasoline taxes are no longer deductible.

11 State and local income		
12 Real estate		
13 General sales (see sales tax tables)		
14 Personal property		
15 Other (itemize) ▶		
16 Total taxes (add lines 11 through 15). Enter here and on line 34 ▶		

Interest Expense (See page 17 of Instructions.)

17 Home mortgage		
18 Credit and charge cards		
19 Other (itemize) ▶		
20 Total interest expense (add lines 17 through 19). Enter here and on line 35 ▶		

Contributions (See page 17 of Instructions.)

21 a Cash contributions for which you have receipts or cancelled checks		
b Other cash contributions (show to whom you gave and how much you gave) ▶		
22 Other than cash (see page 17 of Instructions for required statement)		
23 Carryover from prior years		
24 Total contributions (add lines 21a through 23). Enter here and on line 36 ▶		

Casualty and Theft Losses (See page 18 of Instructions.)

25 Loss before insurance reimbursement		
26 Insurance reimbursement		
27 Subtract line 26 from line 25. If line 26 is more than line 25, enter zero		
28 Enter $100 or amount from line 27, whichever is smaller		
29 Total casualty or theft loss(es) (subtract line 28 from line 27). Enter here and on line 37 ▶		

Miscellaneous Deductions (See page 18 of Instructions.)

30 Union dues		
31 Other (itemize) ▶		
32 Total miscellaneous deductions (add lines 30 and 31). Enter here and on line 38 ▶		

Summary of Itemized Deductions (See page 19 of Instructions.)   A

33 Total medical and dental—from line 10		
34 Total taxes—from line 16		
35 Total interest—from line 20		
36 Total contributions—from line 24		
37 Total casualty or theft loss(es)—from line 29		
38 Total miscellaneous—from line 32		
39 Add lines 33 through 38		
40 If you checked Form 1040, Filing Status box: 2 or 5, enter $3,400; 1 or 4, enter $2,300; 3, enter $1,700		
41 Subtract line 40 from line 39. Enter here and on Form 1040, line 33. (If line 40 is more than line 39, see the Instructions for line 41 on page 19.) ▶		

What are the requirements for an allowance on a medical expense? Basic rule: Qualifying expenses are those that are incurred *primarily* for the prevention or alleviation of a physical or mental defect or illness. Not included in this definition are expenses that benefit the general health of an individual—so even though tennis lessons are helping to keep you fit and that trip to Aruba last winter meant fewer colds, the costs of those are not deductible. They come under the heading of expenses that benefited your general health. Not deductible.

What comes under the 1% of adjusted gross income allowed for medicine and drugs? Amounts paid for medicines and drugs obtained with or without a prescription for the prevention or alleviation of a physical or mental defect or illness. Aspirin to relieve headaches would count, even though it is bought over the counter; but toothpaste bought for dental hygiene purposes does not. Neither do payments for shaving cream or cosmetics. The costs of birth-control pills and birth-control devices prescribed by a physician are deductible. Illegal drugs are definitely not deductible. However, the IRS has ruled that the controversial drug Laetrile, prescribed by a physician and purchased and used by a taxpayer in a locality where its sale and use are legal, is a medical expense.

Can you deduct the costs of a special diet of natural foods and vitamins that your local health-food store manager has advised will increase your pep and vigor? The answer is "No." Generally, the cost of special food or beverages does not qualify. However, if your doctor prescribes food or beverages to be taken specifically for alleviation or treatment of an illness and they are not a part of your nutritional needs—if they are in excess of an ordinary diet—you may include them as medical expenses.

If your vitamins and iron supplements had been prescribed by a doctor, they would be considered a medical expense; without a doctor's prescription, they are not.

A taxpayer sought to deduct the cost of his doctor-prescribed diabetic diet. The deduction was denied because it was ruled a substitute for normal diet. The IRS said that the costs of special foods or beverages taken as substitutes for foods and beverages normally consumed are considered personal expenses and are not deductible.

On the other hand, take the case of a businessman who suffered from hypertension. His doctor prescribed a salt-free diet. Because the businessman's work involved a great deal of traveling, he had to take many of his meals in restaurants. He paid extra charges to the restaurants for preparing salt-free meals for him. The IRS allowed those additional charges as medical deductions.

You may deduct for allowable medical expenses for your dependents and for your spouse if you file a joint return together. If you claim a dependent under a multiple-support agreement, you may claim medical payments you make for the dependent. However, if you are reimbursed by others for any parts of the medical bill, you must deduct those before stating the amount of your claim.

Diane Duffy, sportswear buyer for a department store, helped to support her widowed mother. Her brothers George and Andrew also contributed to their mother's support. All agreed through a multiple-support agreement that Diane would take Mother as a dependent. Mother fell and broke her hip. Mother's medical costs for that tax year were $4,500. Diane wrote the check for the medical payments. George and Andrew each gave Diane $1,500 for Mother's medical expenses. Though Diane had written checks for $4,500 in the way of payments, she had to discount the $3,000 she received from George and Andrew. Her medical deduction for Mother was $1,500. Unfortunately for George and Andrew, they can deduct nothing on their returns for the $1,500 each had contributed because they could not also claim Mother as a dependent.

Did you know that you may take a relative as a

"medical dependent" even though you are not able to get a dependency exemption for that person because he has $1,000 or more in gross income? If you did not know this, you are among millions of other taxpayers who didn't know either. There are stipulations to this, though. You must have furnished more than half the support for your medical dependent and also actually paid his medical bills.

Albert Mann's son Reid is twenty-one. He had just started his first job and had made $2,000 in salary when he broke his collarbone in a motor scooter accident. Doctor and hospital bills amounted to almost $5,000, which Albert paid for him. Albert also supported him to the tune of $4,500 while Reid was out of work as a result of the accident. Albert could not take Reid on a dependency exemption because Reid had made more than $1,000 in gross income. However, Albert could take Reid's medical expenses as a deduction. Albert had met the two "medical dependent" rules: He had contributed more than half to Reid's support and had paid his medical bills.

A divorced spouse paying alimony may agree, according to the divorce decree, also to pay medical expenses to his former wife (or to her former husband). Medical payments would then be deductible as alimony if payments are periodic—not as a medical deduction. However, the spouse receiving the alimony, which must be declared as income and is taxable, may take as a medical deduction the amounts given and used for payment of medical bills.

Tax tip: Though in most cases joint returns save money for married taxpayers in the case of a married couple who are both wage earners with approximately similar incomes, where one has substantial medical expenses, it might be best to file separate returns.

Roger Pritchard had adjusted gross income of $27,000; his wife, Janice, had adjusted gross income of $25,000. Janice went through an emotional upset during the tax year that cost $3,000 in bills for psychiatric care. Had the couple filed jointly, their medical deduction would have been $1,440 ($3,000 less 3% of combined income of $52,000). They figured out their medical deduction filing separately. Janice's medical deduction came to $2,250 on her return ($3,000 less 3% of Janice's income of $25,000).

Many people overlook the fact that the medical deduction allows for transportation if primarily for and essential to medical care. If you use public transportation to get to your doctor, you may deduct the costs of fares. If you use your automobile, you are allowed to deduct 9 cents per mile plus any tolls and any parking fees.

As far as deductibility of long-distance transportation for medical purposes is concerned, if there is a clear medical reason for the trip, plane or train fares might very well be deducted. The cost of food and lodging on your medical trip outside of a hospital or sanitarium would *not* be deductible. Cases wherein the IRS has permitted a long-distance-travel medical deduction include:

A heart disease victim's trip to Florida on doctor's orders

A trip to Florida on doctor's recommendation for a patient whose skin condition required natural sunlight

A trip to California from New York by a patient to visit a physician who was treating him before he moved to New York

The airplane fare for sending a taxpayer's deaf child to a school specializing in sign language

Airplane trips and car rental costs to visit a mentally ill child according to a doctor's recommendation.

In most cases wherein the patient cannot travel without a companion, the companion's transportation would be deductible, too. Cases might include that of a parent escorting a child patient, or a wife accompanying a husband with a severe eyesight problem who is traveling to secure medical help for his problem.

Payments for medical care may be deductible even if the treatments do not have the sanction of the AMA. Thus payments to chiropractors, though the medical profession does not recognize chiropractors, are deductible, as are payments to people who may not have medical training, such as psychologists or psychotherapists. A couple treated for sexual incompatibility were even permitted to deduct the costs for their sex therapy.

Payments for membership in a health club for purposes of physical therapy, if such physical therapy is ordered by your doctor, would entitle you to a medical deduction on your dues if the therapy was for the relief of a specific ailment.

The first time Glenda Richmond tried roller skating she fell and severely injured a knee. Her orthopedist ordered exercise with special weight-lifting machines and whirlpool treatments at a local health club. The cost of yearly dues, $200, was deductible as a medical expense.

In some cases, education costs are deductible as medical care. But the requirements are stiff. The education must be for the alleviation of a physical or mental handicap. That usually means that you or your dependent must be attending a special school that deals specifically with the handicap. Even though one taxpayer with varicose veins was told by her doctor that dancing lessons would relieve her distress, the IRS did not see the cost of the lessons as a medical deduction, though speech training for a stutterer or lipreading for the hard-of-hearing are likely to be deductible as a medical cost. Sending a child to private school that provides ordinary education, even though it is meant to cure, such as sending a child with emotional problems to a military school, will probably not get you a deduction. That is because the military school is not a special school dealing with emotionally disturbed children. If you sent a child with emotional problems to a school with a staff of psychologists, and he received psychological treatment there as well as education, the IRS might permit you to allocate the amount of tuition into education- and psychological-treatment expenses and deduct the costs allocated to psychological treatment.

Devices and supplies bought primarily to alleviate a physical defect or to provide relief for an ailment may be includible as a medical expense. Most people would agree that a wheelchair would be deductible, but may not know that elastic stockings that provide relief for "tired" legs would be deductible, too. Or perhaps contact lenses, besides regular eyeglasses. Bottled water bought to avoid drinking fluorinated city water is not deductible, but installation and monthly cost of a device to add fluoride into home water supply advised by a dentist was declared deductible by the IRS, as were abdominal supports, back braces, orthopedic shoes, a reclining chair (if prescribed by a doctor), special mattress and plywood bedboards for relief of arthritis of the spine, trusses, wigs (advised by a doctor for the mental health of a patient who lost hair through disease), and an air conditioner when necessary for relief in breathing, such as for asthmatics.

A taxpayer, besides requiring special devices and facilities for himself or a disabled or handicapped dependent, might have to go into a capital expenditure for relief. Now, for that capital expenditure to be a medical deduction, it must have as its primary purpose medical relief. Would all of the capital expenditure be deductible? Not in all cases. It might simply be deductible to the extent that its costs exceed the increase in value of the home. For example: Installation of a home elevator might be required for someone with a severe heart problem who could not climb stairs. Installation of the elevator might cost $5,000. A real-estate appraiser estimated that the elevator increased the value of the home by $3,500. The $1,500 above that amount was considered as a medical expense and therefore deductible.

Another example: A taxpayer who had a permanent spinal injury built a pool and put a heater into it and a bubble over it because his doctor ordered him to swim every day to prevent muscles from atrophying. The cost was something like $11,000. An expert real-estate appraiser estimated that the pool enhanced the value of his home by approximately $6,500. That amount was counted as a capital expenditure for the house. The remaining $4,500 was deductible as a medical expense.

Most people know that if they require the services of a trained nurse or an attendant's medical services, the fees are deductible. On the other hand, if you hired someone simply to do the housework, the expense is nondeductible. But what does the IRS say about the case wherein you hire an aid who does both jobs?

Joe Martin, a stroke victim, was partially paralyzed. He hired an aide to help bathe, dress, and groom him. But the aide also did some household chores such as cooking and cleaning. Joe can deduct the part of her wages allocable to nursing services. But the household duties—even though performed by a medical aide—are personal expenses. Since Joe pays the aide $12,000 a year, and the aide spends half her time providing nursing care, Joe has a $6,000 medical-expense deduction.

Suppose your medical aide "sleeps in." Do you get a medical deduction for her room and board? Unless you can show that you had out-of-pocket expenses for lodging beyond your normal expenses, you can't take it as a deduction for that. (An example of out-of-pocket lodging expense might be paying increased rent for an apartment with another room for the attendant.) However, you can claim for your aide's meals. Here's how you do it: First, total food expense must be allocated among the household members. You live alone with your wife. The total family food bill is, say, $4,500. The portion of the food bill allocable to your aide is $1,500 (one third of $4,500). Next, apportion the cost of her food in the same way as her wages were. If she performs nursing duties only half the time, you get a medical-expense deduction for half the cost of her meals, or $750 (one half of $1,500).

Table of Deductible
and Nondeductible Medical Expenses

Deductible Expenses

Abdominal supports
Abortion
Acupuncture
Air conditioning for respiratory problems
Alcoholic inpatient care costs
Ambulance hire
Anesthetist's services
Arches
Artificial teeth, eyes
Autoette-Auto device for handicapped person,
   but not deductible for travel to job or business
Back supports
Birth-control pills or devices prescribed by
   physician
Blood tests
Blood transfusions
Braces
Braille books—excess of cost of Braille works
   over ordinary edition
Cardiographs
Chiropodist
Chiropractor
Christian Science practitioner
Clarinet and lessons advised by dentist for
   treatment of malocclusion
Contact lenses
Convalescent home for medical treatment
Cosmetic surgery

Crutches
Dentist's services
Dermatologist
Drugs
Drug center treatments
Elastic hosiery
Electric shock treatments
Elevator in home for heart patient
Eyeglasses
Guide dogs for blind or hard-of-hearing, and
    training and upkeep
Health and hospital insurance
Hearing aids
Hospital bills
Hydrothermy
Injections as medical treatments
Insulin treatments
Kidney donor's expenses
Laboratory examinations and tests
Legal fees for guardianship of mentally ill
    spouse, where commitment was necessary
Mattress for arthritic patient
Membership in health club if deemed necessary
    by your physician
Nurse—practical or other nonprofessional
    nurse, as well as professional nurse for
    medical services only (includes nurse's board
    and Social Security taxes paid)
Obstetrical expenses
Optometrist
Orthopedic shoes
Oxygen mask, tent
Physicians' fees
Physical exams
Psychiatric care
Psychoanalyst
Psychologist
Radium therapy
Reclining chair, if prescribed by physician
Remedial reading for dyslexic child

Sacroiliac belt

Sex therapy

Special foods or beverages prescribed by doctor
in addition to normal diet, and in no way a
part of normal nutritional need

Special schools for physically and mentally
handicapped child

Splints

Sterilization

Surgical fees

Telephone aids and their repair for
hard-of-hearing

Transportation to doctors, hospitals, clinics,
and for certain prescribed medical reasons

Truss

Ultraviolet ray treatments

Vitamins, if prescribed by physician

Wheelchairs

Whirlpool baths, if prescribed by physician

Wig prescribed by physician for mental health
of person who lost hair from disease

X rays

Nondeductible Expenses

Baby-sitting fees to enable parent to visit doctor

Boarding school fees paid for healthy child
while parent is ill or recuperating, even if
advised by physician

Cosmetics

Dancing or swimming lessons

Diaper service

Domestic help even if prescribed by physician
to ease strain on spouse, except for part of
cost allocated to any nursing duties performed
by domestic

Funeral expenses and plots

Health club membership to promote general
well-being

Illegal operations and drugs

Life insurance premiums and disability
  insurance
Marriage counseling fees
Maternity clothing
Scientology fees
Soap
Stop-smoking program, unless for specific
  ailment and on doctor's advice
Toothpaste
Vacation trips for general well-being
Veterinarian's fees for pet
Weight reduction program, unless for specific
  ailment and on doctor's advice

Keep all bills related to medical expenditures in your tax file. Though we don't wish you ill health, it is surprising how medical (and, by the way, that includes dental) bills pile up. To make record keeping easier, you might open a charge account at a drugstore for drugs and medical supplies. Each month the store will send you an itemized list of those deductibles. The itemizations plus your canceled checks will be helpful in establishing their validity for your deduction.

Of course, when you take your medical deduction, you must subtract any reimbursements on your medical insurance that you got during the year.

CHAPTER 10

Your Home
and Deductions

RIDDLE: When is a home more than just "home, sweet home"?

ANSWER: When you can call it a tax shelter because home ownership can bring tax deductions.

The federal government, recognizing that your home is an investment just as are stocks and bonds, allows you to deduct interest paid on your mortgage. It also does not tax income twice, even if tax paid goes to your local government, so that your property taxes are deductible, too.

Your privately owned house is one of the best investments you have. Private homes have increased in value at a faster rate than most other investments. And if you sell your present home and purchase another, you will pay tax only on the gain on the amount if the adjusted sales price of the old residence exceeds the cost of the new one, providing you meet certain conditions. (If you take a loss on the sale of your home, you cannot, however, deduct the loss.) Here are the rules for reducing capital-gains tax on the sale of your home. You must buy or start building a new residence before or within eighteen months of selling your old residence. Capital gain realized is the amount you come out with after the sale if the adjusted sales price of the old home is more than what you pay for your new home. The government gives you another boost with that adjusted-sale-price bit. Fixing-up expenses to help make your home salable, such as painting, landscaping—anything of that order that is not a capital expenditure, if done within ninety days before you sell the house—will be deducted from the sale price of the house for tax purposes. Also, selling expenses—commissions for real-estate agents, advertising of sale, legal services connected with the sale—can be deducted from the sale price for tax purposes. After those deductions, you will have your adjusted sale price. Here's an illustration of how to figure your gain:

Old home sale price	$120,000
Less selling expenses	7,000
	$113,000
Less fixing-up expenses	8,000
	$105,000
Cost of new home	$100,000
Minus adjusted sale price on old home	105,000
Recognized gain	$ 5,000

If you had come out with no gain—the cost of your new house equaled that of the adjusted sale price of the old—you would pay no capital-gains tax at all. If you paid more for your new house than the adjusted sale price on your old, you would pay no tax either, and you have increased the value of your assets.

Taxpayers fifty-five years of age or over who sell their home after July 20, 1981, have a once-in-a-lifetime exclusion from gross income of $125,000 of the gain realized from the sale of a residence (the home must have been the taxpayer's principal residence for three out of the five years preceding the sale. If you own the home jointly with your spouse and file a joint return in the year your home is sold, only one of you need meet the age requirement of fifty-five or over and the residence and ownership requirement of three out of the last five years. Because you can only claim the $125,000 exclusion once in a lifetime, be wise and use it only if your potential capital gain is greater than $50,000. If it's not, consider waiting until your house appreciates some more.

You may be able to use the sale of a home to help finance your retirement, as did Tom and Peggy Flynn. The Flynns bought their first home twenty-five years ago for $22,000. As their family and income grew, they traded up to bigger and more expensive homes. Each time they traded up, inflation gave them a boost in home values and a good profit to roll over, with taxes deferred into the next house. Their present home is worth $200,000. Because their children are now grown and out on their own, they do not need so large a home. They are also concerned about costs of maintenance, utility bills, and large property taxes while on a fixed retirement income. They plan on selling, realizing a tax-free capital gain of $125,000, and moving to smaller quarters, which will give them savings on maintenance, utility bills, and property taxes. Thus they will have that $125,000 and savings on the smaller home to invest for retirement income.

Congress, cognizant of the need to conserve our resources, has allowed renters as well as homeowners a tax credit in its Energy Act of 1978 (a tax credit differs from a deduction in that a credit is an amount used to reduce the actual amount of tax liability; a deduction is an amount used to reduce gross income to taxable income). The IRS is specific about which energy-conservation items will earn the tax credit. Those items are (a) insulation; (b) storm (or thermal) windows or doors; (c) caulking or weatherstripping; (d) a furnace replacement burner that reduces the amount of fuel used; (e) a device for modifying flue openings to make a heating system more efficient; (f) an electrical or mechanical furnace ignition system that replaces a gas pilot light; (g) a thermostat with an automatic set-back; (h) a meter that shows the cost of energy used.

Form **2119**

Department of the Treasury
Internal Revenue Service

Sale or Exchange of Principal Residence

▲ See instructions on back.
▲ Attach to Form 1040.

1980

25

Note: *Do not include expenses you are deducting as moving expenses on Form 3903.*

Name(s) as shown on Form 1040   Your social security number

		Yes	No
1 (a) Date former residence sold ▲			
(b) Have you ever postponed any gain on the sale or exchange of a principal residence? . . .			
(c) Have you ever claimed a credit for purchase or construction of a new principal residence? . . . (If "Yes," see Form 5405.)			
(d) If you were on active duty in the U.S. Armed Forces or outside of the U.S. after the date of sale of former residence, enter dates. From to			
2 (a) Date new residence was bought ▲			
(b) If new residence was constructed by you, date construction began ▲			
(c) Date you occupied new residence ▲			
(d) If you answered "Yes," to 1(c), did anyone live in your new replacement residence before you did? .			
(e) Were both the old and new properties used as your principal residence?			
(f) Were any rooms in either residence rented out or used for business at any time? . . . . . . (If "Yes," see note in line 7 and attach computation.)			

Part I   Computation of Gain and Adjusted Sales Price

3 Selling price of residence. (Do not include selling price of personal property items.)	3	
4 Commissions and other expenses of sale	4	
5 Amount realized (subtract line 4 from line 3)	5	
6 Basis of residence sold 6		
7 Gain on sale (subtract line 6 from line 5). (If line 6 is more than line 5, enter zero and do not complete the rest of form.) If you bought another principal residence during the allowed replacement period or you elect the one time exclusion in Part III, continue with this form. Otherwise, enter the gain on Schedule D (Form 1040), line 2 or 9. If you intend to replace the residence within the allowed replacement period see instruction B.	7	

Note: *Do not include in line 7 the amount attributable to rented rooms or other business purposes; instead, report separately on Form 4797.*

8 Fixing-up expenses	8	
9 Adjusted sales price (subtract line 8 from line 5)	9	

Part II — Computation of Gain to be Postponed and Adjusted Basis of New Residence

		Yes	No
10 Cost of new residence	10		
11 Gain taxable this year. (Subtract line 10 from line 9. Do not enter more than line 7.) If line 10 is more than line 9, enter zero. Enter any taxable gain on Schedule D (Form 1040), line 2 or 9. If you were 55 or over on the date of sale, see Part III	11		
12 Gain to be postponed (subtract line 11 from line 7)	12		
13 Adjusted basis of new residence (subtract line 12 from line 10) . . .	13		

Part III — Computation of Exclusion, Gain to be Reported, and Adjusted Basis of New Residence

			Yes	No
14 (a) Were you 55 or over on date of sale?				
(b) Was your spouse 55 or over on date of sale? . . . . (If you answered "No" to 14(a) and 14(b), do not complete the rest of form.)				
(c) If you answered "Yes" to 14(a) or 14(b) did you own and use the property sold as your principal residence for a total of at least 3 years (except for short temporary absences) of the 5-year period before the sale? . . . (If you are 65 or over, see instruction C.)				
(d) If you answered "Yes" to 14(c), do you elect to take the once in a lifetime exclusion of the gain on the sale? . . ("Yes," check yes box and complete the balance of Part III. If "No," return to Part II, line 12 above.)				
(e) At time of sale, was the residence owned by: ☐ you, ☐ your spouse, ☐ both of you?				
(f) Social security number of spouse, at time of sale, if different from number on Form 1040 ▶ . . . . . . (Enter "none" if you were not married at time of sale.)				
15 Exclusion: Enter the smaller of line 7 or $100,000 ($50,000, if married filing separately)	15		
16 Part of gain included (subtract line 15 from line 7)	16		
17 Cost of new residence. If you did not buy a new principal residence, enter "None." Then enter the gain from line 16 on Schedule D (Form 1040), line 9, and do not complete the rest of Form 2119	17		
18 Gain taxable this year. (Subtract the sum of lines 15 and 17 from line 9. The result cannot be more than line 16.) If line 17 plus line 15 is more than line 9, enter zero. Enter any taxable gain on Schedule D (Form 1040), line 9 . .	18		
19 Gain to be postponed (subtract line 18 from line 16)	19		
20 Adjusted basis of new residence (subtract line 19 from line 17) . . .	20		

No other energy-conservation items will earn the tax credit, so if that aluminum siding salesman says that you can get a tax credit on siding your house, don't believe him!

The energy-conservation items, furthermore, must be purchased new and have a useful life of at least three years.

The credit is 15% of your expenditure up to $2,000, or a maximum credit of $300 for all devices installed after April 19, 1977, and before 1986. The home energy-conservation tax credit applies to your principal residence only. Energy-conservation measures taken on your vacation home do not qualify for a tax credit. You get no credit for those. Your maximum $300 energy credit on your main residence is cumulative. You do not have to install all your energy-conserving devices in one year. You can spread expenditures over several years up to 1986. If you spend more than $2,000, you get no extra credit. However, if you move and buy or rent another dwelling and install energy-conserving devices in your new place, you can start all over again with your energy-conservation credit. That allowance applies even if you move and install energy-conserving devices in more than one place in one year, providing each is your principal residence.

Even greater tax credit is yours if you install solar, wind, or geothermal energy equipment in a home you are building or in one already built. A credit of 40% of cost—up to $10,000 for a maximum credit of $4,000—may be claimed if you are the original user of the unit and if it has a useful life of at least five years. The energy-conservation-items credit and the renewable-energy-source credit are figured separately. Expenditures for one type of credit does not reduce the other credit. Therefore, if you claimed the top limit on both, you would have a tax credit of $4,000 if the items for which the credit is taken are a proper increase to the basis.

Tenant stockholders in cooperative housing corporations are allowed a proportionate share of the credit.

What do you do when an energy credit is more than your tax? If your credit for this year is more than your tax minus certain other credits, you can carry over the excess energy credit to the following tax year(s).

If you wake up one morning and find your home damaged, you may be eligible for a casualty-loss deduction. Whether you are eligible or not depends on what caused the damage, how much the damage cost, and what reimbursement you get for your loss.

According to the IRS, a casualty is the total or partial destruction of property resulting from an identifiable event of a sudden—or unusual—nature. Included within this definition might be damage or loss caused by hurricane, tornado, flood, storm, fire, smoke, earthquake, riot, vandalism, falling tree, or auto accident. Some of these casualty causes may not be covered by your homeowner's or other insurance, so it's especially important to know how to get a tax break.

Not included under the IRS definition would be damage that results from progressive deterioration. Say your back porch collapses because termites have eaten it away. The damage usually is not deductible since there's no element of suddenness; the termites had been working on that porch for years.

Similarly, damage by moths is not deductible. Nor is damage to shrubbery caused by erosion of soil over a long period of time—especially if the erosion was preventable. On the other hand, damage from erosion resulting from a very heavy storm would be deductible. So might damage to your home caused by subsoil shrinkage due to sudden and severe draught. You could probably claim water damage from pipes bursting after a sudden freeze; you couldn't claim water damage caused by a leaky roof that had long been decaying.

What evidence do you need to prove a casualty loss? It's important to pull together several facts as soon as possible after the casualty. You'll want documents to show:

Form **5695**

Department of the Treasury
Internal Revenue Service

Energy Credits

► Attach to Form 1040.   ► See Instructions on back.

1980

34

Name(s) as shown on Form 1040.

Your social security number

Enter in the space below the address of your principal residence on which the credit is claimed if it is different from the address shown on Form 1040.

Part I: Fill in your energy conservation costs (but do not include repair or maintenance costs). If you have an energy credit carryover from a previous tax year and no energy savings costs this year, skip to Part III, line 16.

A. Answer the following question: Was your principal residence substantially completed before April 20, 1977? . . ☐ Yes   ☐ No

B. If you checked the "NO" box, you CANNOT claim an energy credit for conservation cost. Do NOT fill in lines 1 through 7 of this form.

1 Energy Conservation Items:

a Insulation	1a	
b Storm (or thermal) windows or doors	1b	
c Caulking or weatherstripping	1c	
d A furnace replacement burner that reduces the amount of fuel used . .	1d	
e A device for modifying flue openings to make a heating system more efficient.	1e	
f An electrical or mechanical furnace ignition system that replaces a gas pilot light .	1f	
g A thermostat with an automatic setback . . .	1g	
h A meter that shows the cost of energy used . .	1h	
2 Total (add lines 1a through 1h)	2	
3 Maximum amount	3	$2,000 00
4 Enter the total energy conservation costs for this residence from your 1978 and 1979 Form 5695, line 2.	4	
5 Subtract line 4 from line 3 (If line 4 is more than line 3, do not complete any more of this part. You cannot claim any more energy conservation credit for this residence.) . .	5	
6 Enter the amount on line 2 or line 5, whichever is less.	6	

7 Enter 15% of line 6 here and include in amount on line 15 below . . . . | 7 |

Part II — Fill in your renewable energy source costs (but do not include repair or maintenance costs).
If you have an energy credit carryover from a previous tax year and no energy savings costs this year, skip to Part III, line 16.

8 Renewable Energy Source Items:			
a Solar	8a		
b Geothermal	8b		
c Wind	8c		
9 Total (add lines 8a through 8c)	9		
10 Maximum amount	10	$10,000	00
11 Enter the total renewable energy source costs for this residence from your 1978 Form 5695, line 5 and 1979 Form 5695, line 9.	11		
12 Subtract line 11 from line 10 (If line 11 is more than line 10, do not complete any more of this part. You cannot claim any more renewable energy source cost credit for this residence.) . . .	12		
13 Enter amount on line 9 or line 12, whichever is less.	13		
14 Enter 40% of line 13 here and include in amount on line 15 below	14		

Part III — Fill in this part to figure the limitation

15 Add line 7 and line 14. If less than $10, enter zero.	15		
16 Enter your energy credit carryover from a previous tax year	16		
17 Add lines 15 and 16	17		
18 Enter the amount of tax shown on Form 1040, line 37	18		
19 Add lines 38 through 44 from Form 1040 and enter the total	19		
20 Subtract line 19 from line 18. If zero or less, enter zero.	20		
21 Residential energy credit. Enter the amount on line 17 or line 20, whichever is less. Also, enter this amount on Form 1040, line 45	21		

1. The nature of the casualty and when it occurred. Keep newspaper clippings, police records, insurance correspondence.
2. The direct cause-effect relationship between the casualty and your loss.
3. Your ownership of the property.
4. The original cost of the property, plus any costs of improvement—all minus depreciation. Gather bills, deeds, canceled checks.
5. The fair market value of the property before and after the casualty.
6. The amount of any depreciation or casualty losses claimed on the property in prior years.

What determines the amount of loss? The values of the property before and after the casualty—not the cost of repair—usually set the loss figure. (Sometimes the IRS will accept repair costs as a fair measure of your loss.) The loss cannot exceed your cost less any depreciation claimed.

Before-and-after photographs are good evidence of decrease in value. As a basic safeguard at any time, you should keep an inventory of household goods, including photos and invoices, stored in your safe-deposit box, and keep the list updated.

Also, consider having an appraisal made by an expert. He knows the current market value and has access to pertinent substantiating evidence you probably don't have. His fee is deductible in the year you pay it.

What may you deduct? You may claim all losses—minus $100 for each nonbusiness casualty, and minus any compensation you received from insurance or other sources, such as disaster-relief agencies. Your loss deduction cannot exceed your tax basis in the property.

If a single event, such as a hurricane, severely damages your roof as well as your car, you would absorb the first $100 of damages collectively. On the other hand, if the hurricane damages just your roof and then, later in the year, you have an accident with your auto, each event is treated as a separate casualty. You must absorb the first $100 for each—$200—on your tax return.

If you have a big disaster and your loss is so great that it wipes out all your income for the loss year, you can claim any unused portion of your loss as a deduction for other tax years.

One of the old favorite deductions on home or apartment in the past was the home office. Anyone who could convince the government that he had to bring home work to do after hours took a deduction on his den. Even if he used the Barcalounger in the corner of the living room for perusing stock market pages, he deducted on home expenses because he was engaged in the process of producing income when he was perusing those pages. However, the 1978 law cracked down on the old home-office deduction. The rules are strict: Your home office must be "the principal place of your business," or you must use it exclusively and regularly to meet clients, patients, or customers. The same rules apply to an unattached separate structure adjacent to your home. If you are an artist, say, and your studio is your garage, you must use it *exclusively* for producing your art. You cannot also keep your car in the garage.

The rules for home offices are strict, and we say stick by them unless you want to court trouble, but we also say that if you are self-employed or an outside salesman for whom there is no office at your company headquarters, consider moving your office to your home for a juicy deduction on cleaning costs, heat, light, repairs, depreciation, fire insurance, and outside painting. If one room of a seven-room house is used as your home office, you may deduct one seventh of those home expenses. If you rent, that portion of the rent attributable to that room is deductible. A full deduction—100%—is allowed for costs such as painting, repairs attributable to the home office itself.

What if you are engaged in the production of a second income and you work at home: Would you be able to deduct for a home office? Yes, if again it is the principal place of business for that second income and you use it exclusively and regularly for that purpose.

Amy Thompson is a designer for a sportswear firm. Evenings and weekends she also designs and silk-screens women's scarfs, which she sells to high-fashion boutiques. One room of her four-room apartment is set aside for her scarf business. In that room is her drawing board, her silk-screening equipment, and a desk at which she does her paperwork. Amy may deduct the proportionate share of her rent for her home office.

Richard McCormack is an internal auditor for an insurance firm. He also runs a profitable mail-order business in boat compasses. He keeps his inventory in the playroom of his ten-room house. His wife, Maria, works a few hours between household chores on book-keeping chores at a desk down in the playroom. Their teen-age son and daughter help after school and on weekends by taking packages to the post office. McCormack deducts one tenth or 10% of his heat and lighting bills and home insurance premium bills on his Schedule C. He may also deduct for depreciation on his home office. The furniture, including business machines such as his typewriter, may be depreciated, too.

To back their home-office deductions, both Amy and McCormack keep canceled checks and receipts that refer to their office expenses. They also keep business mail directed to the home office and a record of business phone calls. They note in their business diaries times that business is conducted in the home office.

You don't meet the tests for a home office? Perhaps you can at least deduct part of your home phone bill as a business expense. If, for instance, you can reach certain clients or customers only after regular business hours, and the only practical way to get hold of them is on your home phone, you may allocate that part of your phone bill to business use and take a deduction on it. It is even simpler to keep track of business-related calls if you install a second phone, which you use exclusively for business. You simply deduct all costs related to the second phone number, and remember to file those bills with your income tax information records.

As are casualty losses, thefts are deductible on your tax return, subject to certain rules. (In these days of high crime, almost all of us will have some experience with theft during our lifetime.) If you do have a theft, you are going to have to prove that it was indeed a theft. Mislaid or lost property does not make a theft deduction, unless for mitigating circumstances labeled "mysterious disappearance."

How would you be able to prove that you were the victim of theft? If there is wholesale burglary, of course, you would call the police and report the theft to them. Even if you have a relatively small theft, report it to the police. Though your reporting does not necessarily mean there was a theft—that the article was not just lost—if you did not report the article missing to the police, it seems likely to the IRS that you had just misplaced the article and didn't consider it stolen. Of course, if you have neighbors who saw your house being entered by burglars, statements from them to that effect would certainly help to establish theft.

Theft losses are deductible in the year that they occur. (If you are awaiting insurance reimbursement and that takes you into another year, in that case report the reimbursement as income in the year received.) You will be able to deduct what the articles were worth or their original cost, whichever is the lesser, minus insurance reimbursement, minus $100, which the IRS has you absorb.

It is helpful, too, to hunt up photographs that show the articles that were stolen. Sometimes it can be difficult to find such photos amid your memorabilia. To be sure that they do have photographs of their valuables, many people lay out their jewelry, silverware, and other precious articles, and snap photos of them. (There are even professional photographers who specialize in this service.)

Very often burglars, for no reason apparent to us, also like to destroy your property when they burglarize. Furniture covers and draperies may be slashed, walls defaced, carpets stained with mysterious fluids. You may find that on top of the burglary you will have a casualty loss coming under the heading of vandalism to file for, too.

Deduct your casualty or theft loss on Schedule A of your 1040. You attach Form 4684 to calculate and explain the loss. If you have more than one casualty or more than one theft, you list them separately on this schedule.

Supposing—horrible thought—you have a casualty or theft that is so enormous that it is larger than your income for the year. There's consolation. The IRS allows you a carry-back to three years before your taxable year and a carry-forward for seven years from your taxable year, until your loss is exhausted. Here's what you do: File amended returns for the three previous years, as needed, each with a portion of the loss. You will get a refund on taxes already paid those years. If you still have unused loss from your casualty or theft, you have the coming seven years in which to portion your loss and use it on returns as deductions.

Though you may at present feel snugly ensconced in your present job and in your present home, given the mobility of Americans today it is probable that you will be changing jobs and relocating one or more times during your lifetime. You should know that when this happens you are entitled to a moving adjustment on your return. Here are the expenses you can take off:

1. Travel to the new location
2. Moving household goods and personal effects
3. Premove house-hunting trips
4. Temporary quarters at the new location
5. Disposing of an old residence and acquiring a new one.

Of course, there are qualifications on that deduction. The qualifications involve:

1. Distance to your new job
2. Time on your new job
3. Time you incur moving expenses in relation to your starting work
4. Reasonableness of your expenses.

Let's take those qualifying factors one by one.

What about that distance requirement? The IRS says that your new principal place of work must be at least thirty-five miles farther from your old residence than the old residence was from your former place of work. Say your old job was ten miles from your old home. You get a new job; it is forty-six miles away from your home. Your new job meets distance qualifications. It is thirty-five miles farther than your old job was from your old home.

Now, the IRS uses the phrase "principal place of work." What does it mean by that? If you go to the same office every day it is obvious that that is your principal place of work. What if there is no one place at which you spend most of your working time? In that case, count the miles to the place at which your business activities are centered—for example, where you report for work or are otherwise required to "base" your work. If you have several employers on a short-term basis and report to a union hall for your assignments, count the distance between your residence and the union hall. If you have more than one employer—hold down two or more jobs—count the location of the principal-job workplace in calculating distance. The principal job is determined by most time spent there, most amount of activity you expend there, and most amount of financial remuneration.

First-time job holders are entitled to take a moving deduction if the first job is thirty-five miles away from their home. A young Long Island man fresh out of college lands a job in Denver. Obviously, it is more than thirty-five miles from the house he lived in with his parents. He is allowed a moving deduction on his transportation out to Denver, his trips out to look for a place to live and moving pieces of furniture his parents gave him from their attic, and cost of shipping his clothes, skis, and his dog. He stayed in a motel for a few days before he found his apartment, and was able to deduct his motel bill.

The second requirement for a moving deduction—time on the job—is spelled out explicitly by the IRS. If you are working for someone other than yourself, you must work full time at least thirty-nine weeks during the twelve-month period immediately after your arrival in the area of your new job. It is not necessary that the weeks be consecutive or that you work for one employer, however. You must work full time unless it is customary for your type of employment that it is otherwise. For instance, an actor or a teacher may not work full time all the twelve months of the year. Seasonal workers such as those involved in farming may not work full time all the year either. (However, work contracts should not involve more than six months of off-season periods.) If, through no fault of yours, you cannot work—there is a strike; you are disabled or you even die; there is a disaster—the weeks you don't work will still be included in your work time to meet the thirty-nine-week requirement.

In cases wherein a married couple files a joint return and both spouses are working in the new location, if one spouse leaves the job before the thirty-nine-week requirement is met, but the other spouse remains working full time and meets the thirty-nine-week test, that will be acceptable for the deduction even if that spouse is not the main wage earner.

Notice we said that you or your spouse must be working full time to claim the moving deduction. Part-time work will not make it. That means if you had thoughts of retiring to the Sun Belt and taking a part-time job, you are not entitled to the moving deduction. It might be worthwhile to find another full-time job in the Sun Belt and stick it out for the time requirement in order to claim the moving deduction. (Of course, that plan might not be practical if you are on Social Security.)

If you do not work for someone else, are self-employed or decide to join the ranks of the self-employed and are relocating your business or professional practice, the time requirements differ. You must work on a full-time basis for at least seventy-eight weeks during the twenty-four-month period immediately after your arrival at your new work location. Note that at least thirty-nine of the seventy-eight weeks must be during the twelve-month period immediately after your arrival.

The third requirement for your deduction relating to time you incur moving expenses in relation to your starting work means that your moving expenses must be incurred within one year from the time you first report to your job or business, and the move must have been in connection with the start of work at the new location. However, there may be mitigating circumstances to that one-year rule that the IRS will take into account with an explanation. For instance, you may have a youngster who is in his junior year at high school. It would be a hardship for that youngster not to finish his senior year and graduate with his class. You decide not to move until more than one year is past for the sake of that child. The IRS is not so hardhearted that they will not take that "more than one year" reason into account.

What does the IRS in its fourth requirement for the deduction consider "reasonableness of your expenses" for the deduction? The IRS divides moving expenses into direct and indirect expenses. It allows you $3,000 as an overall deduction, with not more than $1,500 of that allowed for indirect expenses of moving. Direct expenses are those involving the travel costs of your family to the new location and also moving household and personal goods (including pets and your car) to the new address. Traveling costs include food and lodging bills for the day before you depart your old location, food and lodging bills along the route to your new home and at your new location for the day before you move. The IRS does expect you to take the most direct route to your new home when you calculate costs. If, for instance, you are moving cross-country and you decide to go by car and take a circuitous route in order to take in the Grand Canyon, the side trip is not deductible. Otherwise, you calculate the cost of gas, oil, and repairs (or take a flat rate of 9 cents per mile), tolls, and parking fees along the most direct route to your new home.

In figuring the cost of moving household goods and personal goods, don't forget to include the cost of packing and crating, temporary storage if any, and the cost of disconnecting appliances and reconnecting them in your new home.

Family members do not have to travel all at the same time to the new home for you to get the deduction. Separate traveling costs of family members will still get you a deduction for their expenses.

Indirect costs of moving include the cost of premoving house-hunting trips, the cost of selling your old home, the cost of purchasing your new one, and costs of temporary living quarters at your new location.

After you obtain work at your new job, trips that you make (or, say, your wife makes) back and forth from your old home to the new location looking for a house or apartment are deductible, including not only plane, train, and car expenses, but also food and lodging expenses. That even includes trips that were not fruitful in finding a satisfactory place to live.

Costs of meals and lodging at temporary quarters within any thirty consecutive days after you obtain work in your new location are deductible. Members of your family are included in that part of the deduction, too.

The costs of selling your old home—real-estate commissions, attorney's fees, title fees, escrow fees, points or loan-placement charges, state transfer taxes—are deductible indirect expenses. However, because it would be a double deduction if in reducing capital gain on your old home you deducted those expenses, you may not use them also in calculating your moving deduction. However, if you have selling expenses on your old house or buying expenses on your new home that will take you over the $3,000 limit, and you had decided to include them in your moving deduction, put those extra expenses toward reducing capital gain on your selling and buying of your homes.

If you file an individual return, you are entitled to $3,000 for moving expenses. You are limited to $1,500 of that for indirect expenses of moving. Married couples filing joint returns are permitted $6,000, with a limit of $3,000 of that for indirect expenses.

The IRS considers cases of couples who are separated, but still married:

Douglas and Sara Riordan are still married but in the process of divorce, and are separated. They decided to break up their home in Providence, Rhode Island. Douglas obtained a job transfer to Dallas, and Sara has secured a job in Los Angeles. They file separate returns. Each claims a moving deduction. They are each allowed $3,000 for overall expenses, with not more than $1,500 of that for indirect expenses for househunting and temporary quarters.

You deduct moving expenses in the year you paid them or in the year you incurred them. If your employer is reimbursing you for your expenses, you may take your moving deduction in the year you are reimbursed. Of course, you must first declare the reimbursement as income in order to get the deduction.

By the way, the IRS is flexible in what it considers your residence for purposes of deduction. What you call "home, sweet home" may be a trailer, houseboat, or Chinese junk; as long as that is where you permanently reside, it's okay with them.

In this chapter we pointed out that your home is one of the best tax-advantage investments you can make. Our next chapter discusses other types of investments that will give you tax advantages.

CHAPTER 11

Investments
and Deductions

In these inflationary days, it is difficult to put something away out of our earnings; yet you need a nest egg for security against unforeseen disaster. Or perhaps you are a young couple who would like to realize enough for a down payment on a house. Or you may be concerned about the high and ever-increasing cost of college for your children and how you are ever going to build up an education fund that you can fall back on. And the older couple looking forward to retirement has dreamed of having money enough not just for existence, but perhaps to do the traveling that work schedules had previously prohibited.

In order to build up a fund to make your dreams come true, you must put your money into investments that will keep ahead of the current rate of inflation and that are also free of the tax bite, or at least you must manage your investments in such a way that you minimize the tax bite.

Most of you have an investment counselor, and if you don't have one we suggest that you find someone whose advice you feel is reliable. He will know best what your investment needs are and how to handle them. This chapter is only meant to give you a general understanding of investments and the income-tax picture as it relates to investments.

There are investments that give income that is entirely tax free. These would be municipal bonds. The word "municipal" connotes city, but municipal bonds are not just issued by cities. They are also issued by states, counties, villages, territories, and U.S. possessions. State hospitals or universities may sell them. They may emanate from turnpike, tunnel, or bridge authorities; they may also come from housing authorities.

Bonds are essentially IOUs. They are a promise on the part of the issuer to repay the amount invested by a certain date, in return for which you receive regular interest payments. The chief attractions of municipal bonds are safety and the fact that interest income is free from federal tax. And if you are a resident of the issuing locality, interest income often is free from state and local taxes as well.

Costs of municipal bonds are usually determined by the prime interest rate—the minimum interest rate charged by the commercial banks on which all other rates are calculated. Costs of municipal bonds will fluctuate with changes in the prime interest rate. If the interest rate rises, prices of older bonds drop to equalize the return offered. If, on the other hand, the interest rates are heading down, outstanding bonds become more attractive to the investor because their prices are rising.

Municipal bonds are usually considered safer than most other forms of investment because they are backed by the authority of government. There is risk, however, even with some that do look sound. New York City in 1975 did not have the cash to pay off its bondholders. It had to declare a suspension (moratorium) on repayment of notes. Municipal bonds are rated as to safety by a coding system in Moody's and in Standard & Poor's. The best rating is AAA. They range from that down to C. It's best to avoid any risk of default, so it's advisable not to go below an A rating. You should know that while the higher rate denotes a higher degree of safety, usually the higher the rating the lower the rate of return.

Municipal bonds fall basically into two classes: general-obligation bonds and revenue bonds. The distinction is based on the manner in which money is raised to pay interest and to repay principal. General-obligation bonds are backed by the taxing power and general financial resources of the municipality. Revenue bonds rely on revenue raised by the facility. Judge the solidness of general-obligation bonds by their rating and also by what you can find out about the community's record of debt management. Before buying revenue bonds, compare the efficiency of the facility to others, just as you would compare one company in an industry with another as to promise of success.

Most denominations of municipals are in $5,000 units, though you can get them in units of $1,000. We do not advise purchasing municipals, even though they have the advantage of tax-free income, if you have a small amount of discretionary income. In the latter case it is better to stick with a savings bank account, which offers the advantage of greater liquidity—you can easily get your money out in case of emergency, whereas it might take some time to find a purchaser for your bond.

We did say that municipal-bond interest is nontaxable. You don't even state the interest on your tax return. As a matter of fact, there is no place on your tax return to report that income.

You might have thought that Congress closed all tax loopholes with recent tax laws, that tax shelters are dead for all time. Wrong! There are still tax shelters available. Tax shelters provide opportunity for profit yet also reduce or defer current income-tax liability. Congress decided that some tax shelters should be kept to provide private investment in industry that benefits the general public. Tax benefits are the lure for investors. However, tax shelters are not for those in moderate-income strata. Investments in tax shelters can be a risky business (that's one of the reasons Congress gives the tax benefits—to offset risk taken). However, if you are in a high-income group (50% tax bracket) and have a large tax bill and can tie up funds for two years or more, tax shelters might just be for you. Even if you do not meet those qualifications, it's worth reading about them to know what all that talk about "tax shelters" means. The information might just come in handy someday when you may be in a higher bracket.

The favorite tax shelters today are oil and gas, real estate, and equipment leasing. Warning: Before you go into a tax shelter, get to know its management people, or at least get to know their track record in management; don't rely solely on the word of your investment salesman, who may only be interested in making a fast commission. You should also know that a tax shelter does not mean you will never pay taxes on your investment; it means that taxes are deferred to some indefinite date, perhaps to leaner years such as your retirement years, when you will probably be in a lower tax bracket.

Investors in tax shelters are usually limited partners. They provide capital for the investment, while the general partner or partners provide the managerial and operational skills. Tax benefits are prorated and go to the partners of the venture as per agreements.

A venture requiring many partners may be listed with the Securities and Exchange Commission. However, there are many limited partnerships that are perfectly safe that are not listed with the SEC. As we said before, it is up to you to investigate for yourself how sound the management of the investment is.

In all cases, if you are a partner in a tax-sheltered venture, we repeat: All tax benefits will flow to you from the entity on a prorated basis.

We will take each of the types of tax shelters now in favor and describe briefly how they work.

First, oil and gas. You should know some basic facts before we go into the advantages of oil and gas tax shelters. There are three kinds of oil and drilling programs. There is the high-risk exploratory drilling called wildcat drilling. Chances of striking oil are not sure. Drilling is based on speculations (you may know what we mean by wildcat drilling if you have caught one of those old Clark Gable oil-rigger movies on "The Late Show"). The drilling program that drills near already producing wells is less risky. There is a greater chance there will be more oil near already producing ones. These are called development drilling programs. It is best to look for a balance between wildcat and development drilling—the third basic kind of drilling program.

Most oil and gas drilling programs feature first-year tax deductions from 70% to 100%, or 200% or 400%, of the amount you invest. If the drilling operations find oil or gas, your income from the investment will be partially sheltered by the depletion allowance and expenses of drilling, which in some cases is as high as 50% of the net income of the property.

Equipment leasing has gained in popularity in the past couple of years. It is more efficient, business has found, for some other company to buy heavy equipment and for them to lease rather than to buy it themselves. The equipment-leasing partnership buys such industrial equipment as computers, aircraft, railroad cars, ships, pollution-control systems, or machinery. Equipment is leased in agreements that require lessees to pay rent and also maintenance costs of equipment.

Besides the usual amount of 25% or less that comes from investors, sponsors of the leasing company float loans for the additional monies required for purchasing equipment.

The tax advantage for the investor in equipment leasing is that he is allowed to deduct a large amount of depreciation in the first twelve months of his investment, plus miscellaneous up-front expenses and interest on loans. Remember that we said that company deductions are prorated for each investor? Therefore, these deductions are taken right off your personal tax return.

After a few years, depreciation and interest rates are lower, and the lease starts to generate taxable income. But by this time you have had appreciable tax savings. Investing in equipment-leasing programs, then, can be a solution in years when your tax liability is particularly high.

Real estate is the least risky of tax shelters. But whether it will be profitable depends on many factors. Among those are: leverage, interest rates, percentage of occupancy, operating costs, location, and competition. All of these factors have a high degree of variability. Crucial to profitability is efficient management. The previous track record of management will help you in determining whether a particular real-estate venture is sound.

Real-estate offerings fall into four general categories. First there is new, improved real estate. These partnerships build on bare land, tear down old structures, and replace them or buy newly built properties as first owners. It's obvious that this is the riskiest of all the real-estate programs because there is no previous record of how profitable the venture would be. These ventures hope to recover investment in five to seven years through maximum depreciation. Because so much money is needed to start up this operation, cash flow is lean over the first few years.

Existing improved real estate, the second type of real-estate venture, offers tax-sheltered income with minimum risk. These partnerships buy used commercial or residential properties. Because these properties have track records on which you can predicate occupancy rates and revenue rates and any problems involved in maintenance, they are less risky. They offer lower first-year write-offs, but they provide steady cash flow on a tax-sheltered basis, and they have moderate capital-gains prospects.

Federal- and state-assisted housing ventures constitute the third type of program in real-estate investments. The venture company builds or renovates properties for low- or middle-income or elderly tenants with government assistance, such as rent subsidies or loan guarantees. This type of venture usually gives deductions that run over ten or twenty years.

Raw, unimproved land ventures constitute the fourth type of real-estate investment. These programs buy undeveloped land and hold it for sale at a profit that may be taxed at favorable capital-gains rates. Most of the annual cost of carrying the properties is deductible, though amounts may be small in relation to the total investment.

We used the phrase "capital gain" in relation to sale of raw-land real estate. Often we hear of people using the term "capital gain," in relation to their selling their stock on the market. What is capital gain? It is simply the excess of proceeds over the basic cost.

In IRS parlance, a short-term capital gain is made when there is a profit on an asset for *less than* one year. A long-term capital gain is made where there is profit on an asset held for *more than* one year. A capital loss is incurred when an asset is sold at less than cost. A short-term capital loss is incurred when the sale is made *less than* one year after purchase of the asset; a long-term capital loss is incurred when the sale is made *more than* one year after purchase of the asset.

Capital gains and losses are reported in detail on Schedule D of your tax return, and the results are transferred to your 1040.

While short-term capital gains are taxed at the same rate as your ordinary income, long-term capital gains are taxed at a more favorable rate. It's Congress's way to encourage individuals to invest in the economy and keep money in a company long enough for the company to make use of the money. Long-term capital gains are taxed at 40% of the regular rate of ordinary income.

Long-term capital losses are deducted from gains on

your Schedule D and can help to offset tax you might have to pay on gains. Or they may offset ordinary income to the maximum of $3,000 per year. The excess over $3,000 per year can be carried forward over future years under the same rules until the loss amount is exhausted.

Common stock in electric utilities offers an advantage other stocks do not have. Some of their dividends are tax free. To encourage industrial expansion, the government allows utility companies to depreciate plant and equipment faster than these assets actually wear out. In addition, power companies may credit their earnings with a special Allowance for Funds Used During Construction, since it is often many years between the time a utility makes a cash outlay to build a new plant and the time the facility generates revenue.

Dividends to shareholders may be treated as return of capital and therefore given the favorable tax treatment by the federal government. The utility lets you know which part of your dividend is not taxable.

Another way to realize tax benefits on securities income is to transfer the securities to your children. The gift-tax rules enable you to put securities in your children's names while you serve as custodian of the minors' property. True, they will have to pay taxes on gain realized if it is over their exemption of $1,000, but they will be paying in a much lower tax bracket than yours. You could also transfer gifts of money to your minor—up to $3,000 per year if you file a single return, up to $6,000 if you file a joint return. Then later, when market conditions are favorable, invest that money in securities.

Even though the long-term capital-gains tax only has a maximum rate of 20%, it is still enough to keep some people from selling assets that have appreciated. Because we are here to tell you how to pay as little tax as possible, we would like to introduce you to a little-known tax strategy. It is called "the tax-free property swap." Briefly, it means the exchanging of "like-kind" land, buildings, livestock, or municipal bonds to put off taxes on capital gains and, in some cases, to establish losses against your gains.

Let's first take the case of real estate. You own an apartment building in Westchester, N.Y. You exchange it for a medical building in a New Jersey suburb. Since no money changed hands, the deal allows the original owner of the apartment building to defer the tax on the swap. If you wish, you can exchange the medical building, in turn, for another "like-kind" piece of property and swap again for as many times as you desire. The section of the tax code—Section 1031—that applies to the technique puts no prohibition on swapping over and over again.

The section prohibits the tax swap to be used in the case of your own home. However, if you own a ski chalet in Aspen that you manage and rent out and therefore have to inspect periodically, and you have grown tired of cold, you might swap it for winter rental property in Palm Beach. Although the "like-kind" exchange must be made with vacation homes used for business (i.e., full-time rental), you can, by law, occupy the home for ten days a year.

Swaps don't have to be two-way deals in order to qualify under Section 1031. Three-way exchanges can also be tax free, providing they are correctly structured. (Usually a broker or trustee negotiates the deal.) Take an example: Mr. Charles has an office building he wants to swap for Miss Jones's farm, but Miss Jones wants cash for the farm. Then along comes Mr. Smith who wants Mr. Charles's office building. He buys Miss Jones's farm for cash and then swaps the farm for Mr. Charles's office building. In this case, everyone got what he wanted. Mr. Charles qualified for a tax-free exchange, Miss Jones got her cash for the farm, and Mr. Smith acquired the office building he wanted.

Though the law says that you can exchange non-income-producing property—a number of acres of undeveloped land in rural North Dakota, for example—

for productive property—a shopping center in Los Angeles—and it will qualify for tax-free treatment, you may not exchange livestock of different sex such as a cow for a bull because it is not property of "like-kind"!

What about the tax advantages of swapping municipal bonds? Bonds that have lost value on paper can be swapped for similar bonds, thus generating hefty tax write-offs and leaving the investor with little change in his holdings. An experienced broker can generate tax losses to offset clients' ordinary income or to mitigate capital gain on the sale of other investments.

Here's how it works. An investor holds a $25,000 3½% XYZ Turnpike Bond due in 1990. Current market price is $18,000. He sells it and buys a $25,000 3½% ABC Turnpike Bond due in the year 2000. It costs $15,750. Both bonds are rated A. By the exchange, the broker has extended your bond holding ten years, maintained annual income of $875, and maintained par value at $25,000. Furthermore, he reinvested funds and had a return of $2,250 ($18,000 minus $15,750) while establishing a loss of $7,000 on the XYZ Turnpike Bond.

Municipal bonds may also be swapped to achieve a loss and increase interest income, or swapped to achieve a loss and increase interest income with the client investing additional cash. Consult your broker for details on those. If the entire loss is not used or you have no capital gain, you may use the loss to shelter up to $3,000 of this year's income. Any swap losses remaining after these tax applications may be carried forward indefinitely and applied against gains and/or income each year until the loss is used up.

There is a place on your tax return to deduct expenses laid out for your investment program. That place is on Schedule A—Miscellaneous Deductions, alongside "Other (itemize)." You may take off interest for carrying investments. For instance, if you bought AT&T on margin, interest on your margin account may be written off. Brokerage fees are also deductible.

You might subscribe to various publications to keep yourself informed about your investments. Those subscriptions are deductible, as is also your daily newspaper, which carries news of the business world. You may also write off accountant's or lawyer's fees related to investment advice as it concerns taxes.

We have not included in this chapter two of the biggest tax-savings investments you can make: Individual Retirement Accounts and Keogh plans. Since they are related to retirement, we have included them in our next chapter on retirement, pensions, and taxes.

CHAPTER 12

Retirement, Pensions, and Taxes

What is your retirement dream? Leisure for hunting and fishing? Time enough to work on that gadget you are puttering with? A chance to read some of those books you have been meaning to but never had the time for?

Retirement dreams are beautiful, but they can turn into sour reality without financial planning. Even if you are only in your thirties or forties, it's not too early to think about the financial aspects of retirement.

You must ask yourself where the money is going to come from. And you must keep in mind that the rate of inflation is increasing at more than 12% per year! That means that you are going to want as many devices as possible to help you finance your retirement, with as many low-tax or no-tax advantages as possible to counteract that inflation bite.

You are also going to want as many sources of income as possible for retirement years. Though Social Security and your pension are things that you count on for your retirement, you must also supplement them with other sources of income.

What do we see as sources of retirement income?

1. Social Security
2. Pensions from your job
3. Pensions that you set up yourself

4. Annuities
5. Savings
6. Stocks and bonds
7. Real estate
8. Employment during retirement

Let's take those sources of income one by one.

You might have heard people say they are not worried about retirement. "Social Security will take care of that," they say, or, "I'll just live on my Social Security." Well, Social Security was never meant to be a plan to totally support recipients. It was meant to supplement what income a person already had. Even with the increases in Social Security payments, you cannot expect to live on Social Security checks alone.

Take this example: A man who retired at age sixty-five in 1977 after having had maximum earnings each year since 1957 would be getting only a monthly Social Security check of $459.80. His dependent wife, age sixty-five, would increase his benefits by $229.90. That's a total of $689.70 a month. If his wife had worked, she could have drawn benefits either in her own right or as the spouse of her husband.

Social Security payments in your retirement will be supplemented by Medicare benefits. Social Security also entitles you to disability survivor's benefits and to benefits for minor or incompetent children.

If you are or have been self-employed, you have been contributing to your Social Security when you have filed your income tax by filling out Schedule 1040-SE.

It is a good idea, if you are an employee or self-employed, to check on your Social Security benefits as part of your retirement planning. You will want to know whether you qualify for benefits and have a reasonably accurate estimate of what your benefits will be. Write or visit your Social Security Administration office for the postcard "Request for Statement of Earnings." You also might want to ask for the leaflet "Estimating Your Social Security Retirement Check."

It is good to know that your Social Security benefit checks are tax-exempt income. When you receive them you do not have to include them at all on your income-tax form 1040! (However, as we mentioned elsewhere, Social Security payments are counted as dollars toward the support test.)

Your second most dependable source of income is your pension from your job. While Social Security benefits are as secure as our government is (and if our government goes under, what is anything worth, anyway?), your pension from your job is almost as safe, thanks to recent government legislation called the Employee Retirement Security Act of 1974. It was a massive, complete, and very technical overhaul of the entire private-pension system. It set up basic law for pension vesting. Employers must vest an employee 100% after ten years of service. Thus, after ten years, if an employee leaves his job or is fired from his job, he may take with him 100% of the benefits that his employer has contributed to his pension.

The ERISA of 1974 also stated that an employer may not discriminate among his employees in setting up a pension plan—that is, he may not simply set up a pension plan for his officers. Common-law employees must also be included in a pension plan. Employers and trustees must file details of their pension plan annually with the IRS and with the Department of Labor. Severe penalties have been set up for noncompliance with ERISA.

You should be careful to keep track of what is being done regarding your pension plan. Every employer is required to supply each employee with a synopsis of his pension plan annually as amended and is to keep the full plan available for inspection by employees at all times. This pertains to a private-employer plan, or to an employer-union plan where the union is the trustee.

If you are an employee you should know specifically what your pension rights are and what contributions are made for you. It is important for your future welfare to know the facts of your pension plan as regards vesting, distribution, and contribution by your employer.

You should also follow the financial report of the pension trust. See whether or not it is earning for your pension account and what administration costs are (for example, are they excessive?).

You as an employee should also know what your options are if you change jobs and to elect the proper time to take your pension distribution or to leave it with the trust or whether to roll it over into an IRA or another employer/union fund.

You as an employee should know whether or not you can contribute to the trust fund and have the earnings accumulate until your retirement, when you will most likely be in a lower tax bracket.

Many employer plans give the employee the right to contribute his own funds to a maximum (the maximum depends on each particular plan). The earnings on the employee's contribution would not be reportable income until taken.

Of course—and this is good news—employees do not pay tax on any of their employer's contributions to their pension plan until the employee receives his monies.

Usually there is a provision in pension plans to allow an employee to receive a lump-sum distribution of his account balance under certain circumstances (he may become disabled, he may switch jobs, or perhaps he has reached 59½ years of age when he may receive the pension monies). The employee who receives a lump-sum distribution of his pension has several alternatives regarding taxes he would have to pay on his monies.

For one instance, to defer taxes the receiver of the lump-sum distribution may reinvest (roll over) the monies in another qualified retirement plan (if he does this within sixty days of receiving his lump-sum distribution). That would include an individual retirement plan, annuity, or employer plan. If employer contributions are included in the lump-sum distribution, the contributions must be contributed to the new plan to retain their tax-free status.

Phillip Ernst was employed for twenty years as a salesman for a major oil company. Contributions had been made by his employer for the full twenty years he had worked. The contributions were based on his earnings.

Phillip was offered another job in a different industry, which he decided to take. Fortunately, his pension plan did not have any restrictions on his going into the industry he was changing to. The trustees of the old plan informed him that there was $75,000 in his plan vested for him.

His possible options at his age—forty-three years—are: (1) leave the money with the trustees of the old employer pension plan to accumulate earnings free without any additional employer principal contributions and tax free; (2) instruct the trustees to buy an annuity to be payable in later retirement years if that option is available under the trust agreement; (3) take a lump-sum distribution and pay the taxes on the reportable income; (4) roll it into an Individual Retirement Account where someone other than the old employer —trustee—would be responsible for the investments made, and having the option to withdraw and pay the tax and penalty in later years if withdrawn before retirement age.

Suppose that in Phillip's negotiation with his new employer, who also has a qualified pension plan, Phillip finds that he can roll these funds into his new employer's trusteed plan. What should Phillip do?

We assume that Phillip does not need the pension monies to live on. He must evaluate and guess what is going to happen in future years. He must evaluate the performance of his old employer fund, his new employer fund, and the current money market that would be available to him in an Individual Retirement Account (IRA).

Now, there are employees who may not want to roll over their lump-sum distribution. They may want or need their money now. How can they get their money without paying excessively in taxes? There are two methods they might employ.

One method of avoiding high taxes on a lump-sum distribution is to have the entire distribution taxed as ordinary income and take advantage of the special ten-year averaging provision.

Gordon Arnell was forty-one and a computer programmer when he was offered a position with a second computer company. He decided to take it. It was a larger salary and because his children would soon be starting college, he needed that extra salary. Also, because he needed ready money for his children's college, he decided to take a lump-sum distribution on his 100% vested pension with his former employer. In order to avoid excessive taxes, which would have cut into the benefit of his move, he elected the ten-year averaging method for computing his lump-sum distribution.

A second method of taking care of a lump-sum distribution if one is not rolling it over is to separate the distribution into two parts. The portion of the distribution that relates to pre-1974 working years is treated as a long-term capital gain. The balance of the distribution is taxed as ordinary income and is eligible for the ten-year averaging method.

Elaine Starr works for an advertising agency as a buyer of commercial art. She has gained knowledge of sources and customers over the years. She decides to become a self-employed artist's representative. She needs the vested $15,000 in her employer's pension plan for working capital for the new venture. The trustees of the employer plan inform her that of the $15,000 being distributed to her, $6,000 was employer-contributed prior to December 31, 1974, and the balance after that date. She checks with her professional tax preparer and decides that the pre-1974 distribution will be treated as a long-term capital gain, and the post-1975 distribution will be treated as ordinary income. She also elects to take the distribution on January 2 of the following year, since she projects that the first-year earnings of her new business will be meager.

The tax—both federal and state (Caution: some states do not allow ten-year averaging on state income tax)—should be computed both ways: for the ordinary-income ten-year averaging method and for the long-term capital gain, combined with ten-year averaging so that you can see which method results in lower tax cost. Usually, the ordinary-income ten-year averaging method should not be made if you have net long-term losses, either current or carryover, sufficient to offset the pre-1974 capital-gain portion of the distribution.

Although vesting and payouts are mandated by law, there are possible exceptions to those rules. Look at this case:

Dan Whitcomb was employed as a key executive for a merchandising organization located in Philadelphia. There was a special executive pension plan in that firm with a special clause that all contributions would be forfeited if the executives changed jobs in the same industry and went over to a competitor before retirement age. Dan received a solicitation from a West Coast merchandising organization; the new job would be a move upward in status. He elected to forfeit the $100,000 vested with his old employer, which he had to do in taking the new job because his new employer was a competitor. Dan decided that the possibility of going to the West Coast would eventually be more profitable and would offset what he was losing in pension monies with his old firm.

The third source of retirement income is the pension plan that you set up yourself for yourself. The ERISA provides for private pension plans you initiate for yourself. If you are self-employed you may set up a Keogh plan. A Keogh plan allows the self-employed to put aside 15% of their annual earnings, or up to $7,500 per year, whichever is less, in a pension fund. The money invested in your pension plan is deducted from your gross earnings. Thus it is 100% tax deferred, and also the interest earned in a Keogh plan is not taxed currently. You may not touch this money until you are 59½ years old. There is a penalty tax of 10% on the amounts if you dig into them before then, besides paying the regular income tax on the amounts! The law also provides that you must distribute the amounts by age 70½. At the time of distribution the amounts you have put away in the Keogh plan will be taxed as received. However, you have deferred the income into your retirement years, when your income-tax brackets should be much lower. Starting in 1982, Keogh figures will be 15% or up to $15,000.

If you are self-employed and also employ others, ERISA says that you must also cover your employees who have been with you three years or more.

Moonlighters in their own businesses are also eligible to set up Keoghs. Suppose you are employed by a large corporation and are covered under its pension plan. You also work as a free-lance photographer. You do weddings, bar mitzvahs, family parties. You make less than $750 net per year. You can set up a mini-Keogh. Under the mini-Keogh you can invest tax free 100% of your earnings or $750, whichever is less, in a tax-free pension plan. Of course, if you make more than $5,000 per year, go to regular Keogh and invest 15% of your income or $7,500, whichever is less.

You may even set up a pension plan for yourself if you work for someone who does not have a pension plan. The plan for employees that they set up for themselves is called the Individual Retirement Account (IRA). The limit on contributions you may make to the plan is 15% of earnings, with a maximum yearly contribution of $1,500. You can put money in an IRA for a nonworking spouse, which raises the joint maximum contribution to $1,750. As with a Keogh plan, distribution of the pension benefits must not be made before one reaches 59½ without 10% penalty, and interest must be distributed by age 70½. Starting in 1982, every employee may have an IRA of 15% or up to $2,000.

Banks, savings and loan associations, insurance companies, mutual funds, and stockbrokers have plans for Keogh plan and IRA investors. These organizations will act as the trustees for your accounts. In turn, they have to report to the Department of the Treasury each year as to the condition of your account. Thus the IRS is able to keep an eagle eye on whether you have prematurely (before age 59½) dug into your Keogh plan or IRA.

Our fourth source of retirement income is annuities. An individual makes periodic payments or one lump-sum payment to a company, commonly a life insurance firm, which invests the money and contracts to make monthly payments to the individual for the rest of his life, usually starting with his retirement. Some annuities have death benefits. They will pay benefits to the surviving spouse after the death of the original annuitant, and the first $5,000 payment to your surviving spouse is usually tax free.

An annuity might be a good idea for someone who has trouble managing and investing money or does not care to bother with it. However, most annuities do not pay out as much interest as you could get if you invested your money yourself.

Annuities do draw interest during your working years, and that interest is tax free until annuity payments begin. However, again we say that you could invest for yourself in low-tax or tax-deferred investments and draw a higher rate of interest.

Our fifth source of retirement income is savings. Savings accounts are necessary for peace of mind. Experts say that you should have a cushion of at least $10,000 in ready-access saving accounts. As little as $50 banked monthly and compounded semiannually at 6% will help you to reach your $10,000 goal in about twelve years.

Of course, savings account interest and interest on certificates of deposit (they carry higher interest, with penalties for cashing them in before their maturity date) are both reportable and taxed on your 1040.

You may be interested in U.S. savings bonds. E bonds pay interest in a lump sum when they are cashed in. The tax bite on that interest can be great. It may be wise to convert your E bonds to H bonds. You pay taxes on H bonds interest only in the year it is earned. You may spread the tax bite over several years, and if those years are your retirement years you will most probably be in a lower tax bracket.

A sixth source of income for retirement are stocks and bonds—those that grow. Remember with stocks that the first $200 of dividends may be excluded from your income on your 1040 if you own them jointly with your spouse. If you have common stock in utilities, part of your dividend is tax free, as explained in our chapter on investments. We also discussed in that chapter how municipal bonds, though they give less in returns, are tax free.

Real estate is our seventh source of retirement income. We also covered real estate in our chapter on investments. Remember that on income-producing property you have tax benefits of depreciation of buildings.

In talking about real estate, one of the best investments for retirement can be owning the home you live in. Most residences in good neighborhoods increase in value. In the chapter on your home, we explained capital-gain treatment on sale of your home and the once-in-a-lifetime $125,000 exclusion of gain on sale of your home.

An eighth source of income in retirement is a job or business. However, you must be careful not to endanger your Social Security payments by earning more than is allowed under your payments, and also not to boost yourself into a tax bracket that will wipe away the gains you make financially from your job.

There are extra tax breaks when you reach age sixty-five. You will get a double exemption, and if your spouse has reached age sixty-five, a double exemption for her, too. Your Social Security income is tax exempt, as are railroad retirement benefits, veterans' pensions, and disability payments. Partly exempt are pension and annuity payments to which you made a contribution. In most cases, the states, too, give tax breaks for those over sixty-five.

In this chapter we have discussed how you can take advantage of the tax code in preparing for and living in retirement. In the next chapter we tell how surprisingly enough the tax code enables you to take deductions on entertainment.

CHAPTER 13

Deductions and Your Social Life

Many a person's social life had been enhanced in the past by the allowance of business entertainment by the IRS as spelled out in the 1976 tax law. Credit card companies, theaters, restaurants, and country clubs owed much of their revenue to the expense account of the employee and the entertaining of self-employed business and professional people.

Section 162 of the tax code allowed a deduction for all the "ordinary and necessary" expenses paid or incurred during the tax year in carrying on a trade or business. The tax law of 1976 interpreted this as meaning that entertainment expenses were deductible if they were for the entertainment of a customer, prospective customers, suppliers, or employees. Then, shortly before the writing of the 1978 tax laws, the Carter administration proclaimed that business entertaining had gotten out of hand. "'Three-martini lunches' are being subsidized by the government by way of write-offs!" was the cry, ignoring the simple fact that if businessmen depended on three martinis to help haul them through a business deal, their sodden states would devastate our GNP. Exhorted by the Administration to put a stop to the Sodom and Gomorrah-like conditions of conducting business, Congress became inflamed. The cry was to eliminate by 50% all business entertaining. Trim it down to something like a cup of coffee and a slab of apple pie.

Businessmen, restaurant owners, restaurant employees' unions, and theater owners were alarmed. If Congress had its way, the livelihood of thousands would be threatened. Congress cooled down, rethought the matter, and decided to keep just about the same rules for business entertaining in the '78 law as was laid out in the '76 law.

However, the IRS *is* cracking down on what it considers "lavish and extravagant" spending. That description is not defined by the IRS, rather it is deciding what it considers "lavish and extravagant" on a case-by-case basis. Any spending so ruled is nondeductible, even if it meets the test of being "directly related to" or "associated with" the active pursuit of business.

However, the IRS is not so stiff-necked that it does not recognize that businessmen and professionals in certain walks of life do not usually entertain customers in pizza parlors, though it may frown on munificent dinners at four-star restaurants if one is a modest manufacturer of garter belts. (On the other hand, if you are a Hollywood producer, the IRS might allow munificent dinners at four-star restaurants as being consistent with your life-style and with customary mode of entertaining in your industry for your position.)

What are the rules and standards the IRS will use in determining whether your entertaining may come under the heading of a business deduction? Basically, as we stated earlier, the IRS requires that your entertaining must be "ordinary and necessary" for the conduct of business. Your entertainment must be primarily for business negotiation, looking toward income or other business benefit at some specific future time, and business must actually be conducted.

If you are self-employed in a business or profession, obviously your entertaining would be for production of income for that business or professional practice. If you are an outside salesman or an employee who is expected by his employer to entertain business colleagues and are not reimbursed by your employer, entertainment expenses would be deductible to you in determining taxable income.

If your employer has you account to him for your business entertainment and reimburses you for the exact amount, you would not account for business entertainment on your return. That headache goes to your employer on his business return. However, that does not get you off the hook for keeping close records of your business entertainment. Suppose your employer is audited by the IRS, and the IRS disallows some expenses that your employer has reimbursed you for. Say your employer has reimbursed you for dinners at which you entertain, hoping to attract future customers for the business. The IRS says that this sort of entertaining is not necessary for your employer to attract customers. It disallows that expense to your employer. You would then be expected to declare on your next return the amounts you received for those dinners from your employer as income to you!

Suppose the IRS decides to audit *you*. It questions whether your reimbursements were a sneaky way for your employer to hand you a nontaxable bonus. If you have records—your business diary properly filled out and vouchers or receipts for expenditures that show you spent all that money your employer reimbursed you—the IRS will give you a clean bill of health.

You must be prepared to prove your outlay for business entertainment in order to receive the deduction. This is what must go into your business diary:

The date of the business entertainment

The amount of each separate expenditure (incidental items such as taxi fares, telephone calls, and tips may be stated as one total)

The place—the name and address, and the nature of the entertainment

The business purpose—what you expected to gain from it

The business relationship—the name and title of the person or persons entertained and how they relate to your business.

Joseph R. was a sales rep with a leading national producer of chemicals. He was out to land a contract with a large drycleaning chain. He called the buyer for the firm and asked if they could discuss over lunch the possibilities of their purchasing his firm's revolutionary cleaning chemical, which had eliminated the dangers of toxic fumes. Though Joe did not get a firm "Yes" or "No" from the buyer at lunch, he had reasonable expectation of getting business from him. This is the way Joe did his tax accounting in his diary:

Date: Nov. 16

$5.90 incidentals

$25.75—lunch at Gigi's

25th and Broad St., Greenvale, Wis.

Michael Moriarty—buyer, Allied Cleaning Co.

Purpose: to discuss selling Allied our new cleaning chemical.

Joe's diary entry indicates clearly that his lunch was directly related to the conduct of his business. It shows that at the time of the entertainment he had reasonable expectation of deriving some business benefit from the making of the expenditure. It doesn't matter if he does not get the sale for the lunch to be deductible; the fact remains that there was a reasonable expectation that he would. Second, Joe actually did discuss a business deal during the luncheon entertainment. Had a waiter spilled a bowl of soup over Michael Moriarty's head and Moriarty was too upset to discuss business, Joe would still be allowed a deduction for the luncheon because he had intention of discussing business and would have but for circumstances beyond his control. Third, the principal reason for the luncheon was so that Joe could discuss business. It does not matter if more time was spent discussing the latest Jets game than the chemical contract; the fact has been established that business was the principal reason for the business luncheon. Finally, for entertainment to be considered directly related to business, you must show that the expenses for the entertainment were attributable to you and your business associate, which Joe did by entering the name of business associate Moriarty and his business relationship to him in his diary.

Had Joe entertained Moriarty at dinner, say, and told him to bring his wife along and Joe had brought his wife, too, the dinner expenses for the wives would also be deductible. It was reasonably expected that the wives would be there; they always had dinner with their husbands. However, if in addition to wives he had invited several of his friends along to make it a party, his friends' dinner tabs would not be deductible. As a matter of fact, Joe would possibly be losing the whole deduction because by making it a party, he would be casting suspicions on whether it was feasible to discuss business in such a situation.

You would also be allowed a business-entertainment deduction if you could show that your entertainment was, as IRS regulations say, "associated with" the active conduct of your business. To qualify, the entertainment would have to be preceded by or be followed by a discussion of business. If Joe had decided to discuss business with Moriarty over a couple of cocktails and then taken him to a night ball game afterward, both cocktails and the ball game tickets would be deductible. Though they had not discussed business at the ball game, a business discussion had gone on before it. Therefore, Joe's inviting Moriarty to the ball game was "associated with" the active conduct of Joe's business.

It is relatively easy to prove, with substantiation in your diary, entertainment "associated with" your business if it occurs on the same day as the business discussion. However, if the entertainment and the business discussion do not occur on the same day, it might be more difficult to prove your deduction. But not impossible.

Suppose a group of out-of-towners with whom you do business come to your city with their wives. They fly into New York from Pittsburgh late on a Friday. You take them to dinner and the theater and to after-theater drinks Friday night. Saturday morning, the men have a business meeting with you in your office. Your diary should look something like this:

Fri., Jan. 7

Entertained representatives and wives from General Automation, Pittsburgh

Lawrence Anderson, pres. of General, and Mrs. Anderson; Austin O'Connor, vice pres., and Mrs. O'Connor; Mark Olsen, chief engineer, and Mrs. Olsen

$160.35—dinner at LaRoche's, 16 W. 46 St., N.Y.C.

$200.00—theater tickets

$48.00—drinks at Plaza Hotel, 59 St., N.Y.C.

Sat., Jan. 8—9:30 A.M.–1:00 P.M.

Conference at our plant with Anderson, O'Connor, Olsen re installation of machinery in our plant.

Your diary entries have shown the business connection between you and those you entertained. The entries showed that those you entertained were from out of town, and therefore it would seem reasonable that you might entertain them and their wives upon their arrival, then have your business discussion (you state the date, place, and duration of the business discussion) before they fly back to Pittsburgh. Your entertainment, though it did not occur on the same day as your business discussion, preceded it.

Had you decided not to accompany General Automation's officers and wives Friday night and had handed them the theater tickets and told them to charge dinner and drinks to you, the entertainment would not have been deductible. Why? The IRS says you must be present at the entertainment to make it deductible.

Suppose you have a bevy of secretaries and clerical workers who have been loyal and helpful to you in your business. You decide to say "thank you" to them by throwing a party at a local disco. They are invited to bring dates. Is that deductible? Yes, because it is considered to be keeping the goodwill of employees. Don't forget to nail down the deduction with food and liquor receipts.

You may be able to get Uncle Sam to underwrite some of your expenses at a country club, yacht club, or other type of social club. How's that? Your membership may qualify as a business deduction. To qualify, you must use your club more than 50% for business. Remember, 49% won't make it. It must be used at least 51% for business for you to take any deduction at all on your dues. If you use it 51% of the time for business, 51% of your dues will be tax deductible. If you use your club more than that—say, 75% of the time—for business, you may deduct 75% of your dues.

You would enter individual entertainments such as a round of golf at your club in your business diary, just as you did when you took business associates to lunch or dinner at a public restaurant, being careful to note the business discussion that took place during the entertainment, or directly preceded or followed it. The IRS would not expect you to be discussing business while sinking a putt, but would want to see that you did it perhaps at luncheon afterward.

Not only businessmen, but also professional men may deduct the cost of club dues if they meet the more-than-50%-use test for increasing their income. Also taken into consideration by the IRS when concerned with professionals' entertaining are these factors: the nature of the practice; the period of time the professional has been in practice; the number of his clients or patients; the percentage of clients or patients received as referrals as a result of club entertaining; the names of the individuals entertained and the reason why additional income could reasonably be expected from each; whether or not any referrals were actually received from those entertained, and any indication of the effect of the club entertainment on these referrals; the number of times individuals were entertained during the year (inasmuch as repeated entertainment indicates a personal social motive—an IRS "no-no"); and finally, whether or not professionals in the same type of practice in the locality have similar entertainment expenses.

Situations that might make club dues allowable to professional men might be such as the following:

Dan Rowan, a young lawyer, has just joined an established law firm. His success and retention in the firm are dependent on his contributing to the growth of the firm. He joins Eagle Rock Golf Club, which has many members whom he considers to be potential clients. As a result of his participation in the club's activities, he makes several valuable contacts, which lead to an increase in his firm's practice.

Dr. Edward Becker, orthopedist, joined Seaside Yacht Club. He entertained other doctors there, who referred patients to him. Since entertainment of this sort was generally expected of him, as it was of other orthopedists in Dr. Becker's locale, and a substantial number of his patients were referred to him as a result of his entertainments, a tax deduction on his Seaside Yacht Club dues would make it with the IRS.

Besides individual entertainments and club dues, Uncle Sam might allow you a deduction for what it calls an "entertainment facility." What in the world is an "entertainment facility"? The IRS lists under that heading such things as yachts, hunting lodges, fishing camps, swimming pools, tennis courts, ski houses, and airplanes. How can you, if you purchase one, qualify it as a business expense?

Basically, the rules are the same for entertainment facilities as they are for club dues. They must be used at least 51% of the time for business for you to gain any deduction at all. Then, for every percentage of business use over that, you may deduct that percentage on your expenses connected with the facility.

Let's take a yacht as an example. What specifically would be deductible if you use it 80% of the time for business entertaining?

1. 80% of the purchase price
2. 80% of maintenance and repairs, insurance, storage fees
3. 80% of salaries paid to hired hands, workmen
4. 80% of casualty losses, such as windstorm damage, theft, collision
5. 80% of operating costs: gas, oil, tune-ups, phone
6. Depreciation on the yacht—the percentage of the life expectancy of the yacht in any one year, multiplied by your 80%-business-use percentage
7. Loss on sale of the yacht (for example, a yacht that originally cost $50,000 with a life expectancy of ten years is used 80% for business and 20% for personal use; after five years it is sold for $25,000; there is an ordinary profit of $5,000 on the sale of the yacht based on its business use)

8. Cost of food and beverage during business use

It is a good idea when keeping track of your entertainment-facility business deduction to note in your diary not only the days it is used for business, but also the days it is used for personal recreation. Try to keep those business and personal days separate to help further establish use. However, if personal and business use occur on the same day, the IRS will allow business-use deduction for that day.

The following is an example of a yacht used 60% for business, showing a loss on sale:

	100% Total Use of Yacht	60% Business Use of Yacht	40% Personal Use of Yacht
	$40,000	$24,000	$16,000
Cost less 4-year depreciation on 10-year life	−16,000	9,600	No Depreciation allowed
Cost basis of sale	$24,000	$14,400	$16,000
Sale price	20,000	12,000	8,000
Ordinary loss	($ 4,000)	($ 2,400)	No loss allowed

If your idea of fun is gambling junkets to Las Vegas, you will be happy to know that though the IRS requires that you declare your winnings as income (on the 1040 line that asks for "miscellaneous income"), it also allows you to deduct your losses. Catch: Losses can only be deducted against winnings, so that if you lose your shirt at the blackjack tables, or if you haven't even made it with the pinball machines, you cannot take a loss. Be sure to have proof of your gambling losses. Racetrack tickets, casino receipts, etc., will substantiate your claim.

If you had combined your trip to Las Vegas with business you had to do there, you might even qualify for a deduction on transportation and some other expenses. Our next chapter goes into detail about deductible travel and also transportation.

CHAPTER 14

Deductions and Travel and Transportation

Travel to be deductible must meet the same standards as your entertainment deductions. It must be "ordinary and necessary" for the conduct of your business and it must avoid the "lavish and extravagant." As with entertainment, that latter phrase, "lavish and extravagant," is determined on a case-by-case basis. The IRS has no guidelines for that, but we say that if you keep your travel costs consistent with your business position or professional position, chances are you will not run into trouble.

There are other things to know about what the IRS has to say about travel expenses. Look at this:

You are the owner of an exclusive women's dress shop outside Boston. You frequently take the shuttle down to New York to make special purchases for important clients. You leave Boston in the morning and return usually by 10:00 P.M. You have had your lunch and dinner in New York.

What is deductible as business expenses in that example? The costs of your shuttle tickets back and forth to Boston; the costs of transportation to and from the airport and your errands in New York. Your lunch and dinner, too? The IRS says no lunch deduction and no dinner deduction. It says that meals and lodging are deductible only as part of expenses away from home. And this means, it says, "away from home *overnight*." So had you taken a hotel room in New York and slept

137

over, taking the shuttle back the next morning, not only your hotel room but also all your meals would be deductible.

Let's take another example.

You live in a suburb of Cleveland. You are an engineer for a concern whose main office is in Cleveland. As part of your job you must make periodic troubleshooting trips to your concern's plants and units. You travel by auto. Some of the places are quite a distance away. You must be on the road several days and nights to get back and forth to these places. Some of the plants and units are only a day's drive back and forth. Can you deduct all your expenses for these trips? Okay for gas, tolls, and routine maintenance for all your trips. And on trips where you travel for several days, you may deduct meal and motel expenses. However, the IRS says on those that are day trips you may not deduct meals.

Now, if you often make day trips on business, you are losing a lot in tax deductions for meals because of that "overnight" ruling. Our philosophy is, take every deduction even if you have to fight for it. And an IRS ruling is just that—a ruling. It does not have the force of law. IRS rulings can be disputed. You can fight that "overnight" rule as being capricious. After all, you are only making those trips for business reasons— "ordinary and necessary" business reasons. We say take all your expenses on the day trips. Argue your case if you go to audit for it. Enough cases are being won in the courts on the "overnight" ruling to knock it out so that you may very well win your case.

It's not difficult to grasp the idea of the IRS's "overnight" rule. But do you know what the IRS means by the phrase "away from home"? "Home" in IRS language means your principal place of business, employment, or post of duty. For IRS tax purposes, it is not necessarily where you hang your hat at the end of the day.

Why is this important? Because if you are sent on temporary assignment (emphasize the word "temporary") to a city quite a distance from your tax home (IRS translation: your principal place of work—a place too far for daily commuting), you may have to spend a substantial amount of time there, maybe as much as six months. You have to live in a hotel, or perhaps you sublet an apartment. It costs. There are all those restaurant tabs, too. Happy news! Because you are on temporary assignment and away from home—too far to commute—your living costs, lodging, and meals will be deductible to you.

What does the IRS consider "temporary"? The "temporary" test of the IRS is usually (1) your assignment is reasonably expected to last less than one year, or (2) your assignment really does last less than one year. The first case sounds hazy. Let's illustrate:

You are an architect supervising the construction of a major office building in Minneapolis. You work out of the main office of your firm in San Francisco. The building in Minneapolis is expected to be finished in ten months. Materials delivery delays and union labor strikes slow down the job. You wind up being in Minneapolis for sixteen months.

Will you still be able to deduct the costs of your hotel room and meals? Yes, because your original honest estimate was that you were going to be on the job for less than one year.

The courts have taken a more liberal view of what is considered "temporary" in tax cases. The courts reason that your living in a place other than your permanent residence is temporary if it is impractical to move family and possessions lock, stock, and barrel for the time you will be living and working in another locale.

You might take this decision into consideration if you are in the same position as a college professor who is hired for two years at a university too far for him to reach on a commuting basis. If he moves his family, it might mean his taking a large loss on the sale of his house and disrupting his children's education. He decides to keep the family where it is and goes by himself to the new university to work for the two years. He takes a deduction on the apartment he rents and meals at the new university, and fights for his deduction using the court's view as his guideline.

Suppose you work at something that requires continuous travel. You are an actress with a long Broadway run; your permanent residence is in Colorado. Or you teach at a university in Louisiana; you travel to another university seventy miles away to work on your Ph.D. Or you are a salesman who continually travels in the Northeast; you have no main office, but your family lives in Maine. All the foregoing are cases of taxpayers who do not have a principal place of employment that the IRS would call their tax home. The courts have decided in cases such as those that the principal place of *residence* of the taxpayer is his tax home.

If your occupation requires you to travel a great deal, if you must be away from your permanent residence a great deal and incur duplicate living expenses, you might go along with the decision that the courts are coming up with more and more that your tax home is where your permanent residence is, and that therefore your expenses away from there are deductible on your 1040.

What if you combine business and pleasure in one trip to a business or professional convention? If the primary purpose of the trip is to attend the convention, your transportation is deductible as a business expense. Ask yourself if you would have taken the trip if it hadn't been for the convention. Also deductible are meals and lodging while traveling to the convention and expenses of the convention—your room, meals, and bar tabs while at the convention, convention fees, and business entertainment.

Sight-seeing trips before or after the convention are not deductible. But remember, the costs of getting to your convention city and back—the largest costs—can be written off!

In order to deduct those costs, it is up to you to prove that the trip was primarily for business; otherwise nothing at all—zilch, zero—is deductible. How do you do that? Keep a copy of the convention program. Check off the sessions you attended. Take notes of what the speakers had to say. If there is a sign-in book for sessions, sign in. If your deduction is questioned as to whether you actually attended the business sessions of the convention or just went to play golf in the tournament, the secretary of the convention's sponsoring organization will have a record and can send you photostats of your signature in the sign-up book. To establish further proof of the business purpose of your trip, use your business check or business credit card to pay for registration fees, transportation, and hotel bills. Keep receipts for these, too.

What if your convention is in a foreign country? You are a psychiatrist and there is a psychiatric convention in Freud's hometown, Vienna. Can you deduct for that, too? Again the rule: You must be making the trip primarily for business. Though you do intend to do some sight-seeing in Vienna and you also intend to take in Paris before you return home, the IRS will be convinced of your business intent if you go along with their rule of thumb that more than half your time on the trip is spent on business and if you bring back substantial proof from the convention that you were serious about it, instead of simply signing up for it and sitting around lapping up whipped cream and Wiener schnitzel. That means signing up for sessions and taking notes. Of course, if you get yourself invited to speak or to read a paper, so much the better for your business-purpose proof.

Warning: The IRS is allowing only two foreign conventions per person per year. So if you have a choice of conventions in Rome, Tokyo, Athens, Seville, Durban, Bangkok, or Peking, you must narrow your choice down to only two of those conventions for this year. That should not be too much of a hardship when you consider that the government is going to help pick up the tab on the cost of getting there and costs of meals, drinks, and hotel at the convention; and that ruling does not include a convention to San Juan, since Puerto Rico as a commonwealth of the United States does not come under the "two only" rule of foreign conventions.

Combination pleasure and business trips are not just confined to conventions. You might take a trip within the United States or to foreign countries for other business reasons or for educational reasons. If your trip is a combination business-pleasure trip, remember that more than half of it should be accounted for as business in order to prove that business was your primary motive for the trip.

You are a furrier; you travel to Russia and come back by way of Paris and Milan. You took in the Kremlin, the Louvre, and "The Last Supper," but your primary purpose was to buy skins in Russia and to take in the fashion shows in Paris and Milan. You are a doctor who specializes in the treatment of alcoholics. You take a trip to Scandinavia, you take in the fjords, but you visit over twenty-five alcoholism-treatment centers, interviewing directors about their methods of treatment. You are a fourth-grade classroom teacher, involved in a project in your school district to encourage the language arts. You take a trip to Britain; you take in the Tower of London, but you also observe the teaching of English in British schoolrooms. You visit about fifteen schools, taking notes on your observations for a report to your project group back home.

What is deductible? Not only your transatlantic plane fare but also costs of your transportation between cities, as well as costs of hotels, meals, tips, laundry, and expenses of entertaining people you saw on business.

You would like to travel, and you can think of some bona fide business purpose for a trip, but your wife (or husband) would be furious if you left him or her behind. Can you take your spouse along and get a deduction on his/her expenses? Yes, if you can prove that your spouse performed a bona fide business service.

You are a doctor, for instance, attending a medical convention. There are many sessions that pertain to your specialty, kidney transplants. Several of the sessions meet at the same time. You take your husband along to sit in on the sessions and take notes for you while you attend other sessions running at the same time. You are an importer of novelty items. Your wife accompanies you on a trip to the Orient to seek out new sources of supply. She visits certain outlets while you visit others, and she actually negotiates with some of the manufacturers. You are a Los Angeles TV producer. You take your wife with you to New York, where you are wooing backers. Your wife, who is familiar with your business, acts as your secretary, making appointments and taking shorthand notes during business meetings.

What are deductible as business expenses in such cases for your spouse if you take him or her along? Round-trip plane fare, meals, hotels, and any other expenses that would be deductible to you on a business trip.

Even if you can't conjure up a bona fide business reason for your spouse, look at it this way: If you take him or her along and stay in a double room, you may still deduct what it would have cost you to stay in a single room. (A double room costs you $65 per night; a single room would have cost you $45. You may deduct the cost of a single room: $45.) If you are traveling by auto, you may still deduct mileage (20 cents a mile for the first 15,000 miles, and 11 cents a mile for any additional mileage), plus tolls and parking. If you rent a car, the rental is deductible. With your spouse along it costs no more for car expenses, and you still get your deduction, though there is no deduction for your spouse on public transportation if she is just along for the ride.

As we said before, to be deductible as a business trip the trip must meet the "ordinary and necessary" rule and must be taken primarily for business purposes. If you want that trip to pass IRS scrutiny, you must have proof—substantial proof—of its business purpose. Build up that proof before you leave on your trip. To show the whys, the wheres, and who is involved in the necessity of taking your trip, make business appointments ahead of time; write letters to those you propose to see, and keep carbons of those letters. Send letters confirming your phone conversation to those you speak to on the phone regarding your trip. Keep a diary of all your appointments while on the trip. Make notes of your business observations. If you must report to someone when you get back home, keep a copy of your report. Pay trip expenses by check or credit card. Note other expenses daily in your diary. Photographs, if related to your business purpose (for instance, snaps of that new type plant machinery you saw in Lyons), may be helpful.

There is no deduction for your commuting expenses to your job from home and back. But look at this: If you have a home office, attend to some business at home in the morning, and then go on to your business appointment for the day, your commute to the business appointment is deductible.

Woody Lehman is a young accountant. He practices out of his home. Before he leaves his home for the day to visit a client, he does some paperwork in preparation. Then on to the client's office for the rest of the day. He figures he gets a hefty tax deduction each year on commuting expenses by having that office at home, and he is only walking down the hall of his apartment to get to his first stop!

What does Woody base his deduction on? IRS regulations say that transportation costs from your office to business appointments during your workday are deductible business expenses.

Transportation costs to a second job from your first job are also deductible. However, costs of the trip from your second job back to home are not.

Marcia Williams works as an assistant curator in a museum. Her day starts early and ends early. She goes from her museum job to her second job, at the office of an arts news magazine, where she is an editor and where she works for four hours every day. From the magazine office she goes home to her apartment. Marcia deducts taxi fare from her museum job to her magazine job. The fare from the magazine job back to her apartment is not deductible.

Transportation costs to school from work, if you are going to school to improve your skills on the job, are deductible, too.

Gary Upton is manager of administration for the advertising division of a TV network. Twice a week he takes the subway from work downtown to a university, where he is studying for his M.B.A. in marketing, required by his employer in his field. Gary deducts the subway fare from the office to school. However, he may not deduct the subway fare from the university to his home.

Clarice Engle is a legal secretary. On Wednesday nights she takes a pottery course at the same university that Gary attends. Clarice may not deduct her fare to the university. Pottery has nothing to do with improving her skills as a legal secretary, nor is it required by her employer.

In all the allowable cases of deductions for transportation between office and jobs, between one job and another, and between job and school, if you take your auto instead of public transportation, you are permitted 20 cents for the first 15,000 miles, and 11 cents per mile beyond that.

Did you know that there is another aspect of your life that will give you an auto mileage deduction? It is in the charitable aspect of your life, which is discussed in the next chapter.

CHAPTER 15

Charity and Your Tax Deductions

Charity, sweet charity . . . what can be sweeter? The tax deduction that you get for it, especially when you realize that as your tax rate goes up with higher income, the actual cost of giving goes down.

If you itemize your deductions (which, of course, we assume you do, for maximum tax advantage to you), you can—the law says—deduct charitable deductions up to 50% of your adjusted gross income. You may also deduct gifts of certain long-term-gain property at 30% of adjusted gross, which we will go into later.

Now, you just can't hand out money to beggars on the street and claim a charitable deduction. Contributions cannot be made to individuals and count as deductions. Furthermore, the IRS has its list of approved organizations. It even has a publication that lists qualified donees—IRS publication No. 78—which you can send for if you are not sure your pet charity meets the scrutiny of the IRS as a charitable organization. Generally, though, the following categories of organizations will meet the test:

1. A governmental unit such as a government agency, a state university, a police department, or a fire department. The agency may

COST OF A $100 DONATION

Taxable Income	Single	Married, Joint	Married, Separate	Head of Household
$ 2,500	$86	$100	$86	$86
5,000	82	86	82	84
7,500	82	84	79	82
10,000	79	82	76	78
15,000	70	79	63	74
20,000	66	76	57	69
25,000	61	68	51	64
30,000	56	63	46	58
35,000	51	63	46	54
40,000	51	57	46	54
45,000	45	57	41	46
50,000	45	51	41	46
55,000	45	51	36	46
60,000	37	46	36	41
65,000	37	46	36	41
70,000	37	46	36	41
75,000	37	46	36	41
80,000	37	46	36	41
85,000	32	46	32	37
90,000	32	41	32	37
95,000	32	41	32	37
100,000	32	41	32	37
110,000	30	36	30	32
161,300	30	36	30	30
162,400	30	32	30	30
215,400	30	30	30	30

be of the federal, state, city, or town government.

2. Religious organizations. Deductions include dues to churches and synagogues, assessments, and contributions for seats or pews.

3. Charitable organizations such as American Red Cross, Boy Scouts, Girl Scouts, YMHA, YMCA, YWHA, YWCA, heart societies, cancer societies, Salvation Army, CARE.

4. Scientific, literary, or educational organizations. Included are such organizations as hospitals, colleges and universities, historical societies, research organizations, and organizations to combat crime and to promote the general public welfare.

5. Organizations promoting national or international amateur sports competitions, such as the Amateur Athletic Union or the Olympic Sports Committee.

6. Societies for the prevention of cruelty to children or animals.

7. U.S. nonprofit veterans' organizations or auxiliary units.

8. U.S. fraternities or lodges, if contributions are going to be used for religious, charitable, scientific, literary, or educational purposes.

9. Nonprofit cemeteries or burial companies where the contribution is to benefit the whole cemetery and not simply an individual plot.

A charitable deduction you cannot take is one to a foreign charitable organization, unless the contribution is made to an American organization that does charitable work abroad. If you are touring India, for instance, and the abject poverty tugs at your heartstrings and you would like to make a contribution to one of India's charities, remember that you will not be able to claim a deduction for it. But if, say, you made a contribution to the American Red Cross and stipulated that your contribution goes toward funds directed to India, your contribution would be deductible.

Another hard-and-fast rule when it comes to charitable deduction: Your contribution cannot be made to an organization that is directly going to benefit you economically.

A couple sent their son to a private school which, on top of tuition, demanded a donation as a requirement of admission. The IRS denied deduction for the donation to the school because it was of direct benefit to the couple.

A senior citizen was told by a retirement home that if he made a donation to the home he would get a more favorable room. The IRS said nix on the deduction of the donation. It was of direct benefit to the senior citizen.

Contributions are deductible only in the year that you actually wrote the check. If you pledged $500 to your church's building drive one year and gave the church that $500 check in the following year, you deduct the contribution the year you wrote the check, not the year you made the pledge. If you split the paying of your pledge over two years—$250 one year and $250 the next year—you deduct $250 in each year you actually gave the church $250.

If you paid your pledge by credit card, you deduct the amount in the year that you made the charge, regardless of when the bank is paid.

When you go to church, you put a few dollars in the collection plate. Can you deduct that cash? Yes, but unless you have proof of how much you put into the collection plate, the IRS will use its own guidelines. It usually would allow you $78 for the year with unsupported cash donations. If you figure your largess to the church as greater than that, use a church envelope with your name on it. Ask your clergyman for a written accounting of your envelope-enclosed contributions. After all, if you go to church every week and put ten dollars in the collection plate every week, those collection-plate donations would amount to over $500.

You may decide to donate used clothing or household goods to your charity thrift shop and collect a tax deduction. To survive the scrutiny of a possible audit, have the charity list items donated and estimate their value.

According to IRS regulations, your deduction for gifts of property is generally equal to the fair market value of donated property at the time of contribution. The fair market value of the contributed property for purposes of charitable deduction is the price at which the property would change hands at the time of the gift donation between buyer and seller. For instance, the donor of a set of slipcovers in good condition to a thrift shop was given a receipt for $50 for her donation from a worker in the thrift shop who appraised them and felt confident that that was the amount the shop could sell the slipcovers for. The donor can claim a tax deduction of $50 on her next tax return to the charity that runs the thrift shop. She will, of course, file the receipt with her tax-record information should this item ever be questioned on a possible tax audit. The charity thrift shop, for its part, will also have proof that such a donation was made and appraised at $50. Proof of donation and estimate of value are essential for a charitable-contribution claim on your tax return. Your word that you donated a bundle of clothing or your old bedroom set to the Salvation Army is not acceptable to the IRS. It is a good idea to attach a photocopy of valuation with your return.

We have found from our experience lately that many charities are reluctant to involve themselves with the IRS these days on valuation. Charity workers claim it's a hassle, so many charity thrift shops are not giving valuations. Instead, they are asking donors to put their own valuations on donations. How can you figure valuations so that you are not called up by the IRS as being out of line on the one hand, or gypping yourself out of deductible dollars on the other? We might look at a recent case on this subject.

A taxpayer gave used clothing to a church and a school for a rummage sale. There was no valuation given, so he estimated the original cost of the clothing—$525—and deducted 40%. The IRS found that 40% was a bit stiff; they allowed him 20%.

We say that if you can't get an appraisal from the charity, at least make a list of what you donate, item by item, and list original cost. If it is used clothing you know from the foregoing case that you can count on a deduction of at least 20% of original cost. Suppose you donate some items that are brand new—have never been used or worn. Then we say you might take a deduction on those items of 40% of the original cost and be safe. Comment: Charitable deduction on new items donated—40% of original cost on new items is extremely cautious; however, this is what IRS allows without question. We feel it is better to go along with IRS on this than to risk an audit.

What if you inherited an eighteenth-century cloisonné pillbox from Aunt Alida, but you dig only Bloomingdale's chrome? You decide to make a memorial contribution to Aunt Alida by donating the pillbox to charity. The difference between this donation and donations of castoffs is that the pillbox has appreciated in value since Aunt Alida bought it, and you want to make sure that you get credit for the appreciation. You are now claiming a deduction higher than cost.

Again, the IRS demands a properly prepared receipt from the charity receiving the donation. Additional IRS requirements: Your donation must be private personal property (nothing to do with business); you must have owned the item for at least one year; and you must establish the increased value of your donation.

How does one do that? Many charities have expert appraisers on staff for such donations. You can take the charity expert's appraisal, which is free, and, if the charity has a good track record with the IRS on appraisals, it will be acceptable. Or you may hire an independent appraiser. The burden of proving appreciated value rests with the taxpayer. Be careful: The IRS is not stupid and has its own staff of expert appraisers.

Two reputable appraisal associations are the Antique Appraisal Association of America and the American Society of Appraisers. The IRS recognizes that those associations have stiff requirements for membership.

The average fee for a certified appraiser is a minimum of $100, or 1½% base fee. Some appraisers work on a basis of about $50 an hour. After your item or items are written up and appraised, you will receive a copy of the appraisal. The certified appraiser is required to hold on to his copy of the appraisal for five years, a good thing to know if the IRS is checking on tax returns of prior years. The appraisal fee itself is tax deductible, not as a charitable contribution but under miscellaneous deductions, and there is no sales tax on appraisals because appraisal is considered a professional necessity service.

Instead of donating cash, some people might like to donate stock. Now, if you have held the stock only in the short term (less than one year), you will get only a deduction for cost of the stock. So it makes sense to hold off until you can claim a donation on transfer of the stock when it has appreciated over the long term (more than one year). The IRS says that with appreciated stock held over the long term, you may deduct only up to 30% of your adjusted gross instead of the 50% deduction allowed for other charities. Why is that? Because you have made a gain on the stock and have not paid a capital-gains tax. The reduction to 30% of adjusted gross from 50% of adjusted gross for cash donations is to offset the fact that you have not paid a capital-gains tax on your appreciated stock. A good suggestion if you are contributing appreciated property is to seek professional tax counsel to get maximum allowance allowed under law. Remember that excess contributions can be carried forward to future years and used as deductions.

In some cases you may feel that even though some securities have dropped in value below cost, you would like to donate the securities for what they are worth to your favorite charity. Don't. If you donate them, you will only be able to take a deduction at their current cost. Instead, sell them, take a long-term capital loss on your tax return, and then donate the cash from sale of the security to your charity.

Example: You have stock you bought five years ago for $10,000. It is now worth only $2,000. If you donate it to your charity without selling first, you only get a tax deduction of $2,000. Instead, you take a long-term capital loss of $8,000 and then donate the $2,000 realized on the sale of the security.

If you do volunteer work, do not overlook possible charitable deductions for costs incurred in doing your stint for your organization. You may deduct the cost of commutation in doing your volunteer work, and costs of meals, lodging on a trip away from home for the organization, uniforms, telephone calls, and materials and supplies, including stamps and stationery. If you use your car to get to your volunteer job and/or in your volunteer job, you may deduct 9 cents a mile.

Josh Hickson was a member of the National Ski Patrol. As a member of the patrol he was given a free ski-lift ticket. Even better than that were the deductions for his skiing expenses he was able to take as charitable contributions. He was able to deduct 9 cents per mile plus tolls for his trip up to Vermont, rent for his ski chalet, and the cost of all meals while up at the ski area he patrolled. He could also deduct registration fees for patrol meetings and refresher courses, first-aid supplies used in patrol work, annual dues, patrol belts, and patches. He could not deduct his skis, bindings, and ski clothing, but he didn't complain; his ski-patrol activity gave him his skiing for the winter plus a nice deduction of over $2,000!

An *au courant* note in these days of the energy crisis is the increase in donations to charity of "gas guzzlers." A doctor in Los Angeles wheeled his 1970

Cadillac Coupe deVille into a Salvation Army center and handed over the title to a charity worker. The car had brand-new tires and was in good running order. More and more, people are donating their old clunkers that operate but use a lot of gas. Especially numerous are the number of station wagons being donated to charity.

Donators of automobiles usually deduct from their taxes the "blue book" value of the car, usually higher than a car dealer would pay them for the car, so the donators figure they come out ahead by donating their "gas guzzler" to a charity!

Charity and sex seem far apart as aspects of your life, but believe it or not, the sexual aspect of your life may allow for tax deductions too, as we see in the next chapter.

CHAPTER 16

Sex and Taxes

This book promised to go into all aspects of your life and tell how each aspect relates to our topic of saving on taxes. A very important aspect of your life is the expression of your sexuality. At first glance, it seems that there is little regarding sex that is tax deductible. And, admittedly, there is not too much you can deduct on the expression of your carnal desires. However, there are some deductions, and since we are dedicated to not letting any deduction or tax saving go by the boards, we are zeroing in on those few that copulation can garner for you.

Now, the IRS is quite prudish about couples living together without benefit of holy wedlock. If you are living with someone of the opposite sex (we might also say, for gay readers, someone of the same sex) and are not legally married, you may not file in the Married Filing Joint Return category, even if you did exchange vows on the beaches at Pie de la Cuesta beneath a full moon with a lifeguard as your witness. Neither may you take your common-law spouse as an exemption. However, in a revenue ruling, the IRS does say that "parties are married if state of residence recognizes their common-law marriage; if marriage is contracted in a state recognizing it, status is not affected by moving to another state." So if you live in a state that recognizes common-law marriage, you are considered as legally married in the eyes of the IRS as if you had gone before a preacher. You will recall from your American government courses that the federal system states that the law of the states is supreme over that of the federal government.

Deductions directly attributable to your venereal life include those for birth control. Birth-control pills, and devices for birth control such as the diaphragm and the IUD, are medical deductions, as are visits to your physician when he prescribes birth-control pills or birth-control devices. Sterilization operations—tubal ligation for the female and vasectomy for the male—may be counted as medical deductions. Even an abortion, providing the abortion is legal in the state in which it is performed, is a medical deduction. Don't try to deduct it on your tax return for your girlfriend, even though you might have paid the bill for it. It is only deductible on the tax return of the person on whom it is performed, or for his or her dependent.

Perhaps your sex life is not going well. You suffer from what is referred to as sexual dysfunction. You seek the services of a sexual therapist (we mean a certified sexual therapist here, and not a "lady of the evening"). We have seen no case so far arguing the validity of payments for sexual therapists as medical care, but your payments are for diagnosis and cure of a bodily function, aren't they? So take the deduction and fight for it if it is questioned. You are on firm legal ground.

There are expenses you may incur to enhance your sex life—gold lamé slit-down-to-there jumpsuits, Chanel No. 5, satin sheets for women, a Jaguar XKE, Aramis, a quadrisonic sound set with a library of romantic records for men; but unless you have an angle we don't know about, they are *not* tax deductible. Do take heart, though; the dependents that are products of your sex life are worth $1,000 each in exemptions!

You see, though there are not too many deductions you may take for the expression of your sexuality, there are some. Amazingly enough, you may even take tax deductions on taxes. Read the next chapter to find out how you may make the most of your tax deductions on taxes.

CHAPTER 17

Taxes and Deductions

Death and taxes. You have heard all your life that these are two things that no one can avoid. You also might know though, if you have perused Schedule A of your 1040, that some taxes are deductible. Specifically, which taxes are deductible and which are not? What is the most prudent manner of deducting those taxes?

For a tax to be deductible it must fall into one of the following classes:

1. Income tax. That includes state, local—such as city and county—and foreign taxes (taxes imposed by a foreign country on any of its political subdivisions).
2. Real-property tax. Again, this may be state, local, or foreign.
3. Personal-property tax. This is imposed by some, but not all, states and local governments.
4. General sales tax. This tax may be imposed by a state and also by local government.

Let's take state and local income tax. If you received a refund on your taxes last year you probably may make the mistake of including that refund in your gross income. The refund is included in income only if the refund is for a year in which you itemized local income tax. If you included your refund as income, you have raised your gross income. Why is that bad for your tax situation? Because if you have a potential medical deduction stating your refund as income and raising your gross income, you will lose 3% against your medical deduction. Remember, you are permitted a medical deduction for expenses that exceed 3% of your gross income. You will also lose out on a possible part of your charitable deduction because you are permitted 50% of your gross income on charity. The regulations say "No," but try offsetting the refund against the local income-tax deduction for the current year. If you should be questioned, you can show that the refund was reported.

Another strategy you might want to employ is to pay your estimate for state and local taxes in December instead of January. You would do that, of course, only if you wanted to get an additional deduction for the year you are planning.

Rod Michaels has $5,000 in income not subject to withholding. It represents dividends and interest. He had estimated that his state tax on that income is $600. Rod had elected to make four installments of $150 each on April 15, June 15, September 15, and next January 15. He can increase his state income-tax deduction by $150 for the year if he pays the January 15 payment in the preceding December. Rod figures he saves the federal tax on $150, and since he is in the 50% bracket, that $150 deduction means $75 in his pocket.

Real-estate or real-property taxes, whether they are levied by the state, city, or county, are deductible. They generally are not deductible if assessed for local benefits or use and improvements that tend to increase the value of assessed property. For instance, if there is a special tax in your area because new sewers are being installed, and there is a tax to pay for the sewers, that tax would not be deductible. That tax is increasing the value of your assessed property. If the local-benefit tax is for maintenance or repair or for meeting interest charges related to those benefits, it would be deductible. Now, if only a portion of the local tax is for maintenance and repair and interest, make sure that your local authority has broken it down to show those items, because you will be able to deduct what is allocated to those items. Real-estate taxes can be paid in advance to get a larger deduction, but very often real-estate taxes are placed in escrow—that is, the mortgage holder (probably a bank) has a sum from your mortgage payments from which it pays your real-estate taxes and also withdraws interest and principal. Once a year, your bank will send you a breakdown of your mortgage payments. From this notice you will be able to determine how much of your mortgage payments went toward real-estate taxes. Unfortunately, you can deduct only the real-estate taxes (and interest, which is another case). You cannot deduct the rest of your mortgage payments relating to principal, and possibly insurance.

Real-estate taxes are deductible only to the one on whom they are levied (the property owner).

George Willis and his wife, Leah, lived in his mother's home with her. George's mother owned the house, but George paid all the maintenance costs and provided total support on other items for his mother, including payment of the real-estate taxes. However, poor George could not deduct the real-estate taxes on his return because the property was owned by his mother, and thus the taxes were levied on property in her name. Had George's mother signed ownership of the property over to him, he would have been able to deduct the taxes because the taxes would be levied on property he owns.

Personal-property taxes are levied by some states and localities, but not all states and localities. For a personal-property tax to qualify as a deduction it must meet the following tests:

1. The tax must be based on the value of the personal property. A tax based on anything else does not qualify.

Lonnie Milner's state imposes a yearly motor vehicle registration tax of 1% value plus 40 cents per hundred weight. Lonnie paid $28.60 based on value ($1,500) and weight (3,400 pounds) for her auto. She may deduct $15 as a personal-property tax since it is based on the value. The remaining $13.60, based on the weight, is not deductible.

2. The tax must be imposed on an annual basis, even if collected more, or less, frequently.

3. The tax must be imposed on personal property. A tax is considered imposed on personal property even if in form it is imposed on the use of a privilege. Thus an annual tax based on value qualifies as a personal-property tax although it is called a registration fee imposed for the privilege of registering motor vehicles or of using them on the highways.

General sales taxes are taxes that are levied at the same rate on a broad classification of retail items or services. They are deductible. (Selective sales or excise taxes that do not apply to a general range of retail items, such as the selective tax on alcoholic beverages, cigarettes, admissions, or luxury items, are not deductible.)

State sales-tax tables are provided with your tax return for use in figuring your sales-tax deduction according to your income and according to your state percentage of sales tax. Caution here: Those tax tables do not account for extra city or county sales taxes, which you have a right to deduct also. You will have to make an adjustment in the state sales-tax table to figure those other taxes in your general sales-tax deduction. Take this example:

Jed Ambler lives in New York State. He has an adjusted gross income of $20,000. There are four people in his family: himself, his wife, and two children.

According to the state sales-tax table, Jed's deduction for sales tax is $230. That takes into account New York State's 4% sales tax. However, Jed lives in Nassau County, where there is another 3% sales tax, for a total of 7% sales tax. Jed makes the adjustment for Nassau County by dividing the amount on the tax table by 4 and then multiplying by 7 ($230 ÷ 4 × 7 = $403). Thus Jed may deduct $403 on his combined New York State and Nassau County sales taxes.

Actually, the state sales-tax tables are figured very low. We believe you would do even better if you get out your pocket calculator, total all checks made out to department stores, any other store payments where a general sales tax is levied, and restaurant charges on credit cards. From the total of all these checks, take your percentage on state and local taxes. You will most probably find that the result is higher than on the standard sales-tax table.

If you had big-ticket items during the year—you bought new bedroom furniture, you gave your daughter a lavish wedding, you treated yourself to a mink coat—you paid plenty in sales tax. Now the IRS says that the only big-ticket items you can add to the standard sales-tax table are: (1) a car, motorcycle, a motor home, or a truck; (2) a boat, a plane, or a home (including mobile or prefabricated, or materials you bought to build a new home). We feel that is too narrow a definition, so we keep track of big-ticket-item taxes and write "extraordinary items" in one of the blank lines under "taxes" on Schedule A, and follow with the amount of the tax on those "extraordinary items." After all, isn't your daughter's wedding as important as someone else's purchase of a motorcycle? We think so, and whenever an item such as a daughter's wedding has been subject to audit scrutiny, we have fought for and won on the sales-tax deduction.

You might have paid a hefty sum in taxes for hobby equipment. Perhaps without knowing it, what you really have is a second source of income rather than a hobby, or at least a potential source of a second income. If you do, you will find that you will be able to take some lucrative deductions. The next chapter tells when a hobby is a business and what you can deduct on expenses of your hobby-business.

CHAPTER 18

Your Hobby and Deductions

Webster defines a hobby as: "a specialized pursuit that is outside one's regular occupation and that one finds interesting and enjoys doing usually in a nonprofessional way as a source of leisure-time relaxation." Your hobby may be growing geraniums, refinishing furniture, or painting miniatures. Friends comment on how proficient you are at your hobby and that perhaps you ought to sell your work.

Now, if you do sell your work, the IRS says that you must declare the proceeds as income, even if what you get is so small an amount you may consider it just a pittance compared with the money you have spent on equipment. However, there is a happy note: The IRS does allow you to deduct your expenses (only to the extent of your hobby income, though).

In this discussion of hobbies and deduction, let's pretend that photography is your hobby. (In reading, substitute your particular hobby with its particular materials and equipment.) You may have started out with a simple camera, but over the years you have assembled more sophisticated equipment and even built a darkroom in your basement. Mostly you snap photos for your own enjoyment. However, you have done some work for pay on a casual basis—submitted photos for sale at charity shows, did a few children's portraits, occasionally shot a neighbor's wedding, for which you received some compensation. You made

$550 from these small sales of photos in your spare time.

The IRS will allow you to deduct your expenses. However, the deduction on expenses is only to the extent of your income from the sale of your photos. So then, since you made $550, you will be able to deduct only up to $550 in expenses on your hobby.

Because you are now considered to have a profit motive for your hobby—you did sell the pictures, remember?—you are considered to be in business and entitled to take regular business deductions. The IRS stipulates that profits must be realized in two out of five consecutive years. If expenses exceed income, but your intention is to be in business and there is a possibility you will show income in the next five years, deduct your excess expenses over income as a loss on Schedule C.

Even though you may not profit the first year, or in some lean years, you can still take certain business deductions providing you can show that you had "reasonable expectations" of realizing a profit. "Reasonable expectations" is the key phrase, which distinguishes you as a profit-seeking photographer from the casual hobbyist. To qualify for business deductions you have to prove that you have spent a regular portion of your time in pursuit of your photography.

Keep a daily diary describing what you do throughout the year as proof of your hobby-business efforts. In order to avoid confusion, keep a hobby diary separate from your regular business diary. You might have an entry in your hobby diary that looks like this:

June 15
8:00 P.M. to 11:30 P.M.
Darkroom: developed pictures of Clark birthday-party job

Regular entries throughout the year will show that you spent a consistent amount of time and were serious in your efforts.

Also back up your claim of being serious about pursuit of your hobby-business by evidence of your work. Keep your negatives in neat order in filing cabinets. Keep letters relating to acceptance of your work and even letters rejecting your work. If the IRS is given proof that you are serious in your efforts and have a profit motive, you will be able to deduct some of those hobby-business expenses.

You are entitled to engage in more than one business at a time, and the law does allow you to take appropriate deductions.

You will have to file a Schedule C with your 1040. Schedule C is a schedule of profit or loss from business or profession—sole proprietorship. Here are some items you will find on Schedule C and, keeping in mind that we are using the example of photography as a hobby, how you would cope with them:

Method of Accounting: Because most small photography operations report their income on their records and tax returns as income received when cash is received, you will check the box marked "cash."

Inventory: This applies to large businesses where there are hundreds or thousands of inventory items. For the individual photographer, inventory is not a major factor, so this section is usually left blank.

Materials and Supplies: Enter total cost of consumer items—darkroom chemicals, film, matting supplies, paper, etc.

Other Costs: This might include costs for sending out the darkroom work, finishing work, professional matting, enlarging work, and model fees.

Inventory at End of Year: As under the Inventory section, leave blank unless you are a large business.

Depreciation: This would include your auto if used to get to photography jobs, your studio itself, and your equipment (cameras, developing equipment, enlarger, etc.). It would be best for you to use the simplest method of depreciation, which is "straight life." (See the Glossary of Tax Terms for explanation of various methods of depreciation.)

You may obtain from the IRS in Washington, D.C., "Bulletin 'F': Tables of Useful Lives of Depreciable Property." It has a separate category for photography. If your hobby work is photography, as in our example here, look up the life of a 35mm camera. You will see that the IRS considers the life of that camera as ten years; lenses as twenty years; printing and enlarging equipment as ten years. So if you paid $300 for your camera, a ten-year life will give you depreciation of $30 each year for ten years. If you use your camera a lot and feel that its life is only five years or less, then figure depreciation on that basis.

Taxes on Business and Business Property: This includes payroll taxes if you were to hire employees, unincorporated business tax if your state requires you to file on this, and any other special local taxes.

Rent on Business Property: If your studio is outside of your home and you pay rent for your studio, this is self-explanatory. However, if your studio is a part of your home, and providing that your studio is the main place for your business, you may deduct that fraction of the house you use for your studio from overall costs of maintenance. Example: You have a seven-room house; one room is completely devoted to use as a studio. You may deduct one seventh of your lighting bills, heating bills, and painting of or repairs to the exterior of your home. You may not deduct cost of repairs or maintenance for other rooms of the house. All costs for furnishings, repairs, painting, or other maintenance of the studio itself are 100% deductible.

Repairs: This means cost of repairs to your equipment relating to your photography business.

Insurance: Liability coverage, and fire and theft insurance to cover equipment and studio are deductible, as well as compensation insurance if you hire someone.

Commissions: Referral fees and commissions to an agent, if you have one, are 100% deductible.

Interest on Business Indebtedness: Interest on

money borrowed for financing for studio or equipment is 100% deductible.

Bad Debts Arising from Sales or Services: You cannot report this if you are accounting on a cash basis because the cash was never received, so leave this blank.

Other Business Expenses: This sounds rather nebulous, but is important because it can make a big difference on how much tax you will have to pay if you made a pile on your hobby-business. Here is a list of expenses that might go under this heading on your Schedule C: accounting fees, advertising, attorney's fees, automobile expenses used in business, books and periodicals pertaining to your work, cost of courses taken to improve your photography skills or business-procedure skills, cleaning service for your studio, dues to photography societies, entertainment directly related to your photography business, equipment rental, gifts to promote your business (limited to $25 per person per year), postage, stationery, local transportation (bus, subway, taxi), long-distance travel (plane tickets, train and bus fares).

To substantiate your deductions, you must keep records of all expenses. What had started out as a casual hobby has perhaps blossomed into a healthy second business or occupation. You must treat it as seriously and as meticulously as you do your primary business. It does no good merely to list the previous deductions if the IRS decides to question your return. You must show them substantial proof. Keep up your diary of all your business-related expenses. Keeping to the example of a photography business, this is how an entry in your diary might look on one particular day.

Date: May 7
Assignment: Photographs of boats for charter by the Cornell Corporation
Locations: Lockwood Shipyard, Port Lookout, New Jersey

SCHEDULE C
(Form 1040)
Department of the Treasury
Internal Revenue Service

Profit or (Loss) From Business or Profession
(Sole Proprietorship)

Partnerships, Joint Ventures, etc., Must File Form 1065.

▶ Attach to Form 1040 or Form 1041. ▶ See Instructions for Schedule C (Form 1040).

1980

09

Name of proprietor

Social security number of proprietor

A Main business activity (see Instructions) ▶ _____ ; product ▶ _____

B Business name ▶

C Employer identification number

D Business address (number and street) ▶ _____

City, State and ZIP Code ▶

E Accounting method: (1) ☐ Cash   (2) ☐ Accrual   (3) ☐ Other (specify) ▶

F Method(s) used to value closing inventory:

(1) ☐ Cost   (2) ☐ Lower of cost or market   (3) ☐ Other (if other, attach explanation)

G Was there any major change in determining quantities, costs, or valuations between opening and closing inventory? . .

If "Yes," attach explanation.

	Yes	No

H Did you deduct expenses for an office in your home? . . . .

I Did you elect to claim amortization (under section 191) or depreciation (under section 167(o)) for a rehabilitated

certified historic structure (see Instructions) ▶ (_____)

(Amortizable basis (see Instructions) ▶)

Part I Income

1 a Gross receipts or sales . . . . | 1a | |

b Returns and allowances . . . . | 1b | |

c Balance (subtract line 1b from line 1a) . . . . | 1c |

2 Cost of goods sold and/or operations (Schedule C-1, line 8) . . . . | 2 |

3 Gross profit (subtract line 2 from line 1c) . . . . | 3 |

4 Other income (attach schedule) . . . . | 4 |

5 Total income (add lines 3 and 4) . . . . ▶ | 5 |

Part II Deductions

		31	a	Wages		
			b	Jobs credit		
			c	WIN credit		
			d	Total credits		
			e	Subtract line 31d from 31a		
		32	Other expenses (specify):		
6 Advertising			a			
7 Amortization			b			
8 Bad debts from sales or services			c			
9 Bank charges			d			
10 Car and truck expenses			e			
11 Commissions			f			
12 Depletion			g			
13 Depreciation (explain in Schedule C-2)			h			
14 Dues and publications			i			
15 Employee benefit programs			j			
16 Freight (not included on Schedule C-1)			k			
17 Insurance			l			
18 Interest on business indebtedness			m			
19 Laundry and cleaning			n			
20 Legal and professional services			o			
21 Office supplies			p			
22 Pension and profit-sharing plans			q			
23 Postage			r			
24 Rent on business property			s			
25 Repairs						
26 Supplies (not included on Schedule C-1)						
27 Taxes						
28 Telephone						
29 Travel and entertainment						
30 Utilities						

33 Total deductions (add amounts in columns for lines 6 through 32s) . . . . . ▶ | 33 | |

34 Net profit or (loss) (subtract line 33 from line 5). If a profit, enter on Form 1040, line 13, and on Schedule SE, Part II, line 5a (or Form 1041, line 6). If a loss, go to line 35. | 34 | |

35 If you have a loss, do you have amounts for which you are not "at risk" in this business (see instructions)? . . ☐ Yes ☐ No

to complete Schedule C-1—Cost of Goods Sold and/or

Expense Items: Auto mileage—50 miles; tolls—$1.50; parking—$2.75

Lunch: Took Howard Lockwood, president of Lockwood Shipyard, to lunch at Mario's. Discussion about how best to shoot photos and how he would move boats to best camera advantage. Cost of lunch: $22.25.

To back up your diary you must have proof—receipts and canceled checks on expenditures. For auto-mileage expenses, state where you started and where you went. The IRS allows 20 cents for the first 15,000 miles of business use and 11 cents a mile for every mile above that. Ask for receipts at toll booths and parking lots. Also get receipts from restaurants if you don't use your credit card.

If you pay your expenses by check, make a note in the lower left-hand corner of what your expenditure was for.

It helps to keep a careful account of all income and expenditures of this second business of yours in an expense record book especially designated for this business. If your local stationery store does not carry books that are systematized for small businesses, you can order by mail from an office-products supply house. Look for a complete easy-to-keep book with facsimile sheets in each section showing samples of proper entries and explaining each one.

Now, suppose you have completed your Schedule C and find that you have come out with a substantial profit over other years. Your hobby has really paid off and is the flourishing second business you had hoped it would become. Great! you think. But taxes are going to take a big chunk of your profits, and that hurts. This is a case in which income averaging may mitigate that tax bite.

If you have earned income—that includes income from your primary job and any other jobs (or businesses)—four years previous to filing this year's return, you are eligible to file a Schedule G with your

1040, even if your income has been sporadic in the past. Following Schedule G will give you a computation of averageable income. From there, you go on to compute your tax, which will take into account those lean years before your hobby really took off and became a solid source of second income.

Another strategy to lessen the tax bite: Open a Keogh-plan account. Even though your primary work is as an employee for someone else, if you have a business, albeit a second source of income, you are eligible for a Keogh plan. You would be providing for your retirement and deferring income to those years when your overall income will most probably be lower and you will be in a lower tax bracket.

The past several chapters have gone into various aspects of your life and shown you how to shave down the tax bite. Throughout we have emphasized trying to limit spending to tax-deductible items, taking advantage of all deferrals of income, keeping impeccable tax records, and doing tax planning every day. In the next chapter we go into detail as to how to implement this information in filling out the 1040 return itself.

CHAPTER 19

Filing Your
Income-Tax Form

In this chapter we will tell you line by line how to fill out your income-tax form. We are using the long form—the 1040—because this book is basically for those who itemize deductions. However, there may be some of you who would do just as well if you use the short form—the 1040A.

The short form is for you if your total income came solely from wages, salary, bonuses, and tips. It doesn't matter how much income you made last year as long as it was confined to the foregoing. It doesn't make any difference as to your age, marital status, or number of dependents whether you file the short form or the long form. However, you should know that if you use the short form you cannot itemize deductions. You will not be able to claim child-care credit, you cannot report pension income on it, and you also cannot use it if you have more than $400 in dividends or if you are self-employed.

You *must* use the long form if your spouse is filing separately and itemizing deductions.

Never use the short form if your itemized deductions exceed the zero-bracket amount. In that case, it is worth the hassle it may be to fill out the long form with all those supporting schedules.

Supporting schedules that most people need are:

A and B—Itemized Deductions and Interest and Dividend Income

C—Profit (or Loss) from Business or Profession

SE—Computation of Social Security Self-Employment Tax

D—Capital Gains and Losses

E—Supplemental Income Schedule

TC—Tax Computation Schedule

2106—Employee Business Expenses

2441—Credit for Child and Dependent Care Expenses

If these schedules are not sent with your return—and not all of them are—call or write your local income-tax bureau and request that they be sent to you if you think that you will use them.

Form **1040**	Department of the Treasury—Internal Revenue Service **U.S. Individual Income Tax Return** **1980**	
For Privacy Act Notice, see Instructions	For the year January 1–December 31, 1980, or other tax year beginning _____ , 1980, ending _____ , 19 ___	
Use IRS label. Otherwise, please print or type.	Your first name and initial (if joint return, also give spouse's name and initial) Last name	Your social security number
	Present home address (Number and street, including apartment number, or rural route)	Spouse's social security no.
	City, town or post office, State and ZIP code	Your occupation ▶ Spouse's occupation ▶

This part of your 1040 identifies who you are. Don't forget your Social Security number and that of your spouse. If you are filing a joint return, you must also decide which of you will be counted as the spouse. However, take it for granted that your Social Security number, if you have ever filed a tax return before, is linked up with your spouse's by computer. Don't forget to put in your occupation and that of your spouse.

Presidential Election Campaign Fund	▶ Do you want $1 to go to this fund?	Yes ▨ No	Note: Checking "Yes" will not increase your tax or reduce your refund.
	If joint return, does your spouse want $1 to go to this fund? . . .	Yes ▨ No	

Presidential Election Campaign Fund. Check this "Yes" if you want to give to a special fund to pay part of the expenses of the presidential election campaign. Check it "Yes" only if you want to. It doesn't cost you anything. It doesn't get you anything either.

Requested by Census Bureau for Revenue Sharing ▶	A Where do you live (actual location of residence)? (See page 2 of Instructions.) State City, village, borough, etc.	B Do you live within the legal limits of a city, village, etc.? ☐ Yes ☐ No	C In what county do you live?	D In what township do you live?

Requested by Census Bureau for Revenue Sharing. Write in Block A the state and municipality where you live. In Block B check the "Yes" box unless you live in an unincorporated area or outside the municipal limits. In Block C enter the county in which you live. In Block D enter the township in which you live. Note: Separated spouses filing jointly can designate either residence. College students and military personnel must use their college or military addresses.

Filing Status Check only one box.	1	Single	For IRS use only ⸽ ⸽ ⸽
	2	Married filing joint return (even if only one had income)	
	3	Married filing separate return. Enter spouse's social security no. above and full name here ▶	
	4	Head of household. (See page 6 of Instructions.) If qualifying person is your unmarried child, enter child's name ▶	
	5	Qualifying widow(er) with dependent child (Year spouse died ▶ 19___). (See page 6 of Instructions.)	

Filing Status. Your status for the whole year is determined by your marital or living condition as of December 31. For those filing as married, it is cheaper to file jointly (the only exceptions are where there are heavy medical bills and both spouses have income, or possibly when one spouse has a long-term gain and the other a short-term loss). If two people have income of $20,000 each, they have a total income of $40,000. Theoretically, the table divides this in half. It goes back to the $20,000, picks up the tax bracket from there, computes the tax, and then doubles it, so you are actually paying two returns on $20,000. Suppose one made $30,000 and the other made $10,000. What the table does now is go back and pick up the tax on $20,000 and double it. If you filed singly, even though the tax on $10,000 would be less, the tax on $30,000 would be tremendous, so that you average down both at twenty by filing a joint return.

In certain cases, the tax for one filing as a single person is less than one half that of the tax for a person filing as married on a joint return. Prior to 1949, there was only one tax table. California was a community-property state; married Californians were filing as two singles. They had an advantage over states that did not have a community-property law. The U.S. Supreme Court ruled in favor of the community-property law in California and ruled that others in the United States should have the same advantage. The federal government came out with the joint return, which took the joint income and made a joint table, but if you divided it in half and then doubled it, it was the same as the single table at double the amount.

Then in the 1960s, Vivian Kellems instituted a suit against the federal government. She said that she was discriminated against because she was single, that she never had any intention of marrying. The government then issued a table for those filing as single; its rates are a little lower than the table for those filing as married.

Married people filing separate returns will face a higher tax table than those filing singly, jointly, or as the head of household. However, there are people who do not want to file a joint return. These are people who do not want to sign the return of the other, or who may not want to make certain disclosures to the other, or who may be having marital difficulties. It is an expensive way of filing. Also, the maximum tax computation cannot be used with it; this provides that when you reach approximately $52,000 on a joint return, the effective rate of tax is 50%. If you go over that on earned income, you pay no more than that. Your rate can go up to 70% but it has to be on passive income—interest, dividends, etc., not earned income.

Who is an unmarried head of household? A single person who maintains a home for a child or a mother or someone who is a dependent.

Qualifying widow or widower with dependent child: What does this mean? If you are unfortunate enough to become a widow or a widower and you have a dependent child in your home, you are allowed to use the joint tax table for two years after the year in which your spouse died.

Exemptions	6a	Yourself		65 or over		Blind	Enter number of boxes checked on 6a and b ▶
Always check the box labeled Yourself. Check other boxes if they apply.	b	Spouse		65 or over		Blind	
	c	First names of your dependent children who lived with you ▶					Enter number of children listed on 6c ▶
	d	Other dependents: (1) Name	(2) Relationship	(3) Number of months lived in your home	(4) Did dependent have income of $1,000 or more?	(5) Did you provide more than one half of dependent's support?	Enter number of other dependents Add numbers entered in boxes above ▶
	7	Total number of exemptions claimed					

Exemptions. You are allowed exemptions for yourself, your spouse, if you are sixty-five or older, if your spouse is sixty-five or older, or if either of you are blind. You are allowed an exemption for each child you support and other dependents. You must state the relationship of other dependents, the number of months they lived in your home, and state whether the dependents had income of $1,000 or more that is taxable income. Did you provide more than one half their support? Add up the number of dependents. You are entitled to $1,000 exemption for each. If one of your children is a full-time student and you provided one half his support, you can take him as a dependent even if he is forty years old! Twelve semester hours of study for a college student usually means that the person is a full-time student; or if the dependent was in school for five months of the year, he is considered a student.

Income				
Please attach Copy B of your Forms W-2 here.	8	Wages, salaries, tips, etc.	8	
	9	Interest income (attach Schedule B if over $400)	9	
	10a	Dividends (attach Schedule B if over $400) . . . . 10b Exclusion		
If you do not have a W-2, see page 5 of Instructions.	c	Subtract line 10b from line 10a	10c	
	11	Refunds of State and local income taxes (do not enter an amount unless you deducted those taxes in an earlier year—see page 9 of Instructions)	11	
	12	Alimony received	12	
	13	Business income or (loss) (attach Schedule C)	13	
	14	Capital gain or (loss) (attach Schedule D)	14	
	15	40% of capital gain distributions not reported on line 14 (See page 9 of Instructions) .	15	
	16	Supplemental gains or (losses) (attach Form 4797)	16	
Please attach check or money order here.	17	Fully taxable pensions and annuities not reported on line 18	17	
	18	Pensions, annuities, rents, royalties, partnerships, etc. (attach Schedule E)	18	
	19	Farm income or (loss) (attach Schedule F)	19	
	20a	Unemployment compensation (insurance). Total received		
	b	Taxable amount, if any, from worksheet on page 10 of Instructions	20b	
	21	Other income (state nature and source—see page 10 of Instructions)	21	
	22	Total income. Add amounts in column for lines 8 through 21 . . . . ▶	22	

Income. On lines 8 to 21, you enumerate all the sources of your income.

Line 8—Wages, salaries, tips, etc. This figure comes from your W-2. Some employees receive a 1099. Fringe benefits such as educational expenses might have been included on your W-2. Deduct them from your W-2 and explain the elimination on Schedule 2106. If you include them here with your W-2, you may be increasing your taxable income.

Line 9—Interest income (attach Schedule B if over $400). Be careful here. Banks and dividend-paying companies are supposed to supply you with a 1099 if their payments to you are over $10. However, they could get lost in the mail, you could misplace them and forget about them. You are obliged to report that income. That doesn't mean that if it is under $400 you don't report it. It means that if it is over $400 you are supposed to itemize it on your Schedule B. Now some banks where you might have several accounts may send you the total of interest on the several accounts, instead of listing each account with its interest separately. We have not been able to ascertain from the IRS whether or not you can lump interest amounts from the same bank or whether you must list interest for each account from the same bank separately. For safety's sake, list each account with interest separately, even if from the same bank, because the IRS does tie in bank reporting slips with returns. We have gotten numerous requests from the IRS about individual accounts and interest received.

Line 10—Dividends (attach Schedule B if over $400). You have an exemption (exclusion) of $200 per individual. If you are filing a joint return, the first $400 of dividends would not be taxed if dividends are jointly earned.

Line 11—Refunds of state and local income taxes. If you itemized deductions in 1980 and took a deduction for state and local income taxes paid or withheld during 1980, any refund of those taxes you received in 1980 is considered income by the IRS and they tell you to enter it on this line. (If you did not itemize deductions in 1980, you need not report state and local tax refunds.) We agree with what the IRS is telling you to do, but we do not like to show it on line 11 because as we are boosting up our lines 8 through 21, we are knocking out the possibility of a medical deduction. If we know there is no medical deduction because our taxpayer is a member of a corporate plan that pays 100% on medical expenses, we don't care where we are going to put it. However, if we think there is a possibility of a medical deduction, we are not going to use line 11; instead, we are going to net taxes on Schedule A.

Line 12—Alimony received. The spouse who receives alimony must declare the amount here to be included in gross income.

Line 13—Business income or (loss) (attach Schedule C). If you have income from self-employment, enter the amount here after filling out Schedule C. See instructions for Schedule C farther on.

Line 14—Capital gain or (loss) (attach Schedule D). Report all sales and exchanges of capital assets such as stocks, bonds, your house, your car, or whatever you sell at a profit. You may also sell at a loss. If it's a personal item and you have a loss, it's not deductible; but a profit is taxable. See instructions for Schedule D farther on.

Line 15—40% of capital-gain distributions not reported on line 14. If you do not need Schedule D for other capital transactions, enter 40% of your capital-gain distributions for the year here.

Line 16—Supplemental gains or (losses) (attach Form 4797). This is for sale of property, sales or exchanges of assets used in a trade or business.

Line 17—Fully taxable pensions and annuities not reported on line 18. This is a trap if you enter an amount here without looking at Schedule E, because if it is pension money received, there are certain things that should be considered before you voluntarily pay a tax on pensions and annuities: (1) If it was an employer contribution before 1969, it would get capital-gain treatment; (2) If it was because of your retirement and you took a lump-sum settlement, you might be entitled to average the amount over ten years, so you would not want to use the regular table. Where you have this type of thing, you should read the rules very carefully or consult a professional tax preparer. See Chapter 12, "Retirement, Pensions, and Taxes."

Line 18—Pensions, annuities, rents, royalties, partnerships, estates or trusts, etc. (attach Schedule E). For pensions and annuities that are *not* fully taxable. Rents includes rents when you rent out your vacation home, as well as rents on other types of property. The rest of Schedule E is self-explanatory.

Line 19—Farm income or (loss) (attach Schedule F). For farm owners. Schedule F is for listing cash receipts and disbursements, farm deductions, depreciation. The last part is for summary of income and deductions.

Line 20—Unemployment compensation. Report the total amount added to your gross income. Subtract $20,000 if a single return, $25,000 if a joint return. One half of the remainder is taxable.

Line 21—Other income (state nature and source). Here is where you report income you can't find a place for on the 1040 or any of the schedules. (Self-employment income goes on Schedule C.) Income might be from commissions, management fees, director's fees, gambling winnings, prize money, proceeds from lotteries, raffles. Repayment of medical expenses or repayment of other items such as real-estate taxes, if you deducted them in a prior year, go here. Also, amounts your boss gave you as reimbursement for expenses that exceed your expenditures.

Net operating loss from a prior year you are carrying forward would be entered as a minus figure here.

Line 22—Total income. Add amounts in column for lines 8 through 21. This is self-explanatory. This is the grand total of income from all sources.

* * *

Adjustments to Income (See Instructions on page 10)			
23	Moving expense (attach Form 3903 or 3903F)	23	
24	Employee business expenses (attach Form 2106) . .	24	
25	Payments to an IRA (enter code from page 10 .) . .	25	
26	Payments to a Keogh (H.R. 10) retirement plan . . .	26	
27	Interest penalty on early withdrawal of savings . . .	27	
28	Alimony paid	28	
29	Disability income exclusion (attach Form 2440) . . .	29	
30	Total adjustments. Add lines 23 through 29 . . . . ▶	30	

Adjustments to income. This is the important part. We have been honest and reported all our income. Here is where we try to reduce our gross income.

Line 23—Moving expense (attach Form 3903 or 3903 F). This allows you a deduction for moving of household goods and the people in your household and for searching for new quarters, for commissions on selling old home, etc. See Chapter 10, "Your Home and Deductions."

Line 24—Employee business expenses (attach Form 2106). Here is where you take your traveling and entertainment expenses that as an employee you pay for and are not reimbursed for, but that are necessary and ordinary for your job. You also declare what your boss has reimbursed you for.

Line 25—Payments to an IRA. If you are not covered by an employee pension or profit-sharing plan, you are allowed to open up your own retirement account. You can go to a maximum of 15% of your salary or up to $1,500. Take this deduction even if you have to borrow the money to put into an IRA account, because there is a tremendous discount on taxes with IRA. See Chapter 12, "Retirement, Pensions, and Taxes."

Line 26—Payments to a Keogh (H.R. 10) retirement plan. Those self-employed may take 15% of business income or up to $7,500. See Chapter 12, "Retirement, Pensions, and Taxes."

Line 27—Interest penalty on early withdrawal of savings. You may have time deposits on which in past years you declared the interest income. You may have to withdraw the money from your account and are penalized on interest calculated for past years. Here is where you deduct the interest you lost by withdrawing the money before full term.

Line 28—Alimony paid. This is a deduction to the spouse who paid alimony. See Chapter 6, "Divorce, Alimony, and Child Support."

Line 29—Disability income exclusion (attach Form 2440). This exclusion is for people who are retired on permanent and total disability.

Line 30—Total adjustments. Add up all the adjustment figures. Put the total on this line.

| Adjusted Gross Income | 31 | Adjusted gross income. Subtract line 30 from line 22. If this line is less than $10,000, see "Earned Income Credit" (line 57) on pages 13 and 14 of Instructions. If you want IRS to figure your tax, see page 3 of Instructions . . . . ▶ | 31 | |

Line 31—Adjusted gross income. If it is less than $10,000, you may be entitled to earned-income credit.

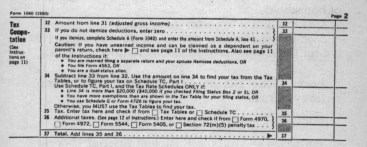

Tax Computation. Here's where we figure how much tax we owe on our adjusted gross income.

Line 32—Amount from line 31 (adjusted gross income). Be sure to copy the correct number from line 31 on the front page of the 1040. Double-check to make sure that you are correct.

Line 33—If you do not itemize deductions, enter zero. Before you forgo itemizing deductions, work out Schedule A to make sure whether your itemizing will give you a lower tax than the zero-bracket amount. If you itemize deductions on Schedule A, put the figure for deductions here. Line 33 lists certain categories of individuals who are required to itemize. Form 4563 is for use by citizens of the United States whose income is from sources within a possession of the United States.

Line 34—Put the result here of your subtraction of deductions. Then go to tax table or use Schedule TC to compute your tax if you file a joint return and your income is over $40,000; if you file as single, married filing separately, or as head of household and if your income is over $20,000, or if you wish to income-average, or if you use Form 4726 (for maximum tax on personal-service income); if your taxable income or personal-service taxable income is $41,500 or over and you are filing as single, $60,000 or over and you are filing as married with a joint return or as a widow or widower, or $44,700 or over and you are filing as head of household.

Line 35—Enter tax after computing.

Line 36—*Additional taxes*. These additional taxes are for those who have to file the following forms:

Form 4970—Tax on Accumulation of Distribution of Trusts

Form 4972—Special 10-Year Averaging Method

Form 5544—Multiple Recipient Special 10-Year Averaging Method

Form 5405—Recapture of Credit for Purchase or Construction of New Principal Residence

Section 72(m)(5) penalty tax—for premature or excessive distribution from a Keogh-plan account

Line 37—*Total*. The GRAND TOTAL of all you owe in taxes.

Credits					
Credits (See instruc- tions on page 12)	38	Credit for contributions to candidates for public office . . .	38		
	39	Credit for the elderly (attach Schedules R&RP)	39		
	40	Credit for child and dependent care expenses (attach Form 2441) .	40		
	41	Investment credit (attach Form 3468)	41		
	42	Foreign tax credit (attach Form 1116)	42		
	43	Work incentive (WIN) credit (attach Form 4874)	43		
	44	Jobs credit (attach Form 5884)	44		
	45	Residential energy credits (attach Form 5695)	45		
	46	Total credits. Add lines 38 through 45		46	
	47	Balance. Subtract line 46 from line 37 and enter difference (but not less than zero) . ▶		47	

Credits. Before we pay our liability, we see if we
have credits against the tax. Credits mean we receive
dollar-for-dollar credits against tax!

*Line 38—Credit for contributions to candidates for
public office*. You may take a tax credit for contributions to candidates for public office, political commit-
tees and newsletter funds of candidates and elected
public officials. To figure your credit, add up the
amounts given. Enter half of the total, but not more
than $25 for a single return, $50 for a joint return.

*Line 39—Credit for the elderly (attach Schedules
R&RP)*. Very few retirees qualify for this credit. The
amount of credit you receive and your eligibility de-
pend on how much Social Security and taxable income
you received. The allowance is very low, but if you
think there is a possibility of qualifying, fill out
Schedules R&RP.

*Line 40—Credit for child and dependent care ex-
penses (attach Form 2441)*. This provides credit up to
$800. If you are married and both spouses are working,
or if you are a head of household or a widow or
widower and you have a child under fifteen years or a
dependent who has to be taken care of, this credit will
help reduce the cost of such expenses as those for a
housekeeper, nursery school, and summer camp. See
Chapter 7, "Your Children and Your Exemptions and
Deductions."

Line 41—Investment credit (attach Form 3468). This
is a credit for investing in certain trade or business
property.

Line 42—Foreign tax credit (attach Form 1116). This is credit for payment of income tax to a foreign country or U.S. possession.

Line 43—Work incentive (WIN) credit (attach Form 4874). Credit given for hiring people under a work-incentive program; also provides credit for hiring people who receive federal welfare payments.

Line 44—Jobs credit (attach Form 5884). This is for employers who increased their business payroll the past year.

Line 45—Residential energy credits (attach Form 5695). Fill out Form 5695 and take those energy credits on your home that we discussed in Chapter 10, "Your Home and Deductions."

Line 46—Total credits. This is the sum of all your credits against tax.

Line 47—Balance. This is the result of subtraction of all your credits from your tax. If the amount is less than zero, enter zero.

Other Taxes (Including Advance EIC Payments)	48	Self-employment tax (attach Schedule SE)	48		
	49a	Minimum tax. Attach Form 4625 and check here ▶ ☐	49a		
	49b	Alternative minimum tax. Attach Form 6251 and check here ▶ ☐	49b		
	50	Tax from recomputing prior-year investment credit (attach Form 4255)	50		
	51a	Social security (FICA) tax on tip income not reported to employer (attach Form 4137) . .	51a		
	51b	Uncollected employee FICA and RRTA tax on tips (from Form W-2)	51b		
	52	Tax on an IRA (attach Form 5329)	52		
	53	Advance earned income credit (EIC) payments received (from Form W-2)	53		
	54	Balance. Add lines 47 through 53 . . . . ▶	54		

Other Taxes. Other taxes are additional tax you might have to pay besides the regular income tax on your adjusted gross income.

Line 48—Self-employment tax (attach Schedule SE). If all your income is from self-employment, you file Schedule SE to determine your Social Security payments. If you receive a W-2 from a job and FICA is withheld and you are also self-employed in another capacity, fill out this form if you earned under $22,900 on that job.

Line 49a—Minimum tax. Attach Form 4625. This is a minimum tax for those who have any of the following tax-preference items:

accelerated depreciation

amortization

reserves for bad debts of financial institution

stock options

depletion

intangible drilling costs

You should attach Form 4625 and enter the tax on this line if you have items of tax preference of more than $10,000 ($5,000 if married filing a separate return) or any tax liability deferred from an earlier tax year.

Line 49b—Alternative Minimum Tax. Attach Form 6251. If you are an individual you may be liable for the alternative minimum tax if your itemized deductions plus your tax-preference items for excluded capital gains and adjusted itemized deduction (itemized deductions exceed 60% of your gross income) are more than $23,300 ($12,700 if married filing separately).

Line 50—Tax from recomputing prior-year investment credit (attach Form 4255). You may be liable for this tax if you held investment credit property for less than seven years and disposed of it before the end of its useful life. You must file Form 4255, which will contain specific instructions for filing.

Line 51a—Social Security (FICA) tax on tip income not reported to employer (attach Form 4137). For those who received $20 or more in any month on tips and did not report the full amount to the employer. File Form 4137 and attach to your 1040.

Line 51b—Uncollected employee FICA and RRTA tax on tips (from Form W-2). If you received tips but not enough wages to cover FICA or RRTA, the amount of tax due will be on your W-2. Write it in here.

Line 52—Tax on an IRA (attach Form 5329). Use Form 5329 and report here taxes on Individual Retirement Accounts.

Line 53—Advance earned-income-credit (EIC) payments received (from Form W-2). Enter total of advance earned-income credit as shown on your W-2 forms.

Line 54—Balance. Add lines 47 through 53. This represents your total for regular income tax and any other taxes you must pay.

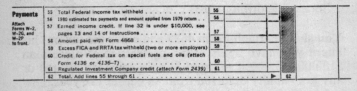

Payments					
Attach Forms W-2, W-2G, and W-2P to front.	55	Total Federal income tax withheld	55		
	56	1980 estimated tax payments and amount applied from 1979 return . .	56		
	57	Earned income credit. If line 32 is under $10,000, see pages 13 and 14 of Instructions	57		
	58	Amount paid with Form 4868	58		
	59	Excess FICA and RRTA tax withheld (two or more employers)	59		
	60	Credit for Federal tax on special fuels and oils (attach Form 4136 or 4136–T)	60		
	61	Regulated Investment Company credit (attach Form 2439)	61		
	62	Total. Add lines 55 through 61 . . . . ▶		62	

Payments. Here is where we deduct payments on tax already made, withheld, or credited.

Line 55—Total federal income tax withheld. Add up all federal tax payments withheld on all your W-2s and put the figure on this line.

Line 56—1980 estimated tax payments and credit from 1979 return. Enter here any estimated payments you made on your 1981 tax, and 1980 credits you applied to your 1981 estimates.

If you and your spouse paid joint estimated tax and now are filing separately, one of you may claim the whole payment, or you may divide it between you.

If you and your spouse filed separate estimated-tax payments but now are filing a joint return, add the amounts you each paid.

If you were divorced during 1980 and had filed joint estimated-tax payments, enter your former spouse's Social Security number on the front of your 1040 in the appropriate box. Write above it the letters "DIV."

If you were divorced and remarried in 1980, enter your present spouse's Social Security number in the box provided on the front of the 1040 and also enter your former spouse's Social Security number in the upper right-hand corner of the 1040 and write "DIV" above the number.

Line 57—Earned-income credit. If adjusted gross income is less than $10,000, you may be entitled to earned-income credit. With your 1040 packet is an earned-income-credit worksheet you should fill out.

Line 58—Amount paid with Form 4868. Form 4868 is for an extension of time to file your 1040. On this line put the amount of payment sent in with the extension to file if you asked for an extension.

Line 59—Excess FICA and RRTA tax withheld (two or more employers). Credit for those who had too much FICA or RRTA tax withheld. If you had two or more employers who paid you a combined total of more than $29,700 in wages, too much FICA or RRTA was probably withheld. Fill out the worksheet with the 1040 packet to determine your credit.

Line 60—Credit for federal tax on special fuels and oils (attach Form 4136 or 4136-T). File Form 4136 if you use gasoline, special fuels, and lubricating oil in your business for computation of credit for federal tax. File Form 4136-T if you are a taxicab owner for this credit.

Line 61—Regulated Investment Company credit (attach Form 2439). If you are a member of a regulated investment trust or mutual fund be sure to take the amount of credit the company will notify you that you may take.

Refund or Balance Due. This part of your return is largely self-explanatory. If you owe money, make out your check to the Internal Revenue Service, and don't forget to put your Social Security number on it to be doubly sure it is credited to you. If you underpaid on your estimated taxes, you will have to fill out a Form 2210, which will help you figure out your penalty. The penalty amount goes on line 66.

However, if you have followed many of the precepts and strategies in this book, the chances are that you will be filling out line 64 and stating the amount of refund coming to you.

Please Sign Here	Under penalties of perjury, I declare that I have examined this return, including accompanying schedules and statements, and to the best of my knowledge and belief, it is true, correct, and complete. Declaration of preparer (other than taxpayer) is based on all information of which preparer has any knowledge.			
	▶ Your signature	Date	▶ Spouse's signature (if filing jointly, BOTH must sign even if only one had income)	
Paid Preparer's Use Only	Preparer's signature and date ▶		Check if self-employed ▶ ☐	Preparer's social security no.
	Firm's name (or yours, if self-employed) ▶ and address		E.I. No. ▶	
			ZIP code ▶	

Please Sign Here. This is the very last part of your return, where you sign that under penalty of perjury that to the best of your knowledge and belief everything in it is true, correct, and complete. If you have declared all your income and followed tax law that we have quoted, you will have a clear conscience and have nothing to be afraid of in signing the return. If it is a joint return, your spouse must sign it, too. Your spouse is also responsible for everything in the return. If you are the spouse signing the return, make sure that you understand everything that goes on the return. The IRS does not accept ignorance as an excuse for a perjured return.

If you have paid a preparer to do your return, he should know that he is required by IRS regulations to sign the return and provide other information where indicated at the bottom of the return.

Our next chapter discusses the most commonly used schedules and tells how to fill them out to your best advantage.

CHAPTER 20

Filling Out
the Tax Schedules

This chapter is an appendix to the previous chapter. Schedules and forms that must accompany many returns are reproduced, and we tell you how to fill them in. As you will readily see, these returns require recorded information to back them up. Remember that precept of ours: Keep impeccable tax records with documentation!

We put the most commonly used schedule first: Schedule A. If you itemize your deductions, you must know how to fill out this schedule accurately.

Schedules A&B—Itemized Deductions AND Interest and Dividend Income

Schedules A&B (Form 1040)
Department of the Treasury
Internal Revenue Service

▶ Attach to Form 1040. ▶ See Instructions for Schedules A and B (Form 1040).

1980

08

Name(s) as shown on Form 1040

Your social security number

Schedule A—Itemized Deductions (Schedule B is on back)

Medical and Dental Expenses (not paid or reimbursed by insurance or otherwise) (See page 16 of Instructions.)

1 One-half (but not more than $150) of insurance premiums you paid for medical care. (Be sure to include in line 10 below.) ▶

2 Medicine and drugs .

3 Enter 1% of Form 1040, line 31 . . .

4 Subtract line 3 from line 2. If line 3 is more than line 2, enter zero . . .

5 Balance of insurance premiums for medical care not entered on line 1 . . .

6 Other medical and dental expenses:
   a Doctors, dentists, nurses, etc. . . .
   b Hospitals. . . . .
   c Other (itemize—include hearing aids, dentures, eyeglasses, transportation, etc.) ▶

Contributions (See page 17 of Instructions.)

21 a Cash contributions for which you have receipts or cancelled checks. . . . .
   b Other cash contributions (show to whom you gave and how much you gave) ▶

22 Other than cash (see page 17 of Instructions for required statement) . . . .

23 Carryover from prior years . . . .

24 Total contributions (add lines 21a through 23). Enter here and on line 36 . . ▶

Casualty or Theft Loss(es) (See page 18 of Instructions.)

25 Loss before insurance reimbursement .

26 Insurance reimbursement . . . . .

27 Subtract line 26 from line 25. If line 26 is more than line 25, enter zero . . .

7 Total (add lines 4 through 6c). . . . .
8 Enter 3% of Form 1040, line 31 . . .
9 Subtract line 8 from line 7. If line 8 is more than line 7, enter zero . . . ▲
10 Total medical and dental expenses (add lines 1 and 9). Enter here and on line 33 . ▲

Taxes (See page 17 of Instructions.)
Note: Gasoline taxes are no longer deductible.

11 State and local income . . . . . .
12 Real estate . . . . . .
13 General sales (see sales tax tables) . . .
14 Personal property . . . . . .
15 Other (itemize) ▲

16 Total taxes (add lines 11 through 15). Enter here and on line 34 . . ▲

Interest Expense (See page 17 of Instructions.)

17 Home mortgage . . . . . .
18 Credit and charge cards . . . . .
19 Other (itemize) ▲

20 Total interest expense (add lines 17 through 19). Enter here and on line 35 ▲

---

28 Enter $100 or amount from line 27, whichever is smaller . . .
29 Total casualty or theft loss(es) (subtract line 28 from line 27). Enter here and on line 37. ▲

Miscellaneous Deductions (See page 18 of Instructions.)

30 Union dues . . . . . .
31 Other (itemize) ▲

32 Total miscellaneous deductions (add lines 30 and 31). Enter here and on line 38 ▲

Summary of Itemized Deductions (See page 19 of Instructions.) **A**

33 Total medical and dental—from line 10 . . .
34 Total taxes—from line 16 . . . .
35 Total interest—from line 20 . . . .
36 Total contributions—from line 24 . . .
37 Total casualty or theft loss(es)—from line 29 .
38 Total miscellaneous—from line 32 . . .
39 Add lines 33 through 38 . . . .
40 If you checked Form 1040, Filing Status box:
2 or 5, enter $3,400
1 or 4, enter $2,300
3, enter $1,700
41 Subtract line 40 from line 39. Enter here and on Form 1040, line 33. (If line 40 is more than line 39, see the Instructions for line 41 on page 19.). ▲

Here we go through a line-by-line breakdown of *Schedule A—Itemized Deductions*.

Medical and Dental Expenses (not paid or reimbursed by insurance or otherwise) *(See page 16 of Instructions.)*		
1 One-half (but not more than $150) of insurance premiums you paid for medical care. (Be sure to include in line 10 below.) ▶		
2 Medicine and drugs .	/////	/////
3 Enter 1% of Form 1040, line 31 . . .	/////	/////
4 Subtract line 3 from line 2. If line 3 is more than line 2, enter zero		
5 Balance of insurance premiums for medical care not entered on line 1		
6 Other medical and dental expenses:		
a Doctors, dentists, nurses, etc. . . .		
b Hospitals		
c Other (itemize—include hearing aids, dentures, eyeglasses, transportation, etc.) ▶		
7 Total (add lines 4 through 6c) . . .		
8 Enter 3% of Form 1040, line 31 . . .		
9 Subtract line 8 from line 7. If line 8 is more than line 7, enter zero		
10 Total medical and dental expenses (add lines 1 and 9). Enter here and on line 33 . ▶		

Line 1—One-half (but not more than $150) of insurance premiums you paid for medical care. Just about everybody can fill this in because almost everybody has Blue Cross, Blue Shield, major medical, or medi-

cal premiums paid on auto insurance or on home-owners' insurance.

Line 2—Medicine and drugs. This means prescribed drugs. For proof you will need your bills as well as canceled checks.

Line 3—Enter 1% of Form 1040, line 31. This is 1% of your adjusted gross income.

Line 4—Subtract line 3 from line 2. If line 3 is more than line 2, enter zero. If the amount you spent for medicines and drugs exceeded 1% of your adjusted gross income, you will have a figure here.

Line 5—Balance of insurance premiums for medical care not entered on line 1. If you spent more than $150 on medical insurance, enter the amount here.

Line 6—Other medical and dental expenses. Consult Chapter 9, "Deductions and Your Health and Physical Maintenance," to see what is deductible, and list the items on line 6.

Line 7—Total (add lines 4 through 6c). Simple addition, but check to see that you are adding up the amounts on the correct lines.

Line 8—Enter 3% of Form 1040, line 31. This is 3% of your adjusted gross income.

Line 9—Subtract line 8 from line 7. If line 8 is more than line 7, enter zero. If costs for doctors, hospitals and appliances, and medical transportation are more than 3% of your adjusted gross income, you will have a figure here.

Line 10—Total medical and dental expenses (add lines 1 and 9). Your total medical and dental expenses. You will probably have at least the $150 of insurance premiums from line 1.

Line 11—State and local income. Includes your withholding and your estimates for the year. You can prepay January 15 estimates to beef up this deduction.

Line 12—Real estate. You can take this deduction only if you have title to the property.

Line 13—General sales (see sales-tax tables). Beware here: Don't use the sales-tax tables the IRS pro-

Taxes *(See page 17 of Instructions.)*
Note: Gasoline taxes are no longer deductible.

11 State and local income			
12 Real estate			
13 General sales (see sales tax tables) . .			
14 Personal property			
15 Other (itemize) ▶............................			
....			
....			
16 Total taxes (add lines 11 through 15). Enter here and on line 34 . . . . ▶			

vides. Check your records. You probably have paid more in sales tax than the IRS gives you credit for. Also, the tax table does not include local taxes. The tax table is computed as state tax. Don't forget to include extraordinarily large taxed purchases—auto, family weddings, furniture, etc.

Line 14—Personal property. Levied in some states and is deductible here.

For further information on deductible taxes, see Chapter 17, "Taxes and Deductions."

Interest Expense *(See page 17 of Instructions.)*

17 Home mortgage			
18 Credit and charge cards			
19 Other (itemize) ▶............................			
....			
....			
....			
....			
....			
....			
20 Total interest expense (add lines 17 through 19). Enter here and on line 35 ▶			

Line 17—Home mortgage. The bank usually sends you a document listing your interest. Be careful to check dates to see that your last payment of the year is included; if it is not, you can still deduct it.

Line 18—Credit and charge cards. Include interest on time payments on these cards.

Line 19—Other (itemize). Interest on car loans, home-improvement loans, personal loans, etc. Beware of insurance loans: The interest is deductible if you pay it. Most policies have an automatic loan provision. If you miss a premium, the insurance company will charge the premium into the cash value of the policy so that it will not lapse. Even if you do not want to pay the premium, pay the interest so that you will get this deduction.

Contributions	(See page 17 of Instructions.)		
21	a Cash contributions for which you have receipts or cancelled checks		
	b Other cash contributions (show to whom you gave and how much you gave) ▶...		
	--		
	--		
	--		
	--		
	--		
	--		
22	Other than cash (see page 17 of Instructions for required statement)		
23	Carryover from prior years		
24	Total contributions (add lines 21a through 23). Enter here and on line 36 . . ▶		

Line 21—Cash contributions for which you have receipts, etc. Make sure that your charities are legal ones. The IRS has a list and they know which are legal. For your church-plate contributions, use an envelope and ask for a receipt. The IRS allows without question only $78 for charity. If you give more, have proof with bills and checks.

Line 22—Other than cash. Secondhand goods; get a value on them from the charity you donate them to. Here you can also take 9 cents per mile in costs of transportation to your volunteer work and any out-of-pocket expenses related to your volunteer work.

Line 23—Carry-over from prior years. See Chapter 15, "Charity and Your Tax Deductions," for explanation of this and other information about charity and contributions.

Casualty or Theft Loss(es)	(See page 18 of Instructions.)		
25 Loss before insurance reimbursement .			
26 Insurance reimbursement			
27 Subtract line 26 from line 25. If line 26 is more than line 25, enter zero . . .			
28 Enter $100 or amount from line 27, whichever is smaller			
29 Total casualty or theft loss(es) (subtract line 28 from line 27). Enter here and on line 37 . ▶			

Line 25—Loss before insurance reimbursement. Casualties are usually acts of God—things you have no control over. Thefts should be reported to the police to back up your claim on this deduction. Line 26 has you subtract the insurance reimbursement, and line 28 shows that you must absorb the first $100 after reimbursement for loss. See Chapter 10, "Your Home and Deductions," for further information on casualty and theft losses.

Line 30 is for deduction of union dues, and line 31 is for deducting other expenses. The latter might include

Miscellaneous Deductions (See page 18 of Instructions.)		
30 Union dues		
31 Other (itemize) ▶ -----------------------------		

---		
32 Total miscellaneous deductions (add lines 30 and 31). Enter here and on line 38 ▶		

education expenses to further you in your job, and costs for uniforms, small tools, safety clothes and equipment, and on-call "beepers" that you provide for your job—in other words, expenses that are ordinary and necessary for your job and that you pick up yourself. Also gambling losses, but not to exceed more than gambling winnings, are deducted here.

Summary of Itemized Deductions (See page 19 of Instructions.)		A
33 Total medical and dental—from line 10 .		
34 Total taxes—from line 16		
35 Total interest—from line 20		
36 Total contributions—from line 24 . . .		
37 Total casualty or theft loss(es)—from line 29 .		
38 Total miscellaneous—from line 32 . .		
39 Add lines 33 through 38		
40 If you checked Form 1040, Filing Status box: 2 or 5, enter $3,400 . . . . 1 or 4, enter $2,300 . . . . 3, enter $1,700		
41 Subtract line 40 from line 39. Enter here and on Form 1040, line 33. (If line 40 is more than line 39, see the Instructions for line 41 on page 19.) . . . . . ▶		

Name(s) as shown on Form 1040 (Do not enter name and social security number if shown on other side)   Your social security number

Part I   Interest Income

1 If you received more than $400 in interest, complete Part I and Part III. Please see page 8 of the instructions to find out what interest to report. Then answer the questions in Part III, below. If you received interest as a nominee for another, or you received or paid accrued interest on securities transferred between interest payment dates, please see page 19 of the instructions.

Name of payer	Amount

Part II   Dividend Income

3 If you received more than $400 in gross dividends (including capital gain distributions) and other distributions on stock, complete Part II and Part III. Please see page 9 of the instructions. Write (H), (W), or (J), for stock held by husband, wife, or jointly. Then answer the questions in Part III, below. If you received dividends as a nominee for another, please see page 19 of the instructions.

Name of payer	Amount

			B

2 Total Interest Income. Enter here and on Form 1040, line 9 . . . . .

4 Total of line 3 . . . .

5 Capital gain distribu- tions. Enter here and on line 13, Schedule D. See Note below . .

6 Nontaxable distribu- tions . . . . .

7 Total (add lines 5 and 6) . . . . . .

8 Dividends before exclusion (subtract line 7 from line 4). Enter here and on Form 1040, line 10a . . . .

Note: *If you received capital gain distributions for the year and you do not need Schedule D to report any other gains or losses, do not file that schedule. Instead, enter 40% of your capital gain distributions on Form 1040, line 15.*

Part III Foreign Accounts and Foreign Trusts

If you are required to list interest in Part I or dividends in Part II, OR if you had a foreign account or were a grantor of or a trans- feror to a foreign trust, you must answer both questions in Part III. Please see page 19 of the Instructions.

	Yes	No
A At any time during the tax year, did you have an interest in or a signature or other authority over a bank account, securities account, or other financial account in a foreign country (see page 19 of instruc- tions)?		
B Were you the grantor of, or transferor to, a foreign trust which existed during the current tax year, whether or not you have any beneficial interest in it? If "Yes," you may have to file Forms 3520, 3520–A, or 926.		

Add up all categories from Schedule A and put the total on line 39. Subtract the proper number on line 40. You are subtracting out (the zero-bracket amount). If you come out with more than the zero-bracket amount, put the figure on line 41. If you come out less than the zero-bracket amount, it means that you would do better with the zero-bracket amount instead of itemizing. You would enter a zero on your 1040, line 33, in figuring your tax computation.

Schedule B is for listing interest and dividend income. You must use it if you:

had more than $400 in interest;
had more than $400 in dividends;
had a foreign account or were a grantor of or transferrer to a foreign trust

On Part I list all taxable interest from all sources. Do not lump accounts together—that is, if you have several accounts in one bank, list each account separately, with interest for each account next to it. Of course, you do not list nontaxable income, such as that from municipal bonds.

On Part II list all dividend income. Include cash and the value of stock, property, or merchandise you received as a dividend. List the name of each payer. Include capital-gain and nontaxable distributions, even though the latter are deducted out on lines 5 and 6.

Schedule D is used to report the sale or exchange of a capital asset. What is a capital asset? Most property you own and use for personal purposes, pleasure, or investment. It could be your house, furniture, car, and stocks and bonds. It might also include a transfer of patent rights. A nonbusiness bad debt can be treated on Schedule D as a short-term capital loss.

If you have a loss on a personal item such as a house or a car, it is not deductible. But if you sell a personal item at a profit, the profit is taxable.

If you have a short-term (one year or less) gain or loss, the entire amount goes on the face of your 1040. If you have a long-term capital gain (held for more than one year), only 40% is added to your ordinary income. If you sell a nonpersonal capital item at a loss, you may deduct $3,000 against ordinary income in the current tax year, and the balance of the loss is carried forward to future years at the rate of $3,000 a year against ordinary income. The loss may always be applied in total against any capital gains you make in future years.

Information from Schedule E—Supplemental Income Schedule—is reportable on your 1040 income section.

Part I deals with pension and annuity income. Here is where you make an allocation between return of your money and your company's money on retirement, or when you receive a lump-sum distribution.

Part II deals with rents and royalties. You report gross rents received, rent expenses, and depreciation of your buildings. Royalties are treated similarly. For instance, if you own a gas royalty (say, a portion of an oil well), you will follow the same procedure as for rents, except that instead of depreciation you have a depletion allowance.

Part III is where you report your share of partnership income, estates or trust income, and/or small-business-corporation income after filling out the various schedules that go with each entity.

This is Schedule C. Here are all the income and expense items for a business or profession. If you have kept good records, you will have the correct numbers at hand for this.

Line E asks you to check your accounting method. If you are on a cash basis, revenues and expenses are recorded on books of account when received and paid, respectively. If you are on an accrual basis, revenues and expenses are recorded as incurred.

Be careful with the income section. You are asked to complete Schedule C-1—Cost of Goods Sold and/or

SCHEDULE D (Form 1040)

Department of the Treasury
Internal Revenue Service

Capital Gains and Losses (Examples of property to be reported on this Schedule are gains and losses on stocks, bonds, and similar investments, and gains (but not losses) on personal assets such as a home or jewelry.)

► Attach to Form 1040.   ► See Instructions for Schedule D (Form 1040).

1980

15

Name(s) as shown on Form 1040

Your social security number

D

Part I Short-term Capital Gains and Losses—Assets Held One Year or Less

a. Kind of property and description (Example, 100 shares 7% preferred of "Z" Co.)	b. Date acquired (Mo., day, yr.)	c. Date sold (Mo., day, yr.)	d. Gross sales price less expense of sale	e. Cost or other basis, as adjusted (see instructions page 21)	f. LOSS if column (e) is more than (d) subtract (d) from (e)	g. GAIN if column (d) is more than (e) subtract (e) from (d)
1						

2 Gain from sale or exchange of a principal residence held one year or less, from Form 2119, lines 7 or 11	**2**		
3 Enter your share of net short-term gain or (loss) from partnerships and fiduciaries	**3**		
4 Add lines 1, 2 and 3 in column f and column g	**4**		
5 Combine line 4, column f and line 4, column g and enter the net gain or (loss)	**5**	
6 Short-term capital loss carryover from years beginning after 1969	**6**	( )

7 Net short-term gain or (loss), combine lines 5 and 6 . . . . | 7 |

Part II Long-term Capital Gains and Losses—Assets Held More Than One Year

8

9 Gain from sale or exchange of a principal residence held more than one year, from Form 2119, lines 7, 11, or 18	9		
10 Enter your share of net long-term gain or (loss) from partnerships and fiduciaries	10		
11 Add lines 8, 9 and 10 in column f and column g	11		

12 Combine line 11, column f and line 11, column g and enter the net gain or (loss) . . . . . . | 12 |
13 Capital gain distributions . . . . | 13 |
14 Enter gain, if applicable, from Form 4797, line 5(a)(1) . . . . | 14 |
15 Enter your share of net long-term gain from small business corporations (Subchapter S) . . . . . | 15 |
16 Combine lines 12 through 15 . . . . | 16 |
17 Long-term capital loss carryover from years beginning after 1969 . . . . | 17 ( )

18 Net long-term gain or (loss), combine lines 16 and 17 . . . . | 18 |

Note: If you have capital loss carryovers from years beginning before 1970, do not complete rest of form. See Form 4798 instead. Otherwise, complete this form on reverse.

Part III Summary of Parts I and II

19 Combine lines 7 and 18, and enter the net gain or (loss) here . . . . | 19 |

20 If line 19 shows a gain—

  a Enter 60% of line 18 or 60% of line 19, whichever is smaller. Enter zero if there is a loss or no
    entry on line 18 . . . . | 20a |

    *If the amount you enter on this line is other than zero, you may be liable for the alternative minimum
    tax. See Form 6251.*

  b Subtract line 20a from line 19. Enter here and on Form 1040, line 14 . . . . | 20b |

21 If line 19 shows a loss—

  a Enter one of the following amounts:
    (i)   If line 7 is zero or a net gain, enter 50% of line 19,
    (ii) If line 18 is zero or a net gain, enter line 19; or,
    (iii) If line 7 and line 18 are net losses, enter amount on line 7 added to 50% of the amount on
        line 18 . . . . | 21a |

  b Enter here and enter as a loss on Form 1040, line 14, the smallest of:
    (i)   The amount on line 21a,
    (ii) $3,000 ($1,500 if married and filing a separate return); or,
    (iii) Taxable income, as adjusted . . . . | 21b |

  Note: *If the loss on line 21a is more than the loss shown on line 21b, complete Part IV to determine
  post-1969 capital loss carryover from 1980 to 1981.*

Part IV Computation of Post-1969 Capital Loss Carryovers from 1980 to 1981
(Complete this part if the loss on line 21a is more than the loss shown on line 21b)

Section A.—Short-term Capital Loss Carryover

22 Enter loss shown on line 7; if none, enter zero and skip lines 23 through 27—then go to line 28 . . . | 22 |

23 Enter gain shown on line 18. If that line is blank or shows a loss, enter zero . . . . 23 |

24 Reduce any loss on line 22 to the extent of any gain on line 23 . . . . 24 |

25 Enter amount shown on line 21b . . . . 25 |

26 Enter smaller of line 24 or 25 . . . . 26 |

27 Subtract line 26 from line 24 . . . . 27 |
   Note: The amount on line 27 is the part of your short-term capital loss carryover from 1980 to 1981
   that is from years beginning after 1969.

Section B.—Long-term Capital Loss Carryover

28 Subtract line 26 from line 25. (Note: if you skipped lines 23 through 27, enter amount from line 21b) . 28 |

29 Enter loss from line 18; if none, enter zero and skip lines 30 through 33 . . . . 29 |

30 Enter gain shown on line 7. If that line is blank or shows a loss, enter zero . . . . . 30 |

31 Reduce any loss on line 29 to the extent of any gain on line 30 . . . . 31 |

32 Multiply amount on line 28 by 2 . . . . 32 |

33 Subtract line 32 from line 31 . . . . 33 |
   Note: The amount on line 33 is the part of your long-term capital loss carryover from 1980 to 1981
   that is from years beginning after 1969.

SCHEDULE E (Form 1040)	Supplemental Income Schedule	1980
Department of the Treasury Internal Revenue Service	(From pensions and annuities, rents and royalties, partnerships, estates and trusts, etc.) ▶ Attach to Form 1040. ▶ See Instructions for Schedule E (Form 1040).	16

Name(s) as shown on Form 1040

Your social security number

Part I Pension and Annuity Income. If fully taxable, do not complete this part. Enter amount on Form 1040, line 17. For one pension or annuity not fully taxable, complete this part. If you have more than one pension or annuity that is not fully taxable, attach a separate sheet listing each one with the appropriate data and enter combined total of taxable parts on line 4.

1a Did you and your employer contribute to the pension or annuity? . . . . ☐ Yes ☐ No

b If "Yes," do you expect to get back your contribution within 3 years from the date you receive the first payment?. . ☐ Yes ☐ No

c If "Yes," show: Your contribution ▶ $ .... d Contribution received in prior years . . . ▲ | 1d | |

2 Amount received this year . . . . | 2 | |

3 Amount on line 2 that is not taxable . . . . | 3 | |

4 Taxable part (subtract line 3 from line 2). Enter here and include in line 18 below . . . . | 4 | |

Part II Rent and Royalty Income or Loss. If you need more space, attach a separate sheet.

5a Are any of the expenses listed below for a vacation home or similar dwelling rented to others (see instructions)? . ☐ Yes ☐ No

b If "yes," did you or a member of your family occupy the vacation home or similar dwelling for more than 14 days during the tax year? ☐ Yes ☐ No

6a Did you elect to claim amortization (under section 191) or depreciation (under section 167(o)) for a rehabilitated certified historic structure (see instructions)?. . . . . ☐ Yes ☐ No

b Amortizable basis (see Instructions) ▶

(a) Property code (describe in Part V)	(b) Total amount of rents	(c) Total amount of royalties	(d) Depreciation (explain in Part VI) or depletion (attach computation)	(e) Other expenses (explain in Part VII)	(f) Net loss	(g) Net income
Property A .						
Property B .						
Property C .						
7 Amounts from Form 4835 . .						
8 Totals . .					(—)	

9 Total rent and royalty income or (loss). Combine amounts in columns (f) and (g), line 8. Enter here and include in line 18 below. **9**

Part III Income or Losses from—

(a) Name	(b) Employer identification number	(c) Net loss	(d) Net income

Partnerships

10 Add amounts in columns (c) and (d) and enter here. . . . . . . **10** ( )

11 Combine amounts in columns (c) and (d), line 10, and enter net income or (loss). . . . **11**

12 Additional first-year depreciation (see instructions for limitations). . . . . **12** ( )

13 Total partnership income or (loss). Combine lines 11 and 12. Enter here and include in line 18 below **13**

Estates or Trusts

14 Add amounts in columns (c) and (d) and enter here. . . . . . . **14** ( )

15 Total estate or trust income or (loss). Combine amounts in columns (c) and (d), line 14. Enter here and include in line 18 below **15**

Small Business Corporations

16 Add amounts in columns (c) and (d) and enter here. . . . . . . **16** ( )

17 Total small business corporation income or (loss). Combine amounts in columns (c) and (d), line 16. Enter here and include in line 18 below **17**

Part IV

18 TOTAL income or (loss). Combine lines 4, 9, 13, 15, and 17. Enter here and on Form 1040, line 18 . ▶ **18**

19 Farmers and fishermen: Enter your share of gross farming and fishing income applicable to Parts II and III **19**

E

Schedule E (Form 1040) 1980

Part V — Property Reported in Part II

Property Codes	Kind and location of property
A	
B	
C	

Part VI — Depreciation Claimed in Part II. If you need more space, use Form 4562.

(a) Description of property	(b) Date acquired	(c) Cost or other basis	(d) Depreciation allowed or allowable in prior years	(e) Depreciation method	(f) Life or rate	(g) Depreciation for this year
Total additional first-year depreciation (Do not include in items below. See instructions for limitations.) →						
Property A						
Totals (Property A)					→	
Total additional first-year depreciation (Do not include in items below. See instructions for limitations.) →						
Property B						
Totals (Property B)					→	
Total additional first-year depreciation (Do not include in items below. See instructions for limitations.) →						

Totals (Property C) . . . .

Part VII Expenses Claimed in Part II

Expenses (Description)	Properties		
	A	B	C
Taxes			
Insurance			
Interest			
Commissions . . .			
Other (list) ▲			

SCHEDULE C (Form 1040)

Department of the Treasury
Internal Revenue Service

Profit or (Loss) From Business or Profession

(Sole Proprietorship)

Partnerships, Joint Ventures, etc., Must File Form 1065.

▶ Attach to Form 1040 or Form 1041. ▶ See Instructions for Schedule C (Form 1040).

1980

09

Name of proprietor

Social security number of proprietor

A Main business activity (see Instructions) ▶ _____ ; product ▶ _____

B Business name ▶

C Employer identification number

D Business address (number and street) ▶ _____
City, State and ZIP Code ▶

E Accounting method: **(1)** ☐ Cash **(2)** ☐ Accrual **(3)** ☐ Other (specify) ▶

F Method(s) used to value closing inventory:

(1) ☐ Cost **(2)** ☐ Lower of cost or market **(3)** ☐ Other (if other, attach explanation)

G Was there any major change in determining quantities, costs, or valuations between opening and closing inventory? . . . .

If "Yes," attach explanation.

H Did you deduct expenses for an office in your home? . . . .

I Did you elect to claim amortization (under section 191) or depreciation (under section 167(o)) for a rehabilitated certified historic structure (see Instructions) . . . .

(Amortizable basis (see Instructions) ▶ _____)

	Yes	No
G		
H		
I		

Part I Income

1 a Gross receipts or sales	1a	
b Returns and allowances	1b	
c Balance (subtract line 1b from line 1a)	1c	
2 Cost of goods sold and/or operations (Schedule C–1, line 8)	2	
3 Gross profit (subtract line 2 from line 1c)	3	
4 Other income (attach schedule)	4	
5 Total income (add lines 3 and 4) . . . . ▶	5	

Part II Deductions

6 Advertising			31 a Wages . . .		
7 Amortization			b Jobs credit . .		
8 Bad debts from sales or services .			c WIN credit . .		
9 Bank charges			d Total credits .		
10 Car and truck expenses . . .			e Subtract line 31d from 31a .		
11 Commissions			32 Other expenses (specify):		
12 Depletion			a		
13 Depreciation (explain in Schedule C–2)			b		
14 Dues and publications . . .			c		
15 Employee benefit programs . .			d		
16 Freight (not included on Schedule C–1)			e		
17 Insurance			f		
18 Interest on business indebtedness .			g		
19 Laundry and cleaning			h		
20 Legal and professional services .			i		
21 Office supplies			j		
22 Pension and profit-sharing plans .			k		
23 Postage			l		
24 Rent on business property . .			m		
25 Repairs			n		
26 Supplies (not included on Schedule C–1)			o		
27 Taxes			p		
28 Telephone			q		
29 Travel and entertainment . .			r		
30 Utilities			s		

33 Total deductions (add amounts in columns for lines 6 through 32s) . . . . ▶ | 33 | |

34 Net profit or (loss) (subtract line 33 from line 5). If a profit, enter on Form 1040, line 13, and on Schedule SE, Part II, line 5a (or Form 1041, line 6). If a loss, go on to line 35 . . . . | 34 | |

35 If you have a loss, do you have amounts for which you are not "at risk" in this business (see Instructions)? . . ☐ Yes ☐ No

SCHEDULE C–1.—Cost of Goods Sold and/or Operations (See Schedule C Instructions for Part I, line 2)

1 Inventory at beginning of year (if different from last year's closing inventory, attach explanation) .	1	
2 a Purchases	2a	
b Cost of items withdrawn for personal use	2b	
c Balance (subtract line 2b from line 2a)	2c	
3 Cost of labor (do not include salary paid to yourself)	3	
4 Materials and supplies	4	
5 Other costs (attach schedule)	5	
6 Add lines 1, 2c, and 3 through 5	6	
7 Inventory at end of year	7	
8 Cost of goods sold and/or operations (subtract line 7 from line 6). Enter here and on Part I, line 2 . ▶	8	

SCHEDULE C–2.—Depreciation (See Schedule C Instructions for line 13)
If you need more space, please use Form 4562.

Description of property (a)	Date acquired (b)	Cost or other basis (c)	Depreciation allowed or allowable in prior years (d)	Method of computing depreciation (e)	Life or rate (f)	Depreciation for this year (g)
1 Total additional first-year depreciation (do not include in items below) (see instructions for limitation) ▶						
2 Other depreciation:						

3 Totals

4 Depreciation claimed in Schedule C–1 . . . . **4**

5 Balance (subtract line 4 from line 3). Enter here and on Part II, line 13 . . . . ▶ **5**

SCHEDULE C–3.—Expense Account Information (See Schedule C Instructions for Schedule C–3)

Enter information for yourself and your five highest paid employees. In determining the five highest paid employees, add expense account allowances to the salaries and wages. However, you don't have to provide the information for any employee for whom the combined amount is less than $25,000, or for yourself if your expense account allowance plus line 34, page 1, is less than $25,000.

Name (a)	Expense account (b)	Salaries and wages (c)
Owner		
1		
2		
3		
4		
5		

	Yes	No
Did you claim a deduction for expenses connected with:		
A Entertainment facility (boat, resort, ranch, etc.)?		
B Living accommodations (except employees on business)?		
C Conventions or meetings you or your employees attended outside the U.S. or its possessions? (see Instructions)		
D Employees' families at conventions or meetings?		
If "Yes," were any of these conventions or meetings outside the U.S. or its possessions? . .		
E Vacations for employees or their families not reported on Form W–2?		

Operations. This schedule starts with opening inventory of your business. You add purchases and then reduce them for items taken for personal use. Add on labor, materials and supplies, and any other costs. You must submit a scheduled list of other costs. Finally, subtract your closing inventory. Remember, cost of goods sold includes cost of labor if in manufacturing.

Deductions from income are listed in alphabetical order. That should cause you no trouble except perhaps the deduction for depreciation. You must fill out Schedule C-2 for that. You start with cost or other basis. That would mean the original cost or what the item is valued at. Your method of computing depreciation could be straight-line, or by units of production, by declining balance, or by sum of the years digits. Life or rate is determined by the estimated life of the asset. Depreciation for the tax year is determined by method and life or rate and computation resulting from that.

On the following two pages, Schedule 2106—Employee Business Expenses—is the schedule you must fill out if you are taking the adjustment of income known as employee business expenses on your 1040, line 24.

Part I is where you take travel and entertainment expenses that as an employee you pay out of your own pocket and for which you are not reimbursed by your employer. On this return you must also state what your employer does reimburse you for.

Part II is for those employee expenses listed on Schedule A in the way of small tools, etc., you provide for yourself for the job. You might subscribe to periodicals relating to your job. A nurse, for example, might list scissors and other supplies that she owns.

Also note Part III, for those who have educational expenses relating to their job.

Schedule G—Income Averaging—is fairly explicit. Use this schedule when there is an increase of average income of more than $3,000 over the base-period taxable income over the past four years. Your average income is obtained by adding the past four years and taking 30% of the past four years' income, then subtracting it from the current tax year's income. If the current tax year's income is more than $3,000 over the base-period taxable income over the past four years, using this Schedule may drop your tax bracket for this year. From this form you would insert your tax liability on Schedule TC.

Form 4726—Maximum Tax on Personal Service Income—is used by those of you who have earned income over the 50% tax bracket. From this form you would go to Schedule TC and insert your tax liability.

Schedule TC—Tax Computation Schedule—we use basically when we want to employ another way of computing tax other than use of the tax tables. For instance, if you want to use income averaging with Schedule G, or if you use Form 4726—Maximum Tax on Personal Service Income—you will use the tax computation schedule to help compute your tax. You would also use the tax computation schedule if your income is higher than the tax tables go. That would be $40,000 if married filing a joint return, and $20,000 for everyone else.

Another case in which you should use Schedule TC is if your personal exemptions exceed the number provided in the tax tables.

Form 2441—Credit for Child and Dependent Care Expenses—must be filled out if you claim the credit on line 40 on the face of your 1040. Read Chapter 7, "Your Children and Your Exemptions and Deductions," and the directions on the form, which are quite explicit. You should have no trouble with this.

Schedule SE—Computation of Social Security Self-Employment Tax—is where you figure your Social Security tax. It is the same tax as if you had FICA deducted on the job. It is not calculated at the same rate.

First, you would fill out your Schedule C—Profit (or

Form **2106**

Department of the Treasury
Internal Revenue Service

Employee Business Expenses

(Please use Form 3903 to figure moving expense deduction.)

▶ Attach to Form 1040.

1980

Your name		Social security number	Occupation in which expenses were incurred
Employer's name		Employer's address	

Instructions

Use this form to show your business expenses as an employee during 1980. Include amounts:

● You paid as an employee;
● You charged to your employer (such as by credit card);
● You received as an advance, allowance, or repayment.

Several publications, available from IRS, give more information about business expenses:

Publication 463, *Travel, Entertainment, and Gift Expenses.*
Publication 529, *Miscellaneous Deductions.*
Publication 587, *Business Use of Your Home.*
Publication 508, *Educational Expenses.*

Part I.—You can deduct some business expenses even if you do not itemize your deductions on Schedule A (Form 1040). Examples are expenses for travel (except commuting to and from work), meals, or lodging. List these expenses in Part I and use them in figuring your adjusted gross income on Form 1040, line 31.

Line 2.—You can deduct meals and lodging costs if you were on a business trip away from your main place of work. Do not deduct the cost of meals you ate on one-day trips, when you did not need sleep or rest.

Line 3.—If you use your own car in your work, you can deduct the cost of the business use. Enter the cost here after figuring it in Parts

IV, V, and VI. Base the cost on your actual expenses (such as gas, oil, repairs, depreciation) or on a mileage rate.

The mileage rate is 20 cents a mile up to 15,000 miles. After that, or for all business mileage on a fully depreciated car, the rate is 11 cents a mile. A car whose cost is being figured under the mileage rate is considered to have a useful life of 5 years. If in any year actual expenses are claimed using a useful life of less than 5 years, use of the mileage rate after that shorter useful life will be limited to 11¢ per mile. (For depreciation, see Publication 463.)

Figure your mileage rate amount and add it to the business part of what you spent on the car for parking fees, tolls, interest, and State and local taxes (except gasoline tax).

Line 4.—If you were an outside salesperson with other business expenses, list them on line 4. Examples are selling expenses or expenses for stationery and stamps. An outside salesperson does all selling outside the employer's place of business. A driver-salesperson whose main duties are service and delivery, such as delivering bread or milk, is not an outside salesperson. (For outside salesperson, see Publication 463.)

Line 5.—Show other business expenses on line 5 if your employer repaid you for them. If you were repaid for part of them, show here the amount you were repaid. Show the rest in Part II.

Part II.—You can deduct other business expenses only if (a) your employer did not repay you, and (b) you itemize your deductions on Schedule A (Form 1040). Report these expenses here and under Miscellaneous Deductions on Schedule A. Examples are union or professional dues and expenses for tools and uniforms. (For details, see Publication 529.)

You can deduct expenses for business use of the part of your home that you exclusively and consistently use for your work. If you are not self-employed, your working at home must be for your employer's convenience. (For business use of home, see Publication 587.)

If you show education expenses in Part I or Part II, you must fill out Part III.

Part III.—You can deduct the cost of education that helps you keep or improve your skills for the job you have now. This includes education that your employer, the law, or regulations require you to get in order to keep your job or your salary. Do not deduct the cost of study that helps you meet the basic requirements for your job or helps you get a new job. (For education expenses, see Publication 508.)

Part V.—If you trade in a car you used in business for a new one you also used in business, fill out lines 1 through 15. If you paid cash for the new car or traded in a car not used in business, fill out only lines 10 through 15. Refigure the basis for depreciation each year in the future that your percentage of business use changes.

PART I.—Employee Business Expenses Deductible in Figuring Adjusted Gross Income on Form 1040, Line 31

1 Fares for airplane, boat, bus, taxicab, train, etc. . . . .

2 Meals and lodging . . . .

3 Car expenses (from Part IV, line 21) . . . .

4 Outside salesperson's expenses (see Part I instructions above) ▲ . . . .

5 Other (see Part I instructions above) ▲ . . . .

6 Add lines 1 through 5 . . . .

7 Employer's payments for these expenses if not included on Form W–2 . . . .

8 Deductible business expenses (subtract line 7 from line 6). Enter here and include on Form 1040, line 24 .

9 Income from excess business expense payments (subtract line 6 from line 7). Enter here and include on Form 1040, line 21

PART II.—Employee Business Expenses that are Deductible Only if You Itemize Deductions on Schedule A (Form 1040)

1 Business expenses not included above (list expense and amount) ▲ . . . . . .

2 Total. Deduct under Miscellaneous Deductions, Schedule A (Form 1040). . . . . . .

PART III.—Information About Education Expenses Shown in Part I or Part II

1 Name of educational institution or activity ▲

2 Address ▲

3 Did you need this education to meet the basic requirements for your job? . . . . ☐ Yes ☐ No

4 Will this study program qualify you for a new job? . . . . ☐ Yes ☐ No

5 If your answer to question 3 or 4 is No, explain (1) why you are getting the education and (2) what the relationship was between the courses you took and your job. (If you need more space, attach a statement.) ▲

6 List your main subjects, or describe your educational activity ▲

PART IV.—Car Expenses (Use either your actual expenses or the mileage rate)

	Car 1	Car 2	Car 3
	___ months	___ months	___ months
A. Number of months you used car for business during 1980.			
B. Total mileage for months in line A.	___ miles	___ miles	___ miles
C. Business part of line B mileage.	___ miles	___ miles	___ miles

Actual Expenses (Include expenses for only the months shown in line A, above.)

	Car 1	Car 2	Car 3
1 Gasoline, oil, lubrication, etc.			
2 Repairs			
3 Tires, supplies, etc.			
4 Other: (a) Insurance			
(b) Taxes			
(c) Tags and licenses			
(d) Interest			
(e) Miscellaneous			
5 Total (add lines 1 through 4(e)).			
6 Business percentage of car use (divide line C by line B, above).	%	%	%
7 Business part of car expense (multiply line 5 by line 6).			
8 Depreciation (from Part VI, column (h)).			
9 Divide line 8 by 12 months.			
10 Multiply line 9 by line A, above.			
11 Total (add line 7 and line 10; then skip to line 19).			

Mileage Rate

12 Enter the smaller of (a) 15,000 miles or (b) the combined mileages from line C, above.	· · ·	___ miles
13 Multiply line 12 by 20¢ (11¢ if car is fully depreciated) and enter here.	· · ·	
14 Enter any combined mileage from line C that is over 15,000 miles.	· · ·	___ miles
15 Multiply line 14 by 11¢ and enter here.	· · ·	
16 Total mileage expense (add lines 13 and 15).	· · ·	

17 Business part of car interest and State and local taxes (except gasoline tax) . . . .

18 Total (add lines 16 and 17) . . . .

Summary:

19 Enter amount from line 11 or line 18, whichever you used . . . .

20 Parking fees and tolls . . . .

21 Total (add lines 19 and 20). Enter here and in Part I, line 3 . . . .

PART V.—Basis for Depreciation of Car Used in Business (See instructions on front)

Trade-in of Old Car:

1 (a) Total mileage at trade-in		miles
(b) Business mileage		miles
(c) Business percentage . . . . (divide line (b) by line (a)) . . .		%
2 Purchase price or other basis		
3 Trade-in allowance		
4 Difference (subtract line 3 from line 2) .		

New Car:

10 Purchase price or other basis . . . . . .

11 Estimated salvage value . . . .

12 Difference (subtract line 11 from line 10) . . . .

5 Multiply line 4 by percentage on line 1(c) . . . .

6 Gain or (loss) on previous trade-in . .

7 Balance of lines 5 and 6 (subtract gain or add (loss)) . . . .

8 Depreciation allowed or allowable . .

9 Gain or (loss) on business part (Subtract line 7 from line 8 for gain; or line 8 from line 7 for (loss)). . . . .

13 Multiply line 12 by the percentage on line 6 of Part IV. . . . .

14 Enter gain or (loss) from line 9 . . . .

15 Basis for depreciation (Balance of lines 13 and 14: subtract gain or add (loss)) . . . . . .

PART VI.—Car Depreciation

Make and model of car (a)	Date acquired (b)	Basis (from line 15, Part V) (c)	Age of car when acquired (d)	Depreciation allowed in previous years (e)	Method of figuring depreciation (f)	Rate (%) or life (years) (g)	Depreciation this year (h)

SCHEDULE G (Form 1040)

Department of the Treasury
Internal Revenue Service

Income Averaging

▶ See instructions on back.
▶ Attach to Form 1040.

1980
21

Name(s) as shown on Form 1040

Your social security number

Base Period Income and Adjustments

	(a) 1st preceding base period year 1979	(b) 2d preceding base period year 1978	(c) 3rd preceding base period year 1977	(d) 4th preceding base period year 1976
1 Enter amount from: Form 1040 (1977, 1978, and 1979)—line 34 Form 1040A (1977 and 1978)—line 10 Form 1040A (1979)—line 11				
2 a Multiply $750 by your total number of exemptions in 1977 and 1978 . . .				
b Multiply $1,000 by your total number of exemptions in 1979				
3 Taxable income (subtract line 2a or 2b from line 1). If less than zero, enter zero . .				
4 Income earned outside of the United States or within U.S. possessions and excluded under sections 911 and 931				
5 On your 1980 {2 or 5 enter $3,200} in column Form 1040, if {1 or 4 enter $2,200} (d) you checked box {3 enter $1,600} . .				
6 Base period income (add lines 3, 4 and 5) .				

Computation of Averageable Income

7 Taxable income for 1980 from Schedule TC (Form 1040), Part I, line 3 . . .	7
8 Certain amounts received by owner-employees subject to a penalty under section 72(m)(5)	8
9 Subtract line 8 from line 7	9

10 Excess community income . . . . |10|	
11 Adjusted taxable income (subtract line 10 from line 9). If less than zero, enter zero		**11**
12 Add columns (a) through (d), line 6, and enter here . . . . |12|	
13 Enter 30% of line 12		**13**
14 Averageable income (subtract line 13 from line 11)		**14**

If line 14 is $3,000 or less, do not complete the rest of this form. You do not qualify for income averaging.

G

Computation of Tax

15 Amount from line 13		**15**
16 20% of line 14		**16**
17 Total (add lines 15 and 16)		**17**
18 Excess community income from line 10		**18**
19 Total (add lines 17 and 18)		**19**
20 Tax on amount on line 19 (see caution below)		**20**
21 Tax on amount on line 17 (see caution below) . . . . |21|	
22 Tax on amount on line 15 (see caution below) . . . . |22|	
23 Subtract line 22 from line 21 . . . . |23|	
24 Multiply the amount on line 23 by 4		**24**
	Note: *If no entry was made on line 8 above, skip lines 25 through 27 and go to line 28.*	
25 Tax on amount on line 7 (see caution below) . . . . |25|	
26 Tax on amount on line 9 (see caution below) . . . . |26|	
27 Subtract line 26 from line 25		**27**
28 Tax (add lines 20, 24, and 27). Enter here and on Schedule TC (Form 1040), Part I, line 4 and check Schedule G box		**28**

Caution: Use Tax Rate Schedule X, Y or Z from the Form 1040 instructions to figure your tax on lines 20, 21, 22, 25 and 26. Do not use the tax tables.

Form **4726**	**Maximum Tax on Personal Service Income**	**1980**
Department of the Treasury Internal Revenue Service	▶ See instructions on back. ▶ Attach to Form 1040 (or Form 1041).	31

Name(s) as shown on Form 1040 (or Form 1041)   Identifying number

Do not complete this form if—(a) Taxable income or personal service taxable income is:

    $41,500 or less, and on Form 1040, you checked box 1,

    $60,000 or less, and on Form 1040, you checked box 2 or box 5,

    $44,700 or less, and on Form 1040, you checked box 4,

    $28,300 or less, and this is an Estate or Trust return (Form 1041);

    (b) You elected income averaging; or

    (c) On Form 1040, you checked box 3.

Personal Service Income		Deductions Against Personal Service Income	
1 Total personal service income	**1**	**2** Total deductions against personal service income	**2**

3 Personal service net income—Subtract total of line 2 from total of line 1 . . . . **3**

4 Enter your adjusted gross income **4**

5 Divide the amount on line 3 by the amount on line 4. Enter result as a percentage. If more than 100%, enter 100%. Round to nearest 4 numbers. **5**

6 Enter your taxable income	**6**
7 Multiply the amount on line 6 by the percentage on line 5 . . .	**7**
8 Enter the total of your 1980 tax preference items other than capital gains . . .	**8**
9 Personal service taxable income. Subtract line 8 from line 7 . . .	**9**
10 If: on Form 1040, you checked box 1, enter $41,500. . . . on Form 1040, you checked box 2 or box 5, enter $60,000. . . . on Form 1040, you checked box 4, enter $44,700 . . . you are filing Form 1041, enter $28,300. . . .	**10**
11 Subtract line 10 from line 9. If line 10 is more than line 9, do not complete rest of form .	**11**
12 Enter 50% of line 11	**12**
13 Tax on amount on line 6* **13**	
14 Tax on amount on line 9* **14**	
15 Subtract line 14 from line 13	**15**
16 If the amount on line 10 is: $41,500, enter $13,392 . . . . $60,000, enter $19,678 . . . . $44,700, enter $13,961 . . . . $28,300, enter $9,839	**16**
17 Add lines 12, 15, and 16. This is your maximum tax	**17**

*Use Tax Rate Schedules from Form 1040 or Form 1041 instructions.

SCHEDULE TC
(Form 1040)

Department of the Treasury
Internal Revenue Service

Tax Computation Schedule

▶ Attach to Form 1040.

1980

Name(s) as shown on Form 1040

Your social security number

Part I Computation of Tax for Taxpayers Who Cannot Use the Tax Tables

Use this part to figure your tax if:

- Your income on Form 1040, line 34, is more than $20,000 and you checked Filing Status Box 1, 3, or 4 on Form 1040.

- Your income on Form 1040, line 34, is more than $40,000 and you checked Filing Status Box 2 or 5 on Form 1040.

- You had more exemptions than were shown in the Tax Table for your filing status.

- You figure your tax using Schedule G (Income Averaging) or Form 4726 (Maximum Tax on Personal Service Income).

1 Enter the amount from Form 1040, line 34	**1**	
2 Multiply $1,000 by the total number of exemptions claimed on Form 1040, line 7 . . .	**2**	
3 Taxable income. Subtract line 2 from line 1. (Figure your tax on this amount by using the Tax Rate Schedules or one of the other methods listed on line 4.)	**3**	
4 Income tax. Enter tax and check if from: ☐ Tax Rate Schedule X, Y, or Z, ☐ Schedule G, or ☐ Form 4726. Also enter on Form 1040, line 35	**4**	

Part II Computation for Certain Taxpayers Who MUST Itemize Deductions

If you are included in one of the groups below, you MUST itemize. If you must itemize and the amount on Schedule A (Form 1040), line 40, is more than your itemized deductions on Schedule A, line 39, you must complete Part II before figuring your tax.

Note: If your earned income is more than your itemized deductions, you don't have to fill in Schedule A. Just enter your earned income in Part II, line 3, of this schedule, unless you are married filing a separate return and your spouse itemizes deductions. Generally, your earned income is the total of any amounts on Form 1040, lines 8, 13, and 19. See page 11 of the instructions for Form 1040 for more details.

line 3, of this schedule. If this is the case, don't complete Part II. Go back to Form 1040, line, 33, and enter $0. Then go to Form 1040, line 34.

C. You file Form 4563 to exclude income from sources in U.S. possessions. (Please see Form 4563, and Publication 570, Tax Guide for U.S. Citizens Employed in U.S. Possessions, for more details.)

You MUST itemize your deductions if:

A. You can be claimed as a dependent on your parents' return and had interest, dividends, or other unearned income of $1,000 or more and had earned income of less than $2,300 if single (less than $1,700 if married filing a separate return).

B. You are married filing a separate return and your spouse itemizes deductions. (There is an exception to this rule. You don't have to itemize if your spouse must itemize only because he or she is described in **A** and enters earned income instead of itemized deductions on Part II, described in **A** and enters earned income instead of itemized deductions on Part II.

D. You had dual status as a nonresident alien for part of 1980, and during the rest of the year you were either a resident alien or a U.S. citizen. However, you don't have to itemize if at the end of 1980, you were a nonresident alien married to a U.S. resident or citizen and file a joint return reporting your combined worldwide income.

		TC	

1 Enter the amount from Form 1040, line 31 . . . . | **1** | ▨ |

2 If you checked Form 1040, Filing Status Box: $\begin{cases} \text{2 or 5, enter \$3,400} \\ \text{1 or 4, enter \$2,300} \\ \text{3, enter \$1,700} \end{cases}$ . . . . | **2** |

3 Enter the amount from Schedule A, line 39 . . . . | **3** |

Caution: *If you can be claimed as a dependent on your parents' return, see the Note above. Be sure you check the box below line 33 of Form 1040.*

4 Subtract line 3 from line 2 . . . . | **4** |

5 Add lines 1 and 4. Enter here and on Form 1040, line 34. (Leave Form 1040, line 33 blank. Disregard the instruction to subtract line 33 from line 32. Follow the rest of the instructions for Form 1040, line 34.) . . . . | **5** |

The example below may help you to complete *Part II.*

Example.—Walter Green, a single individual, is claimed as a dependent on his parents' return. Walter's adjusted gross income, Form 1040, line 31, is $4,000. Of this amount, $1,500 was earned income from a summer job and $2,500 was unearned income that he received as a beneficiary of a trust. Because Walter is being claimed as a dependent on his parents' return and has unearned income of $1,000 or more and earned income of less than

$2,300, he must use Part II of Schedule TC. Walter knows that his total itemized deductions are only $500. Since this is less than his earned income ($1,500), he does not have to complete Schedule A. Walter enters $2,300, the zero bracket amount for a single individual, on line 2 of Part II and his earned income on line 3. He completes Part II as shown below and enters the total of $4,800 on Form 1040, line 34. He then figures his tax using the Tax Tables as explained in the instructions for lines 34 and 35 on page 12.

1 Adjusted gross income . . .	. .	$4,000
2 Zero bracket amount for a single individual . .	. .	$2,300
3 Earned income . . .	1,500	
4 Subtract line 3 from line 2 . .	. .	800
5 Add lines 1 and 4. Enter here and on Form 1040, line 34.	. .	$4,800

Note: *If Walter's itemized deductions are more than his earned income, he must complete Schedule A first.*

Form **2441**

Department of the Treasury
Internal Revenue Service

Credit for Child and Dependent Care Expenses | 1980

▶ Attach to Form 1040.   ▶ See Instructions below.   27

Name(s) as shown on Form 1040

Your social security number

---

1 See the definition for "qualifying person" in the instructions. Then read the instructions for line 1.

(a) Name of qualifying person	(b) Date of birth	(c) Relationship	(d) During 1980, the person lived with you for:	
			Months	Days

2 Persons or organizations who cared for those listed on line 1. See the instructions for line 2.

(a) Name and address (If more space is needed, attach schedule)	(b) Social security number, if applicable	(c) Relationship, if any	(d) Period of care		(e) Amount of 1980 expenses (include those not paid during the year)
			From Month—Day	To Month—Day	

To Figure Your Credit, You MUST Complete ALL Lines That Apply

3 Add the amounts in column 2(e).	**3**	
4 Enter $2,000 ($4,000 if you listed two or more names in line 1) or amount on line 3, whichever is less . .	**4**	
5 Earned income (wages, salaries, tips, etc.). See the instructions for line 5. An entry MUST be made on this line.		
(a) If unmarried at end of 1980, enter your earned income . . . . ▲	**5**	
(b) If married at end of 1980, enter your earned income or your spouse's, whichever is less . .		
6 Enter the amount on line 4 or line 5, whichever is less	**6**	
7 Amount on line 6 paid during 1980. An entry MUST be made on this line . . . . ▲	**7**	
8 Child and dependent care expenses for 1979 paid in 1980. See instructions for line 8	**8**	
9 Add amounts on lines 7 and 8.	**9**	

10	Multiply line 9 by 20 percent.	**10**	
11	Limitation:		
	a Enter tax from Form 1040, line 37 . . . . . . **11a**		
	b Enter total of lines 38, 39, and 41 through 43 of Form 1040 . . . **11b**		
	c Subtract line 11b from line 11a (if line 11b is more than line 11a, enter zero) . . .	**11c**	
12	Credit for child and dependent care expenses. Enter the smaller of line 10 or line 11c here and on Form 1040, line 40 .	**12**	

13 If payments listed on line 2 were made to an individual, complete the following:

		Yes	No
(a) If you paid \$50 or more in a calendar quarter to an individual, were the services performed in your home?			
(b) If "yes," have you filed appropriate wage tax returns on wages for services in your home (see instructions for line 13)? . . .			
(c) If answer to (b) is "yes," enter your employer identification number . . . . . ▲			

General Instructions

If you or your spouse worked or looked for work, and you spent money to care for a qualifying person (see below), this form might save your tax.

What is the Child and Dependent Care Expenses Credit?—This is a credit you can take against your tax if you paid someone to care for your child or dependent so that you could work or look for work. You can also take the credit if you paid someone to care for your spouse. The instructions that follow list tests that must be met to take the credit. If you need more information, please get Publication 503, Child and Disabled Dependent Care.

For purposes of this credit, we have defined some of the terms used here. Refer to these when you read the instructions.

Definitions

A qualifying person can be:

• Any person under age 15 whom you list as a dependent. (If you are divorced, legally separated, or separated under a

written agreement, please see the Child Custody Test in the instructions.)

• Your spouse who is mentally or physically not able to care for himself or herself.

• Any person not able to care for himself or herself whom you can list as a dependent, or could list as a dependent except that he or she had income of \$1,000 or more.

A relative is your child, stepchild, mother, father, grandparent, brother, sister, grandchild, uncle, aunt, nephew, niece, stepmother, stepfather, stepbrother, stepsister, mother-in-law, father-in-law, brother-in-law, sister-in-law, son-in-law, and daughter-in-law. A cousin is not a relative for purpose of this credit.

A full-time student is one who was enrolled in a school for the number of hours or classes that is considered full time. The student must have been enrolled at least 5 months during 1980.

What Are Child and Dependent Care Expenses?

These expenses are the amounts you

paid for household services and care of the qualifying person.

Household Services.—These are services performed by a cook, housekeeper, governess, maid, cleaning person, babysitter, etc. The services must have been needed to care for the qualifying person as well as run the home. For example, if you paid for the services of a maid or a cook, the services must have also been for the benefit of the qualifying person.

Care of the Qualifying Person.—Care includes cost of services for the well-being and protection of the qualifying person.

Care does not include expenses for food and clothes. If you paid for care that included these items and you cannot separate their cost, take the total payment.

Example: You paid a nursery school to care for your child and the school gave the child lunch. Since you cannot separate the cost of the lunch from the cost of the care, you can take all of the amount that you paid to the school.

This example would not apply if you had school costs for a child in the first grade or

(Continued on back)

SCHEDULE SE (Form 1040)

Department of the Treasury / Internal Revenue Service

Computation of Social Security Self-Employment Tax

▶ See Instructions for Schedule SE (Form 1040).
▶ Attach to Form 1040.

1980
23

SE

Name of self-employed person (as shown on social security card) | Social security number of self-employed person ▶

Part I — Computation of Net Earnings from FARM Self-Employment

Regular Method

1 Net profit or (loss) from:

a Schedule F (Form 1040)	1a	
b Farm partnerships	1b	
2 Net earnings from farm self-employment (add lines 1a and 1b)	2	

Farm Optional Method

3 If gross profits from farming are:

a Not more than $2,400, enter two-thirds of the gross profits . . . . . .
b More than $2,400 and the net farm profit is less than $1,600, enter $1,600 .

	3	

4 Enter here and on line 12a, the amount on line 2, or line 3 if you elect the farm optional method .

	4	

Part II — Computation of Net Earnings from NONFARM Self-Employment

Regular Method

5 Net profit or (loss) from:

a Schedule C (Form 1040)	5a	
b Partnerships, joint ventures, etc. (other than farming)	5b	
c Service as a minister, member of a religious order, or a Christian Science practitioner. (Include rental value of parsonage or rental allowance furnished.) If you filed Form 4361 and have not revoked that exemption, check here ▶ ☐ and enter zero on this line . . .	5c	
d Service with a foreign government or international organization	5d	
e Other (specify) ▶ _____	5e	
6 Total (add lines 5a through 5e)	6	

7 Enter adjustments if any (attach statement, see page 29 of Instructions)	7	
8 Adjusted net earnings or (loss) from nonfarm self-employment (line 6, as adjusted by line 7) . .	8	
Note: If line 8 is $1,600 or more or if you do not elect to use the Nonfarm Optional Method, skip lines 9 through 11 and enter amount from line 8 on line 12b.		
Nonfarm Optional Method		
9 a Maximum amount reportable under both optional methods combined (farm and nonfarm) .	9a	$1,600 00
b Enter amount from line 3. (If you did not elect to use the farm optional method, enter zero.) .	9b	
c Balance (subtract line 9b from line 9a)	9c	
10 Enter two-thirds of gross nonfarm profits or $1,600, whichever is smaller	10	
11 Enter here and on line 12b, the amount on line 9c or line 10, whichever is smaller . . .	11	

Part III Computation of Social Security Self-Employment Tax

12 Net earnings or (loss):		
a From farming (from line 4)	12a	
b From nonfarm (from line 8, or line 11 if you elect to use the Nonfarm Optional Method) .	12b	
13 Total net earnings or (loss) from self-employment reported on lines 12a and 12b. Do. (If line 13 is less than $400, you are not subject to self-employment tax. Do not fill in rest of schedule)	13	
14 The largest amount of combined wages and self-employment earnings subject to social security or railroad retirement taxes for 1980 is	14	$25,900 00
15 a Total "FICA" wages (from Forms W–2) and "RRTA" compensation	15a	
b Unreported tips subject to FICA tax from Form 4137, line 9 or to RRTA	15b	
c Add lines 15a and 15b	15c	
16 Balance (subtract line 15c from line 14)	16	
17 Self-employment income—line 13 or 16, whichever is smaller	17	
18 Self-employment tax. (If line 17 is $25,900, enter $2,097.90; if less, multiply the amount on line 17 by .081.) Enter here and on Form 1040, line 48	18	

Loss) from Business or Profession. The bottom-line figure on your Schedule C will give you the basis for computation of your Social Security tax.

If you have self-employment income from a partnership, you are required to fill out this Schedule SE, too. In that case, your income from your partnership income-tax return (Schedule K-1—Partner's Share of Income, Credits, Deductions, etc.) would be the basis for your computation of your Social Security contribution.

CHAPTER 21

Amending Your Return

Do you recall that in the first chapter we told you the purpose of this book was to show you how to get a refund through taking the biggest and the most deductions on your 1040? We also told you that it is up to you to see that you get a refund. No one can do it for you.

We laid down four basic rules to follow, based on our experience with clients who always seem to get a refund, or at least minimal tax bills.

1. IF IT ISN'T A DEDUCTION, DON'T SPEND IT.
2. TAKE ADVANTAGE OF ALL DEFERRALS OF INCOME.
3. KEEP IMPECCABLE TAX RECORDS WITH DOCUMENTATION.
4. DO TAX PLANNING EVERY DAY.

Then we went into various facets of your life and showed you how they may include tax deductions for you. We showed you that regardless of your marital status you do have some options on how to file your return for maximum tax benefits. One bachelor client learned through us that instead of filing as a single, he could file as head of household—because he supported a younger sister who lived with him—and he received a refund.

A working woman with a fourteen-year-old son

231

spent a considerable sum to send him to summer camp. She was delighted to learn that she was entitled to child-care credit for the camp expenses. She made a mental note of that for the future and filed amended returns for the past years, claiming child-care credit.

A building contractor, who with his two brothers completely supported his parents, learned about the multiple-support agreement, which entitled each of them to take a turn in taking exemptions for their parents.

A mother and father with a son who was a discipline problem discovered that by transferring him from the military academy to which they had sent him to a school that had a staff psychologist, they could prorate school costs between academic and psychological services and take a medical deduction on the school's psychological services for their son.

A young executive who was transferred from one city to another learned that he could avoid capital-gains tax on the sale of his old home by buying another home within two years.

We showed you under what circumstances you can enhance your social life and do some traveling and still deduct expenses on those activities. We told you how your hobby, if turned into a second source of income, can be expense free. We even told you how your sex life has built-in tax deductions! Other taxes, we informed you, can be deductible on your federal return. In Chapter 12, "Retirement, Pensions, and Taxes," and in Chapter 11, "Investments and Deductions," we emphasized one of our precepts: taking advantage of all deferral on income.

You are tax-wise by now. You will keep explicit records after this, and you will adjust your life where you can to take advantage of tax laws. You will keep explicit records as documentation. It's great to be tax-savvy for the future, but we also promised you that you can do something to recoup on past returns for omissions before you had all the knowledge you gained in this book.

The first thing we do when we take on a new client is to examine his previous years' tax returns. Invariably, we find for lack of knowledge he has overpaid on his taxes and very often could have gotten refunds. We sit right down and amend his returns for the past three years. According to tax law, you have three years from the time you filed a return to amend it.

There is nothing complicated or mysterious about amending a return. You don't have to be a CPA to do it. Simply get in touch with your local IRS office (its phone number and address are in the telephone book) and request that a Form 1040X be sent you. This form is titled: Amended U.S. Individual Income Tax Return.

Technically, what you are doing when you amend your original return is redoing it, or reworking the deduction and recalculating the tax with the omitted deductions on it. Form 1040X asks for your original figures, the net change, and the corrected amount. State reasons why credit or refund is claimed on the back of the 1040X.

You might have received a refund on your original return. However, after reading this book you may find that there were even more deductions you were entitled to, so you decide to amend that original return. If you do—and why shouldn't you?—note that on line 20 you are to tell how much refund you received on your original return. This is subtracted from the refund due on your amended return. The refund on your original return, if you have not yet received it, will be sent separately and be considered separately from the refund on your amended return.

It usually takes two to three months for the IRS to process an amended return, so do not be discouraged if your check is not in next week's mail.

Important: If you are amending your federal return, there is a good chance that your state return can be amended too for a refund!

1040X Amended U.S. Individual Income Tax Return

(Rev. November 1980)

Department of the Treasury
Internal Revenue Service

Please print or type

This return is for calendar year ▶ 19_____ , OR fiscal year ended ▶ _____ , 19_____ .

Your first name and initial (If joint return, also give spouse's name and initial)	Last name	Your social security number

Present home address (Number and street, including apartment number, or rural route)		Spouse's social security no.

City, town or post office, State, and ZIP code		

Enter below name and address as shown on original return (if same as above, write "Same"). If changing from separate to joint return, enter names and addresses used on original returns. (Note: You cannot change from joint to separate returns after the due date has passed.)

a. Service center where original return was filed

b. Has original return for the year being changed been audited? . . . . ☐ Yes ☐ No
If "No," have you been advised that it will be? . . . . ☐ Yes ☐ No
If "Yes," Identify IRS office ▶

c. Filing status claimed. (Note: You cannot change from joint to separate returns after the due date has passed.)
On original return . . ▶ ☐ Single ☐ Married filing joint return ☐ Married filing separate return ☐ Head of Household ☐ Qualifying Widow(er)
On this return . . . ▶ ☐ Single ☐ Married filing joint return ☐ Married filing separate return ☐ Head of Household ☐ Qualifying Widow(er)

Income and Deductions

	A. As originally reported or as adjusted (See instructions)	B. Net change—Increase or (Decrease)—explain on page 2	C. Correct amount
1 Total income (see instructions).			
2 Adjustments to income (see instructions) . . .			
3 Adjusted gross income (subtract line 2 from line 1)			
4 Deductions (see instructions)			
5 Subtract line 4 from line 3			

Note: If this return is for 1977 or later and you use the tax tables, do not complete line 6 or take the general tax credit. Instead, enter on line 8, the tax on the income you reported on line 5.

6 Exemptions from page 2, line 5 . . . .
7 Taxable income (subtract line 6 from line 5) . . .

Tax Liability

8 Tax (see instructions) (method used in column C _____) . .
9 Credits (such as residential energy credits, credit for the elderly—see instructions) .
10 Subtract line 9 from line 8 . . . .
11 Other taxes (such as self-employment tax, minimum tax—see instructions) . . .
12 Total tax liability (add line 10 and line 11) . . .

Payments

13 Federal income tax withheld and excess FICA and RRTA tax withheld
14 Estimated tax payments . . . .
15 Earned income credit . . . .
16 Credits for Federal tax on special fuels, regulated investment company, etc.
17 Amount paid with Form 4868 (application for automatic extension of time to file) .
18 Amount paid with original return, plus additional tax paid after it was filed . . .
19 Total of lines 13 through 18, column C . . . .

Refund or Balance Due

20 Overpayment, if any, as shown on original return . . . .
21 Subtract line 20 from line 19 (see instructions) . . . .
22 BALANCE DUE. If line 12, column C is more than line 21, enter difference. Please pay in full with this return . .
23 REFUND to be received. If line 12, column C is less than line 21, enter difference .

Please Sign Here

Under penalties of perjury, I declare that I have filed an original return, and that I have examined this amended return, including accompanying schedules and statements, and to the best of my knowledge and belief this amended return is true, correct, and complete. Declaration of preparer (other than taxpayer) is based on all information of which the preparer has any knowledge.

▲ Your signature   Date   ▲ Spouse's signature (if filing jointly BOTH must sign even if only one had income)

Paid Preparer's Use Only

Preparer's signature and date ▲   Check if self-employed ☐   Preparer's social security no.
Firm's name (or yours, if self-employed) and address ▲   E.I. No. ▲   ZIP code ▲

BE SURE TO COMPLETE PAGE 2

Form 1040X (Rev. 11-80)

Part I Exemptions (See Form 1040 or Form 1040A Instructions)

If exemptions are unchanged or are decreased, do not complete lines 6 and 7.

	A. Number originally reported	B. Net change	C. Corrected number
1 Exemptions—yourself and spouse, 65 or over, blind			
2 Your dependent children who lived with you			
3 Other dependents			
4 Total exemptions (add lines 1 through 3)			
5 Multiply $1,000 ($750, if 1978 or prior) by the total number of exemptions claimed on line 4. Enter this amount here and on page 1, line 6			

6 Enter first names of your dependent children who lived with you, but were not claimed on original return:

Enter number ▲ [ ]

7 Other dependents not claimed on original return:

(a) Name	(b) Relationship	(c) Number of months lived in your home	(d) Did dependent have income of $1,000 ($750, if 1978 or prior) or more?	(e) Did you provide more than one half of dependent's support?

Enter number ▲ [ ]

Part II Explanation of Changes to Income, Deductions, and Credits

Enter the line reference from page 1 for which you are reporting a change and give the reason for each change. Attach applicable schedules.

Check here ▶ [ ] If change pertains to a net operating loss carryback, an investment credit carryback, a WIN credit carryback, or a jobs credit carryback.

CHAPTER 22

Your Tax Return
and the IRS Obstacle Course

After you have finished your tax return, and it has been mailed, it runs the IRS obstacle course. Ninety-three million '80 returns were screened by October. It was then that most of the audit notices went out for that year, but you can still be nabbed for audit on your '80 return this year or later.

Let's follow the IRS processing of returns to see why. Initial scrutiny of returns takes place at one of ten IRS regional processing centers: Cincinnati, Ohio; Atlanta, Georgia; Fresno, California; Ogden, Utah; Austin, Texas; Kansas City, Missouri; Andover, Massachusetts; Brookhaven, New York; Memphis, Tennessee; Philadelphia, Pennsylvania. Here is where obvious errors are spotted: unsigned returns, missing W-2s, faulty arithmetic, etc. On the second step, the center inspectors give "eyeball checks" for unallowable deductions. Third step: Returns transfer to the center computer where they are put through twice by two different operators as a double check against error. Fourth: Your tax return travels to the main IRS computer center in Martinsburg, West Virginia, for final processing. There, selection of returns for audit are made and also clearance for refunds. (Note: A refund does not mean that you might not be audited later on.) Five-year records of your returns are kept on tape in Martinsburg. Microfilm records there go back to the early 1960s.

Individual as well as corporation and excise tax returns are identified for audit under a special, secret computer program. (The formula for the screening is so secret that though a Washington State couple is suing under the Freedom of Information Act to make it public, there is little hope that they will win their suit.) The computer program makes use of thirty-eight to fifty classification criteria. Any income-tax return that meets one of these programmed criteria is identified for audit. The identified returns are then made available to district employees designated as classifiers who are selected from experienced tax technicians and revenue agents. They screen and select those returns they judge to be most in need of examination.

Only about 2% of all returns are actually audited. Small consolation if you are one of the 2%! What are the chances that you will be audited? If you don't itemize, your odds are less than 1 out of 100. (However, don't let that stop you from itemizing if that is the cheapest route for you.) At the other end of the audit odds is the chance of someone with income of $50,000 or more. For these people the odds are 1 out of 11 of being audited.

Top targets are doctors and other self-employed professionals who do not have taxes withheld: particularly dentists, lawyers, engineers, architects. Real-estate brokers and funeral directors are also top targets. Include too in that category of top targets those who use tax shelters and employees who get a lot of tips (waiters, waitresses, taxicab drivers, etc.).

The audit criteria used by the computer and in the manual screening of returns by classifiers can be placed in these general categories:

1. *Type of error*.
   This is the identification of items on the return that either appear to be incorrectly treated or reported, or which are very unusual. For tax purposes, an item may be considered unusual in at least four different ways: (1) its dollar amount in

relation to other items on the return; (2) its description on the return; (3) its very presence on the return; or (4) its complete absence from the return.

2. *Size of income.*

The IRS claims that the larger-income returns yield the highest tax adjustment and, on examination, show a high frequency of change. It believes that there is a general correlation between size of income and the accounting and reporting complexity involved in filing large-income returns. Furthermore, it finds taxpayers in the high-income brackets have more involved and varied financial activities than those in lower income brackets. It therefore follows that there is a wider margin for error in reporting by upperclass taxpayers and a greater chance that such returns will produce changes upon examination.

3. *Type of business taxpayer is engaged in.*

The type of business a taxpayer is engaged in often determines the complexity of laws involved. For example, the laws applying to a businessman who gains income from natural resources would be much different from those that pertain to someone who is engaged in retailing. Also, as we discussed earlier, certain occupations lend themselves more easily to tax evasion.

4. *The return as a whole.*

Transactions having to do with gains and losses through sales and exchanges of property, returns with itemized deductions far in excess of the standard deduction, income from rents and royalties, or interest and dividends imply activities not directly related to a taxpayer's occupation, and thus may lead to erroneous reporting.

The agent who examines your return before contacting you is told to look for unusual and unfamiliar items. Here is a list of various items he might want to verify.

1. Exemptions claimed for children not residing with you or exemptions for persons other than children.
2. Excessive refunds due to exclusions under the law without adequate explanation (sick pay exclusions, for example).
3. Schedule "C" items:
   a. Disproportionate gross profit percentage;
   b. Inadequately explained business losses;
   c. Disproportionate bad-debt deductions for indicated volume of sales. Bad debts claimed by cash-basis taxpayers;
   d. Disproportionate repairs to depreciable assets;
   e. Amortization of emergency facilities;
   f. Net operating loss deduction;
   g. Inappropriate or disproportionate travel and entertainment expenses;
   h. Inadequate description and analysis of any depreciation deduction taken;
   i. Other income offset by farm losses;
   j. Investment income (interest and dividends) disproportionate to other income;
   k. Recapture of investment credit on disposition of property;
   l. Treatment of gain on disposition of assets where accelerated depreciation is claimed.
4. Disproportionate or inadequately explained deductions and exclusions from gross income.
5. Use of income-averaging formula.
6. Unexplained or apparent unreasonable deductions from gross rents and royalties.
7. Capital-gain and -loss schedules indicating capital-gain treatment for noncapital assets; sale for nominal consideration; use of capital-loss carry-overs; installment report-

ing of gains; and problems of "unstated interest" in installment sales.

8. Gains and losses from other than capital assets and discounts on obligations of buyer.
9. Disproportionate amount of income vs. number of exemptions claimed.
10. Casualty losses inadequately explained as to method of loss determination.
11. Deductions for dependents outside immediate family or living apart from taxpayer.
12. Excessive refunds.
13. Inadequate or incomplete schedules or responses to questions on return.
14. Required schedules not furnished, such as Multiple Support Declaration.
15. Business vs. nonbusiness treatment of bad debts.
16. Separate filing by spouse indicated.
17. Employee's moving expenses.
18. Recovered amounts deducted in prior years, such as bad debts, medical expenses, state income and other taxes, losses, etc., must be included in income in the year of recovery.

The IRS's Audit Technique Handbook provides some guidelines for questions that might arise during the audit. Your examiner will pay attention to these guideline questions and also may have others that pertain to your particular case.

The occupation line of the tax return is of significance to the examiner primarily because of its relationship to other items which are or should be on the return. Examples of such interrelationships: If you are a waiter or cab driver, is income from tips reported on the return? Does the occupation of salesman coupled with name of employer indicate whether there is an allowance for expense deductions or whether they should be deducted as an employee business expense or as an itemized deduction? (A salesman at a local retail store usually should not claim entertainment expenses. An automobile salesman's business expenses should usually appear only as an itemized deduction.) Does the salesman who is involved in out-of-town travel and is furnished a car use it for personal use? A wife who is listed as a housewife usually is not eligible for the child-care credit.

On the matter of exemptions and deductions, your agent will question a return that lists dependent children but no wife as to whether a separate return is being filed by her. This item is significant to him with respect to the right to use the standard deduction or the tax table, the top limitation of the standard deduction, or the right to compute the tax under the joint-return provisions. Is the taxpayer really contributing more than 50% support in nonmultiple-support cases? Is there documentation of that support claim? The agent would ask the age of the dependent to determine whether the dependent might be collecting Social Security. He would also question as to whether welfare payments, relief, and incidental earnings of the dependent are used for his support. He will question the taxpayer as to the age of his youngest child. Sometimes he may find that a child born after the end of the taxable year but before the filing date is claimed as an exemption; however, the child only qualifies as an exemption if born before January 1 of that year.

Your agent will have a number of questions to ask regarding income. One will be whether a wife worked during the year. Frequently, when the wife earned less than $600 during the year, the income is omitted from the tax return under a mistaken belief that the wife is a dependent. He will ask if the taxpayer received any Christmas or other bonuses during the year and, if so, whether it was included on his W-2 form. If a taxpayer's occupation is such that he had a number of employers during the year, did he list all his income on his return? Did he include all his W-2s? The agent might ask the taxpayer to account chronologically for all his employment throughout the year. The examiner may, in determining tip income of a waitress, ask her restaurant owner for the year's receipt total, divide by the average number of waitresses, and then assume 15% of that as her tips for the year. He might establish a cab driver's tip income by applying 15% to his individual bookings or meter readings. If listed salaries show that a husband and wife are working for their own closely held corporation, the examiner will seek to determine whether the corporate return has been selected for examination. If it has not, he will probe to see whether the wife is actually working for the corporation. If she did no work, it may mean the corporation return will be examined too!

In cases where a taxpayer takes disability income exclusion (Form 2440), the agent will scan the form for such errors as failure to include in income the benefits received from all sources—employers, insurance companies, unions—or for exclusion of payments that are not in income because they are specifically not taxable. (Example: A worker covered by the Railroad Retirement Act may attempt to exclude it on the tax return.) In the case of a salesman reporting sick pay, the agent will seek to determine whether the amount is actually a salary. (In some cases, the amount may be the weekly "draws" against his earned commissions. His employer may not even have an accepted plan.)

The agent will look into the case of an employee's claiming travel and entertainment deductions for a schedule of expenses completed on Form 2106—Employee Business Expenses. Agents figure that employees are generally reimbursed by their employers for these expenses. If there is any question as to the reimbursement, or as to whether the taxpayer was obligated to incur those expenses, the examining office will ask the taxpayer to secure a letter from his employer. For the letter to pass inspection with the auditor, it should state whether the employee was reimbursed or not and, if so, how much and whether the amount is included on his W-2. In order to determine the maximum amount that could have been spent for entertainment, the agent will total all funds received from salaries, commissions, drawings on account, investments, and savings. Then he will subtract estimated amounts spent for living expenses, actual savings, and investments. He will determine expenses allowable for automobile operation by the approximate total mileage involved. This can be ascertained by referring to any repair bills from the beginning through the end of the year, because quite often the bill will reflect the mileage reading. He can also determine allocation between business and personal use by referring to automobile insurance policies, which usually state whether other members of the family operate the automobile.

The agent will not limit audit of dividend income reported by the taxpayer to information documents attached to the return. The agent will look for classification, time of receipt, and total reported. The agent will study the taxpayer's broker's monthly statements to check carefully for dividends credited to his account. He will refer to his IRS manual for corporations that issue wholly or partly nontaxable dividends and check with the taxpayer's holdings.

The agent will want to verify interest income. If interest-bearing securities were sold during the year, he will check to see if any interest should have been reported. Where bonds have been acquired with interest in default, he will determine whether any interest received which accrued after the purchase date is reflected as interest income. He will analyze brokerage account statements to see whether interest charged on margin account has been netted against interest or dividend income (it must be claimed as an itemized deduction). In the analysis, he will determine whether interest paid to carry tax-exempt securities has been deducted. He will ask the taxpayer whether he has cashed any government bonds, held any matured government bonds, or had any savings accounts during the taxable year. He will look for other interest income often erroneously omitted from returns: interest on paid-up insurance policies and interest on prior year tax refunds. If property was sold in prior or current years and a purchase-money mortgage constituted part payment, interest income should be reflected in the return. A common error is to regard all collections on account of the mortgage as principal until it is fully paid.

Gains and losses from sale or exchange of property involve the agent in verification of selling price, expenses of sale, the adjusted basis of the property, and the holding period. He will analyze brokerage "bought" and "sold" slips, and the broker's monthly statements for the purchase or sales price, the commissions, the transfer taxes (federal and local), and accrued interest. He will scrutinize documents for holding periods of the capital asset because the IRS Code varies its treatment of gains and losses according to whether they are short-term or long-term. In the case of personal residence sales, he will scan the closing statement as the best source for checking the transaction. He will try to obtain the purchase and sale statements from the taxpayer or the other party or the mortgagee. He may inspect the filing of plans and permits to make material renovations or additions at local building departments to determine facts relating to capital additions to the property.

In the cases of taxpayers declaring income from pensions and annuities, the agent will want to determine: (1) the investment in the contract or the cost of the annuity; (2) tax-free cost recovery in the past; (3) the expected return; (4) payments received during the taxable year. He may ask for a statement from the employer or insurance company as to the cost of the pension or annuity paid by the taxpayer.

The Audit Technique Handbook for IRS Agents indicates what the auditor should look for when scrutinizing itemized deductions. He will divide charitable contributions into two classes: those fully substantiated, and those paid in cash with no substantiation available. He will compare names of suspicious charities with the IRS's list of exempt organizations. He will ascertain that pledges have actually been paid, since otherwise they are not allowable. In determining amounts paid in cash and not substantiated, he will ask himself whether the total of contributions claimed seems reasonable in relation to the amount available from which contribution could have been made. He will take into consideration how much available cash would be left out of gross income less the other deductions claimed on the return, personal living expenses, income taxes withheld, and any estimated tax payments.

Agents will examine carefully contributions to schools which the taxpayer's dependents attend in order to determine whether the deduction claimed actually represents cost of tuition. He will also keep in mind that many charities conduct rummage or auction sales or regularly offer for sale personal property that has been donated. Many times, valuable items such as color televisions, jewelry, furs, paintings, etc., are disposed of at or near their fair market value. It is illegal for the taxpayer to make out the check to the charity and deduct such purchases as contributions to the organization.

The agent will expect documentary substantiation for deductions of interest paid. He will examine the terms of the interest agreement and analyze payments to establish that principal payments have not been included as interest. He will take care to distinguish between interest and the discount given on the principal, since the Code provides that the discount be amortized over the term of the loan. He will eliminate life insurance premiums or other charges normally added to time-payment contracts.

The examiner will verify from actual receipts or mortage statements appropriate amounts paid on real-estate taxes as well as the name of the registered property owner. In cases where the property was recently acquired or sold, he will check to see that taxes were prorated.

The IRS's Audit Technique Handbook explains that the audit of medical expenses of a sizable amount usually does not present a problem to the examiner because receipts and other records of payment can be secured for the larger doctor bills and hospital expenses. However, the Handbook does caution against double deductions being claimed or against accepting unreceipted bills. It tells the auditor to be aware that deductions are sometimes claimed when the taxpayer actually pays the total medical bill and subsequently receives an insurance settlement of all or part of the medical expenditures made. It warns that problems also arise in connection with the audit of amounts claimed for drugs and prescriptions. If such amounts appear unreasonable, he is told to make an attempt to tie them in with specific illnesses. Pharmaceutical charges appearing on a hospital bill, the Handbook says, should be segregated and included in medicine and drugs for the purpose of applying the 1% limitation. Care should be exercised, it continues, in the analysis of medicines and prescriptions in order to prevent the inclusion of various nondeductible expenses which are sometimes listed as medicine, such as toothpaste, toothbrushes, and other toilet articles. It cautions that premiums paid on a medical insurance policy which has elements of expense reimbursement as well as loss-of-earnings recovery are only partially deductible, and that premiums paid on life insurance with incidental health insurance benefits are not deductible. Also, since various employers pay part of health insurance costs, the deduction claimed should be verified as actually having been paid by the taxpayer.

In calculating the correct amount allowable for a fire, storm, or other casualty-loss deduction, the Handbook says the examiner should consider the difference between the fair market value of the asset before and after the casualty or the adjusted basis, whichever is less. From this amount must be deducted any insurance or other compensation received or recoverable. The examiner, the Handbook warns, must exercise care to determine that the repair or replacement claimed only restores the property to substantially the same condition as before the casualty, and that any repair or replacement that results in improving the property beyond the condition that existed before the casualty would not be an acceptable measure for the deduction. In the case of theft, the auditor must verify that a theft in fact did occur before a deductible loss can be okayed. He should look for a police report. In both casualty and theft deductions, the agent must determine any allowance on insurance recovery.

We have given you many instances and examples that may result in your return being flagged for audit. In the next chapter we tell you how to prepare for, conduct yourself during, and survive an audit.

CHAPTER 23

How to Survive a Tax Audit

April 15 has come and gone and you managed to scrounge up the figure in the 1040 Balance Due column, or perhaps you were the happy recipient of a tax refund. Then wham! A letter comes in the mail:

INTERNAL REVENUE SERVICE
DISTRICT DIRECTOR

DEPARTMENT OF THE TREASURY
Tax Year(s) 19___

Date: Feb. 6, 198_

Day and Date of Appointment:
Time:
Place of Appointment:

Smith, John and Mary
5 Plymouth Place
New York, N.Y. 10010

Room Number:
Appointment Clerk:

We are examining your federal income tax return for the above year(s) and find we need additional information to verify your correct tax. We have, therefore, scheduled the above appointment for you.

The letter will go on to tell you that if you filed a joint return, either you or your spouse may keep the appointment, or you may have an attorney, a CPA, an individual enrolled to practice before the IRS, or a qualified unenrolled individual (whoever might have done your return for you) represent you, providing they have filed the IRS's Authorization and Declaration form (Form 2848-D).

The letter goes on to tell you to bring records you used as a basis for items checked. (See items sheet, for example.) Attached to the letter might be a blue notice that will tell you in more specific detail what records to bring for each item to be examined. (See illustration of notices as examples.) They give you seven days in which to reply to their request for you to meet at your nearest IRS branch.

Or you may get a mail audit. Your letter might go something like this:

> We are examining your federal income tax return for the year shown above and find we need additional information from your records to determine your tax liability. We will review your records as quickly as possible and return them to you after we have completed the examination.

If you have acted legally and have substantial proof of your transaction or transactions in question, you have every chance of emerging from the audit "with a clean bill of health."

Before we go on to discuss more about your audit, we would like to tell you a little about a special type of audit called the Taxpayer Compliance Measurement Program audit. Those chosen for this type of audit are selected at random, not because they are suspected of wrongdoing. They must substantiate *every* line of their 1040s. They may even be required to produce their marriage licenses if they claim marital status or their children's birth certificates if they claim children for exemptions! Every deduction, every income-adjustment item, must be substantiated with records.

These research audits are conducted on individual tax returns every three years and fifty thousand returns are selected.

To make up an unbiased random sampling, IRS statisticians flip open a book of random numbers—the page is chosen at random—and with closed eyes pick a multiple-digit number on the page. Taxpayers whose Social Security numbers have the same ending digits as the number chosen are the people whose returns are tapped for the research examinations. Selected individuals are then subjected to the grueling audit. The information on their original tax returns, along with any tax change that is proposed as a result of the research audits, is entered on special IRS check sheets and computer tapes. This is the information that forms the statistical data base of the mathematical formulas the IRS uses to score all individual tax returns.

Do not risk the ire of your auditor by disregarding an audit letter requesting an interview at an appointed date and time. If you are unable to go at that time, call the auditor and arrange another date—promptly.

Read the audit letter carefully to make sure you understand the items being questioned. If you don't understand what is being asked for, or being questioned, call your auditor. He would rather you call before the appointment and be prepared, than arrive confused and unprepared, thus wasting his time and yours. When you call him and when you go to the audit, do not bring up any other items on your return other than those he has requested for discussion. You may very well get yourself hung up on an item and find that you are making trouble for yourself.

Do some homework before your audit. Get out your return and see how you answered the questioned item. Also, get out all records pertaining to the item. For instance, if child-care credit is questioned—you deducted the cost of camp for your fourteen-year-old—gather all the information that relates to the Child Care Credit form. Hunt up the canceled check made out to your child's camp, a copy of the camp's brochure to prove it exists, and your receipt for the camp's fee from the director. You might also include your child's birth certificate to prove that he was under fifteen and therefore you were still entitled to child-care credit.

Be fully prepared for your audit. Unlike criminal court, you are considered guilty until you prove your innocence, and the burden of proof is on you!

Please bring the records to support the following items reported on your tax return and its schedules:

- ☐ Alimony Payments
- ☐ Automobile Expenses
- ☐ Bad Debts
- ☐ Capital Gains and Losses
- ☐ Casualty Losses
- ☐ Child and Dependent Care Expenses
- ☐ Contributions
- ☐ Education Expenses
- ☐ Employee Business Expenses
- ☐ Exemptions
- ☐ Interest Expense
- ☐ Medical and Dental Expenses
- ☐ Moving Expenses
- ☐ Rental Income and Expenses
- ☐ Sale or Exchange of Residence
- ☐ Sick Pay or Disability Income Exclusion
- ☐ Taxes
- ☐ Uniforms, Equipment, and Tools

Please bring evidence such as accounting ledgers and journals, bank statements, and canceled checks to support the following items shown on Schedule C:

☐ All Business Expenses

☐ Bad Debts

☐ Cost of Goods Sold

☐ Depreciation

☐ Gross Receipts

☐ Insurance

☐ Interest

☐ Rents

☐ Repairs

☐ Salaries and Wages

☐ Taxes

☐ Travel and Entertainment

☐

☐

☐

☐

Please bring evidence such as accounting ledgers and journals, bank statements, and canceled checks to support the following items shown on Schedule F:

☐ All Farm Expenses

☐ Depreciation

☐ Feed and Seed Purchased

☐ Fertilizers, Lime

☐ Gross Receipts

☐ Insurance

☐ Inventories

☐ Labor Hired

☐ Machine Hire

☐ Other Farm Income

☐ Repairs and Maintenance

☐ Supplies Purchased

☐ Taxes

☐

☐

☐

Information
Guide

Medical and Dental Expenses

To help us complete the examination of your return, please include the following with your records:

1. Cancelled checks, receipts, etc. for all medical and dental expenses. Identify the person for whom each expense was incurred.

2. Itemized receipts for drugs and medicine. Cancelled checks alone are not acceptable because they may include payment for drugstore items that are not deductible. Identify the person for whom the drugs and medicine were purchased.

3. Record of any expense reimbursed or paid directly by insurance.

4. Insurance policies on which you claimed a deduction for premiums paid. Include cancelled checks or other receipts for payment of these premiums.

Department
of the
Treasury
Internal
Revenue
Service

Notice 87
(Rev. 6-74)

Information
Guide

Employee Travel and Entertainment Expenses

To help us complete the examination of your return, please include the following with your records:

1. Statement from your employer showing:
(a) Employer's reimbursement policy.
(b) Amount and kind of expense reimbursed, charged, or provided.
(c) Specific expenses not covered by reimbursement policy.
(d) Territory assigned to you and a brief outline of your duties.

2. Explanatory statement from your employer if you are required to provide an office in your home or elsewhere or to use your home telephone in connection with your employment. Furnish receipts or canceled checks to verify these expenses.

3. Copies of expense vouchers submitted to your employer for reimbursement.

4. Receipts and records of expenses for business purposes:
(a) Lodging and meals while away from home.
(b) Gifts.
(c) Promotional items.
(d) Entertainment.

5. Verification of automobile expenses for business purposes:
(a) Invoice of purchase or lease of vehicles.
(b) Receipts for oil, gas, repairs, etc.
(c) Records of business mileage and total mileage.

Department
of the
Treasury
**Internal
Revenue
Service**

Notice 93
(Rev. 8-76)

GPO 907-412

Department
of the
Treasury

**Internal
Revenue
Service**

Information   Notice 94
Guide   (Rev. 6-70)

Moving
Expenses

To help us complete the examination of your
return, please include the following with
your records:

1. Cancelled checks or receipts to verify amounts
of moving expenses you paid.

2. Names and relationship to you of members of
your household who moved with you.

3. Computations showing number of miles by
direct route from your old residence to:
(a) your new place of employment, and
(b) your old place of employment.

4. Name and address of each employer since
moving to new place of employment and period
of time employed by each.

5. Statement from your employer of the allowance
or reimbursement paid you for moving expenses.
Show amounts by types of expense, such as
transportation fares, meals and lodging, automobile expense, transportation of household and
personal property, etc.

Information
Guide

Interest Expenses

To help us complete the examination of your return, please include the following with your records:

1. Receipts, canceled checks, or statements from creditors showing amounts of interest paid and names of payees. If the checks cover principal and interest payments, be able to show the amount representing interest.

2. Payment books on installment purchases or contract on purchase, and evidence of payments made on the contract.

3. Land contract for land contract interest or mortgage receipts.

Department
of the
Treasury
Internal
Revenue
Service

Notice 89
(Rev. 6-78)

Information Guide

Capital Gains and Losses

To help us complete the examination of your return, please include the following with your records:

Stock Sales

1. Brokerage vouchers establishing the purchase price and sales price of stock sold.

2. If you sold securities on which you had a return of capital during the holding period of the stock, provide records showing adjusted basis of stock.

3. If you claim worthless securities, provide verification of dissolution of the corporation.

4. For stock held in a liquidated or defunct corporation, provide verification of liquidation and liquidation distribution.

Other Property

1. Closing statements on purchase of property.

2. Verification of capital improvements to property.

3. If you reported gain or loss from sale of property, furnish:

(a) Records which show terms of sale and expense of sale.

(b) Copy of closing statement or settlement sheet.

4. If sale involved rental or other business property, furnish copies of your income tax returns for the 2 years before the year of sale.

5. If you reported gain or loss from repossession, furnish:

(a) Copy of your income tax return for the year of the original sale.

(b) All contracts or legal documents involved.

(c) Verification of repossession costs.

Department of the Treasury Internal Revenue Service

Notice 102 (Rev. 6-74)

* GPO: 1975-621-742/5025. R3

Information
Guide

Child Care

To help us complete the examination of
your return, please include the following
with your records:

1. If your marital status changed during the year, for
each period you were married, furnish—
(a) Dates of marriage.
(b) Your earnings in each period.
(c) Amount of child care you paid during each period.

2. (a) Amounts you paid for household services for the
entire year.
(b) Amounts you (or, if married, you and your spouse)
paid for the care of a qualifying individual during any
period of the year.

3. (a) Names and addresses of persons or
organizations you paid for child care.
(b) Copies of canceled checks or receipts to verify
child care costs.

4. If you paid for care of a disabled dependent, furnish
information showing that:
(a) The dependent was physically or mentally unable
to care for self.
(b) The dependent or spouse was cared for in your
household.

Department
of the
Treasury
Internal
Revenue
Service

Notice 99
(Rev. 7-77)

**Information
Guide**

Alimony
Payments

To help us complete the examination of your
return, please include the following with
your records:

1. Copy of divorce decree, separate
maintenance decree, or other written document which specifies the basis for alimony
payments.

2. Current name and address of divorced or
separated spouse.

3. Canceled checks or receipts to verify payments you made. If you do not make alimony
payments directly, please furnish documents
showing the source of the payments. Examples of such documents are insurance
policies, endowments, and annuity contracts.

Department
of the
Treasury
Internal
Revenue
Service

Notice 98
(Rev. 8-76)
GPO 907-411

Information
Guide

Uniforms, Equipment, and Tools

To help us complete the examination of your return, please include the following with your records:

1. Explanation of how the expense claimed relates to your employment.

2. A statement from your employer if your employment required this expense.

3. Cancelled checks or receipts to verify the expense claimed.

Department
of the
Treasury
Internal
Revenue
Service

Notice 97
(Rev. 6-74)

**Information
Guide**

Casualty
Losses

To help us complete the examination of your return, please include the following with your records:

1. Insured property:

A copy of insurance report showing:

(a) Date and nature of loss or damages claimed.

(b) Amount of damages claimed on insurance.

(c) Amount of coverage carried.

(d) Date and amount of claim paid by insurance.

2. Uninsured property:

Any fire or police department reports on fire losses, theft losses, or losses from accidents. If you are unable to obtain a copy of the fire or police department report, furnish the name or number of the precinct or police station where the accident or theft was reported.

3. If available, photographs showing extent of loss.

4. Fair market value of property before and after the casualty, or estimate of damage from qualified estimator or adjuster.

5. Cost or other basis of property and date you acquired the property.

Department
of the
Treasury
**Internal
Revenue
Service**

Notice 96
(Rev. 7-74)

GPO : 1975 O - 107-029

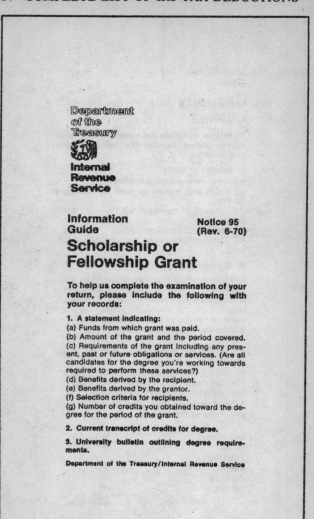

**Department
of the
Treasury**

**Internal
Revenue
Service**

**Information
Guide**

Notice 95
(Rev. 6-70)

Scholarship or
Fellowship Grant

To help us complete the examination of your
return, please include the following with
your records:

1. A statement indicating:

(a) Funds from which grant was paid.

(b) Amount of the grant and the period covered.

(c) Requirements of the grant including any present, past or future obligations or services. (Are all candidates for the degree you're working towards required to perform these services?)

(d) Benefits derived by the recipient.

(e) Benefits derived by the grantor.

(f) Selection criteria for recipients.

(g) Number of credits you obtained toward the degree for the period of the grant.

2. Current transcript of credits for degree.

3. University bulletin outlining degree requirements.

Department of the Treasury/Internal Revenue Service

**Information
Guide**

Education
Expenses

To help us complete the examination of your
return, please include the following with your
records:

1. Document showing period of enrollment in
educational institution or participation in educational activity, and number of hours of instruction
each week.

2. Document showing principal subjects studied, or
description of educational activity.

3. Canceled checks or receipts to verify amounts
you spent for:
(a) Tuition and books.
(b) Meals and lodging while away from home
overnight.
(c) Travel and transportation.
(d) Other educational expenses

4. Statement from your employer explaining:
(a) Whether the education was necessary for you
to keep your employment, salary, or status.
(b) How the education helped maintain or improve
skills needed in your employment.
(c) How much educational expense reimbursement
you received. (Show this by types of expense.)

5. Brief description of the nature of your employment during the year.

6. Complete information about any scholarship
or fellowship grant you or your dependent received
during the year.

7. Teachers Only: a statement showing:
(a) Type of teacher's certificate under which you
taught.
(b) Date certificate was issued.
(c) List of subjects taught.

Department
of the
Treasury
**Internal
Revenue
Service**

Notice 91
(Rev. 8-76)

Information Guide

Taxes

To help us complete the examination of your return, please include the following with your records:

For real estate and personal property taxes:
1. Canceled checks or receipts for taxes paid.
2. If you sold or purchased real property, a copy of the settlement statement.
3. Identification of any special assessments deducted as taxes, and an explanation of their purpose.

For sales tax:
1. Receipts for sales taxes paid on a car, truck, boat, airplane, mobile or prefabricated home, or building materials you bought to build a new home.
2. If you paid more sales tax on items not listed above than the amount shown for your income in the Optional State Sales Tax Tables (See Form 1040 instructions), verification of purchases on which sales tax was paid.

For gas tax:
Verification of nonbusiness miles driven or of your gas purchases, with figures to show how you computed the gas tax.

For State and local income taxes:
1. Copies of state and local income tax returns.
2. Canceled checks or receipts showing taxes paid. (Amounts of State and local income tax refunds you received or that were credited to you you may be taxable to you in the year received or credited. This is generally the case if you claimed the tax as an itemized deduction in a previous year.)

Department of the Treasury
Internal Revenue Service

Notice 88
(Rev. 7-78)

Should you bring along an accountant? If you use an accountant for your tax return it is wise to ask him to attend the audit. Give him plenty of notice so that he can fit the date into his schedule. He will brief you before the audit as to what to bring and how to conduct yourself. If you feel that the audit will be too nerve-racking for you, it's more than you can take, or if you will be out of town at that time, you may give your accountant power of attorney to represent you without your being there.

If you do go to the audit, dress in your usual business clothes. It is imprudent to wear extravagant jewelry. Why flaunt your wealth in front of an IRS agent who is, if you are very comfortable, making a fraction of what you are?

Don't, repeat *don't* be a wise guy. Agents do not appreciate "smart-alecky" or snide remarks or jokes about the IRS or the tax structure. Do not embark on speeches about how the government is wasting your tax money. What the government does with your tax money is not within your agent's province. They have seen those types before and, frankly, it bores them and they do resent the waste of their time. They are for the most part fairly pleasant, intelligent, courteous people who are just doing their jobs.

Remember: If you can show him that the contested item comes within the tax rules, or that you actually incurred a deduction expense, you will have no difficulty.

Be honest. Don't try any slick tricks. One taxpayer we know was questioned on his medical deduction. He presented, among others, a large check made out to Dr. John Lloyd. His auditor turned over the check to read the endorsement on the back. It read: John Lloyd, D.V.M. "Your dog," said the auditor, "does not qualify you for a medical deduction," and discounted that check. Our friend did not realize what his auditor had, that D.V.M.—Doctor of Veterinary Medicine—had given away the fact that the check was payment for his dog's treatment and not for a human member of his family!

Then there was another case of a taxpayer who had no proof for a large medical deduction. She claimed she had undergone an appendectomy and volunteered to show her scar. Her auditor declined her offer, stating that the scar would not prove to him what year the operation had taken place and that he would have to discount the deduction unless she could produce her surgeon's canceled check.

An outside salesman had a rather large business-entertainment deduction. When questioned about it, he confidently produced his business diary. The trouble was, amounts were all in nice even numbers. In "doctoring" his diary, he had forgotten to include sales taxes, something that the perceptive agent picked up on immediately.

Unless you have committed absolute fraud on the return, your agent will come to some sort of agreement with you about what he will allow and what he will disallow on it, according to his interpretation of tax regulations. If you agree with his findings, he will ask you then and there at the audit to sign an agreement form. This IRS form (No. 870) will show any increase or decrease in your tax liability. If you agree to more tax, you'll have to pay 12% interest per year on the increase. On the other hand, if it was happily discovered during the audit that you made an overpayment, you are usually entitled to receive 12% interest on your tax overpayment.

Suppose you don't agree with your auditor's conclusions. You think the auditor is in error, or you dispute his interpretations of tax law as applied to your situation. You must still prove you're right, but you do have recourses beyond this stage.

If your audit took place at an IRS office, you may request an immediate meeting with a supervisor to state your case. If agreement is reached, your case will be closed.

If agreement is not reached at this meeting, or if the unagreed examination was made outside of an IRS office, the IRS will send you (1) a transmittal letter notifying you of your right to appeal the proposed adjustments within thirty days; (2) a copy of the examination report explaining the proposed adjustments; (3) an agreement or waiver form; and (4) a copy of the IRS publication on appeal rights.

If after receiving the examination report you decide to agree with the examiner's findings, sign the agreement or waiver form and pay any additional amounts you may owe plus interest on the additional tax.

However, if you still dispute the IRS's decision according to the last examination, you may take your case to an appeals office in your region. Address your request to the district director, who will send your request to the appeals office. A conference will be set up for you in order to present your view. If agreement is still not reached after this conference, you may take your case to court.

You may skip the appeals procedure if you like and go directly to court after the examination report.

You may go to the United States Tax Court, the United States Court of Claims, or your United States District Court. None of these courts have any connection with the IRS.

To take your case to the Tax Court, first you must ask the IRS to issue a formal letter called a statutory notice of deficiency. You have 90 days from the date this notice is mailed to you to file a petition with the Tax Court (150 days if addressed to you outside the United States). The Tax Court hears cases only if the tax has not been assessed or paid. You must be sure that your petition to the Tax Court is filed in time or else the IRS will hold you responsible for the tax and pursue you for collection.

The Tax Court is presided over by a corps of judges who are rotated. The court will schedule your case for a location convenient to you. You may represent your-

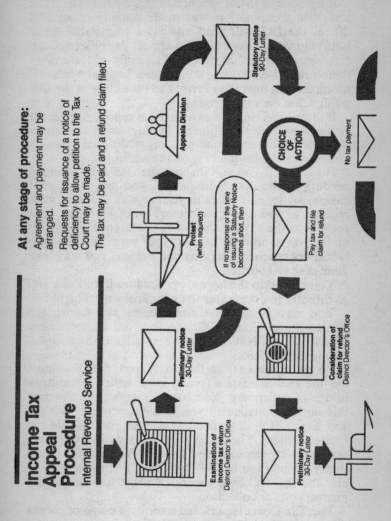

Income Tax Appeal Procedure

Internal Revenue Service

At any stage of procedure:

Agreement and payment may be arranged.

Requests for issuance of a notice of deficiency to allow petition to the Tax Court may be made.

The tax may be paid and a refund claim filed.

Examination of income tax return
District Director's Office

Preliminary notice
30-Day Letter

Preliminary notice
30-Day Letter

Consideration of claim for refund
District Director's Office

Protest
(when required)

Appeals Division

If no response or the time of issuing a Statutory Notice becomes short, then

Statutory notice
90-Day Letter

CHOICE OF ACTION

Pay tax and file claim for refund

No tax payment

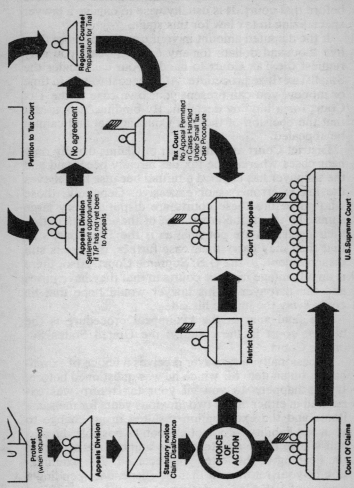

self or be represented by anyone admitted to practice before that court. It is usually wise to engage a lawyer specializing in tax law for this stage.

If the disputed amount in your case is not more than five thousand dollars for any one tax year, you may request the Tax Court to handle your case under the Small Tax Case procedure. At little cost to you in time or money, you can present your own case to the Tax Court for a binding decision. By binding, it is meant that the decision of the Tax Court is final and cannot be appealed.

District Court and the Court of Claims usually only hear cases wherein the tax has already been paid and the taxpayer has claimed a refund because he believes the tax is erroneous or excessive. Generally, those who go before these courts are disputing very large sums. To them, the advantage of these courts is that their decisions are not final as is the Tax Court's so that they may carry their case further, if there is still disagreement, to the U.S. Supreme Court. Also, there is an advantage in these courts in that they have juries and the taxpayer or his lawyer would hope that he could sway the jury to his side.

The final step in the tax-appeal procedure is the highest court in the country: the United States Supreme Court.

Occasionally, a taxpayer receives a notice of examination on an item for which he was questioned before. If this happens to you—if your tax return was examined in either of the two previous years for the same items and the examination resulted in no change to your tax liability—contact as soon as possible the person whose name and telephone number are shown in the heading of the letter you received. The examination of your return will then be suspended, pending a review of IRS files to determine whether or not they should proceed in the investigation.

Suppose the IRS finds you owe more tax. What penalties can the IRS impose? First, there is interest on your tax deficiency figured at a 12% annual rate. In addition, you can be liable for:

• Late filing. If you didn't get a time extension you'll be assessed 12% annual interest charge of the tax due each month (or any part of each month) your return is unpaid. You will be excused if you can show "reasonable cause" for your delay. If you are entitled to a refund on your return there is no penalty at all.

• Insufficient payment. If you filed on time, but did not pay all the tax due, the IRS can assess you for .5% per month for each month you don't pay the deficiency up to a total penalty of 25% of the underpayment. "Reasonable cause" may excuse you from this penalty.

• Insufficient estimated tax. Penalty is 12% annually of underpayment for period of underpayment.

• Negligent or intentional underpayment. There is a 5% penalty based on underpayment.

• Fraudulent underpayment. Penalty is 50% of total underpayment PLUS possible criminal penalties including imprisonment!

What does the IRS consider criminal tax evasion? Don't worry if you have claimed minor cash contributions you can't prove or don't have all the records for travel and entertainment expenses. You won't go to jail. However, if you failed to report substantial amounts of income or deductions are for fictitious expenses—especially if you have done this over a period of years—you are guilty of criminal fraud. Also criminal is the claiming of fictitious dependents or the filing of several different returns for the same refund. Willful failure to file any tax return is a crime, too, even if you intended to file later.

What's the penalty for criminal tax evasion? A maximum of up to five years' imprisonment and a fine of $10,000 for each year of tax evasion. However, if a citizen makes a "voluntary disclosure" of tax evasion prior to any audit contact from the IRS, it's generally their unofficial policy to let taxpayers make amends without prosecution.

You say you don't have the money for your taxes, but you don't want to go to jail for tax evasion? File anyway and work out payment with the IRS. That way, though you pay some penalty, you are not in criminal violation.

Glossary
of Tax Terms

Even though you suspect that you and the IRS are both speaking English, there often seems to be a discrepancy in what you mean and what the IRS means for a word or a phrase. What has happened is that over the years since the income tax has been in existence, the IRS has, as have so many other government agencies, developed a language all its own. To help you understand words and phrases the IRS uses and what they mean in tax terms, we have prepared a glossary of tax terms.

A

Adjusted gross income—Income from all sources, minus the following if they apply: moving expenses, employee business expenses, payments to an IRA, payments to a Keogh plan, interest penalty due to early withdrawal of savings, alimony paid.

Alimony—Separate maintenance or periodic payments of a fixed amount for an indefinite period, or payments of an indefinite amount for either a fixed or an indefinite period. Does not include child support.

Audit—A systematic investigation of procedures and records to determine conformity with prescribed regulations. The IRS has the right to examine your returns for the past three years—six years in case of fraud. There is no statute of limitations for a failure to file.

B

Birth and dependency—If a child is born during the year, even if it is on December 31, and you provide more than half the child's support, you get a dependency exemption. If a child was born to you and only lived momentarily, you still get an exemption. The child is considered to have lived if the state of birth issued a birth certificate for him or her. You cannot claim an exemption for a stillborn child.

Blindness—You are allowed an additional $1,000 exemption for blindness if you were blind on the last day of the year. If you are totally blind, you attach a statement to your return to that effect. You are also allowed the exemption if you are partially blind. Partial blindness would be: (1) you cannot see better than 20/200 with glasses; or (2) your field of view is not more than 20 degrees. You must submit with your return a certified statement from an eye doctor or registered optometrist that that condition exists.

Bunched income—Income that is for the most part received in one year for work, but which work was, for the most part, done over several previous years. This might refer to income from personal services, musical or literary work, or from back pay to an employee. In order to avoid excessive tax in the year the income is received, the taxpayer would file Schedule G—Income Averaging.

Business income—Income from a trade, business, or profession. If you are the sole proprietor of a trade or business, or if you are a professional in your own practice, you report your income on either the accrual or the cash basis. You may report your business income on the accrual basis even if you report your non-business income on the cash basis.

C

Capital expenditures (in support tests)—Big-ticket items that must be included in figuring total support.

They might be furniture, appliances, automobiles, or such.

Carry-over—The capital loss for one year that may be deducted at a rate of not more than $3,000 per year against ordinary income for the next succeeding years, or completely against capital gains as they arise.

Casualty—This is the complete or partial destruction or loss of property resulting from an identifiable event that is damaging to property and is sudden, unexpected, or unusual in nature. Casualty damage might come from a hurricane, accident to your automobile, mine cave-in, sonic boom, or vandalism.

Child, yours—Your child means your son, stepson, daughter, stepdaughter, a child who was placed with you by an authorized placement agency for adoption, or a foster child who was a member of your household for your entire tax year. In order for you to take an exemption for your child, he must be under nineteen at the end of the year or a full-time student of any age.

Child-care credit—This is 20% of expenses that you paid for the care of a child or care of a dependent so that you could be employed. The amount is subject to limitation. The credit is limited to $400 for one child, $800 for more than one.

Community-property state—State in which property is considered owned equally by husband and wife. Community-property states are: Arizona, California, Idaho, Louisiana, Nevada, New Mexico, Texas, and Washington.

Custody (of child)—This is usually determined by decree of divorce or separate maintenance, but if not established in the decree it usually means that the parent who has physical custody of the child for the greater part of the year has custody of the child for the tax year.

D

Death (and member-of-household test)—If a person died during the year, but was a member of your household for the entire part of the year preceding death, the person will have met the member-of-household test.

Death of spouse—If your spouse died within the two tax years preceding the year for which your return is being filed, you may be entitled to use the Married Filing Joint Return tax table. You must not be remarried and must have a dependent child to file as a qualifying widow or widower.

Decree of annulment—This holds that no valid marriage ever existed. You must file as an unmarried individual for the tax year in which you obtain the annulment; then you must file an amended return for any year in which you filed as married within the annulled marriage, and refile under another category.

Deduction—An amount that may be subtracted from one's adjusted gross income.

Dependent—A person who qualifies you for the $1,000 exemption if the following five tests are met: (1) support test; (2) gross-income test; (3) member-of-household or relationship test; (4) citizenship test; (5) joint-return test.

Depreciation—Expensing the cost of a fixed asset by allowing for diminishing worth due to wear and tear and the aging process. Methods of depreciation used on tax returns: straight-line method, declining-balance method, and sum-of-the-digits method.

E

Earned-income credit—Credit applied against your tax liability if your earned income or adjusted gross income, whichever is larger, is less than $10,000.

Employee compensation (other than wages, salaries, tips)—This includes fees, commissions, bonuses, disability retirement income, payments to insurance companies not included on your W-2, fair market value of meals and living quarters if given by your employer as a matter of your choice and not for his convenience, and strike and lockout benefits paid by a union from union dues.

Estimated tax—The total of your expected income tax and self-employment tax for the following calendar year minus your expected withholding.

Exclusion—Subtraction of up to $100 on the 1040 of ordinary dividends received from qualifying domestic corporations. The exclusion goes up to $200 if you and your spouse owns stocks jointly and file a joint return.

Extension—A taxpayer may get an automatic extension of time to file his income-tax return by filing an application on Form 4868 by the return due date. The extension application must show the estimated tax due and be accompanied by a check for the estimated tax owed. Further extensions will only be allowed for six months from the return due date and must be because of severe hardship that prevents filing of a return.

F

Fellowship—An amount granted an individual for his or her benefit as an aid in the pursuit of study or research. If it is not used as compensation for services, the amount of the fellowship may be excluded from income on the tax return.

FICA—Federal Insurance Contributions Act, also known as Social Security and also as old-age benefits. Includes federal disability benefits and widows' and children's benefits as well as retirement benefits.

Foreign-tax credit—Credit against your United States income tax claimed for foreign income taxes paid to a foreign country or United States possession. Instead of taking foreign taxes as a credit, you may alternatively take them as an itemized deduction.

Form W-2—A wage and tax statement that shows total wages and other compensation paid and the income tax and Social Security tax withheld during the calendar year.

Form W-2G—A statement showing the amount of net winnings on gambling and the amount of tax withheld (20% of gross proceeds).

Form W-2P—A statement showing the amount of pension or annuity paid during the year and tax withheld on payments.

Form W-4—A form provided by your employer on which you indicate your marital status and the number of withholding allowances you are claiming.

Full-time student—A person who is enrolled for the number of hours or courses considered by the educational organization to be full-time attendance. The student may be taken as a dependent by his or her parents if attendance is full time for five months of the year, regardless of the earnings of the student.

G

Gross income—All income that is taxed. Excluded from this are: certain specified gifts and inheritances, death benefits, interest on state obligations, certain injury and sickness compensation, and Social Security benefits.

H

Head of household—A taxpayer who is unmarried on the last day of the tax year and either (1) paid more than half the cost of maintaining a home that is the principal residence for the entire year for a dependent parent; or (2) paid more than half the cost of maintaining a home that is the principal residence for the entire year for himself and his unmarried child, grandchild, foster child, stepchild, or other dependent relative.

I

Interest income (taxable)—Interest received from the following sources is fully taxable: bank accounts, loans, notes, bonds (except state and local government bonds), building and loan accounts, credit union accounts, U.S. savings bonds, and refunds of tax. If interest totals more than $400, sources and amounts must be listed on Schedule B.

Investment credit—A credit of 10% of investment in newly acquired machinery or equipment used in your business. This also may apply to the building of certain property. File Form 3468 to claim credit.

IRA—Individual Retirement Account. This is open to employees who are not covered by a qualified retirement plan. Contributions to an IRA may be deducted from gross income. You are allowed to contribute each year the smallest of the following: (1) actual amount of contribution to an IRA; (2) $1,500; or (3) 15% of your compensation.

J

Joint return—A return filed by the husband and wife together. You may file a joint return even if one of you had no income or deductions. Usually the tax is lower if a joint return is filed. A joint return splits the joint income reported and uses a lower tax rate. You must be married on the last day of the tax year (December 31) and living as husband and wife or living together in a common-law marriage that was recognized by the state where the common-law marriage began; married and living apart but not legally separated under a final decree of divorce or separate maintenance; or separated under an interlocutory decree of divorce. If your spouse died during the year, you may still file as married for the entire year.

Joint-return test (for dependent)—You are not allowed an exemption for a dependent if he or she files a joint return with spouse unless your married dependent is not required to file a return but does so only to obtain a refund of taxes withheld.

K

Keogh plan (pension)—Plan for self-employed individuals. An individual may contribute 15% of net self-employment income or $7,500 per year, whichever is less, and invest in a retirement plan known as a Keogh plan. The amount of contribution is tax deductible and the earnings are not taxed until withdrawn for retirement income, or earlier.

L

Long-term capital gain—A gain on the sale or exchange of property held for investment and held for more than one year.

Long-term capital loss—A loss on the sale or exchange of capital assets or property held for investment and held for more than one year.

M

Maximum tax—A tax-rate limit of 50% on the personal-service income of an individual. The limit applies if: (1) you are single with personal-service taxable income of more than $40,200; (2) you are married filing jointly with personal-service income of more than $55,200; (3) you are a qualifying widow or widower with personal-service taxable income of more than $55,200. The maximum tax rate does not apply if: (1) you are married and do not file a joint return with your spouse; (2) you elect income averaging.

Medical insurance premiums—Payments for medical insurance. The IRS includes premiums paid for supplementary Medicare coverage in determining items of support and in calculating medical deduction.

Medicare benefits—Medicare benefits are divided into two categories: basic and supplementary. Both are excluded from the gross income of the person receiving benefits. Basic benefits are considered to be support provided by the person for himself as akin to Social Security payments. Supplementary benefits are not included in support either because they are considered as medical insurance payments.

Minimum tax—An additional tax imposed on taxpayers who have tax-preferential items such as accelerated depreciation, stock options, large itemized deductions, and intangible drilling costs. This is in addition to the regular income tax.

Multiple-support agreement—A group of individuals who contribute more than one half the support of a dependent agree that one of them, who must have contributed more than 10% of the mutual dependent's support, gets to take the dependent as an exemption. Each of the others must file a statement that they are not taking the dependent for an exemption that year. The person claiming the exemption files with his return Form 2120—Multiple Support Declaration.

P

Penalty—The IRS imposes a penalty of one half of 1% of the unpaid taxes for each month or part of month beyond the due date for tax payment. The maximum penalty is limited to 25%. There is also a negligence penalty: 5% of a deficiency, and 50% for a fraud penalty.

Personal-service income—Any amount that is earned income or that is received as a pension or annuity resulting from an employer-employee relationship or from tax-deductible contributions to a retirement plan. Usually the tax limit on personal-service income is 50%.

Personal-service net income—Personal-service income less any adjustments that are attributable to that personal-service income, such as trade or business expenses, Keogh plan or IRA contributions, or net operating losses.

R

Refund—Monies coming to you as a result of overpayment of income and Social Security taxes.

Residential energy credit—There are two distinct energy credits to residential energy credit: (1) expenditures for home energy conservations; (2) expenditures for renewable energy source property. Each is subject to its own conditions and limitations.

RRTA—Railroad Retirement Tax Act. This refers to retirement benefits for railroad employees.

S

Scholarship—An amount paid or allowed to or for a student at an educational organization to aid in the pursuit of studies. Is not counted in the student's support.

Self-employment tax—Tax on self-employment income. The rate is 9.3% for old-age and survivors' benefits and hospitalization. This tax is in addition to regular income tax on self-employment income.

Separate return—An individual return for a married person. Each spouse reports only own income, own exemptions, and own deductions on a separate return.

Short-term capital gain—A gain on the sale or exchange of property held for investment for one year or less.

Short-term capital loss—A loss on the sale or exchange of property or capital assets held for investment for one year or less.

Single—Never married; formerly married, with a final decree of divorce; not involved in a common-law marriage in a state that recognizes common-law marriage if the arrangement was begun in a state that recognizes common-law marriage.

T

Tax credit—An amount used as payment of tax owed.

Tax-exempt income—Income that does not have to be included on the tax return: Social Security benefits, welfare benefits, life insurance proceeds, Armed Forces family allotments, nontaxable pensions, nontaxable interest.

Total support—To determine whether you have contributed more than half to the support of a dependent, you must first total all support furnished by him or her, you, and others. Total support encompasses: (1) fair rental value of lodging furnished the dependent; (2) all items of expenses paid for the dependent, such as clothing and medical care; (3) a proportionate share of expenses that cannot be attributed directly to the dependent, such as food for the household.

Z

Zero-bracket amount—This amount is the deduction built into the tax tables. It is $3,400 for married taxpayers filing jointly, $2,300 for single taxpayers and heads of households, and $1,700 for a married taxpayer filing separately. Itemized deductions are in excess of the zero amount.